THE ADVENTURES OF KIMBLE BENT

LECTOR HOUSE PUBLIC DOMAIN WORKS

THE ADVENTURES OF KIMBLE BENT

JAMES COWAN

ISBN: 978-93-5342-722-1

First Published: 1911

LECTOR HOUSE LLP
E-MAIL: lectorpublishing@gmail.com

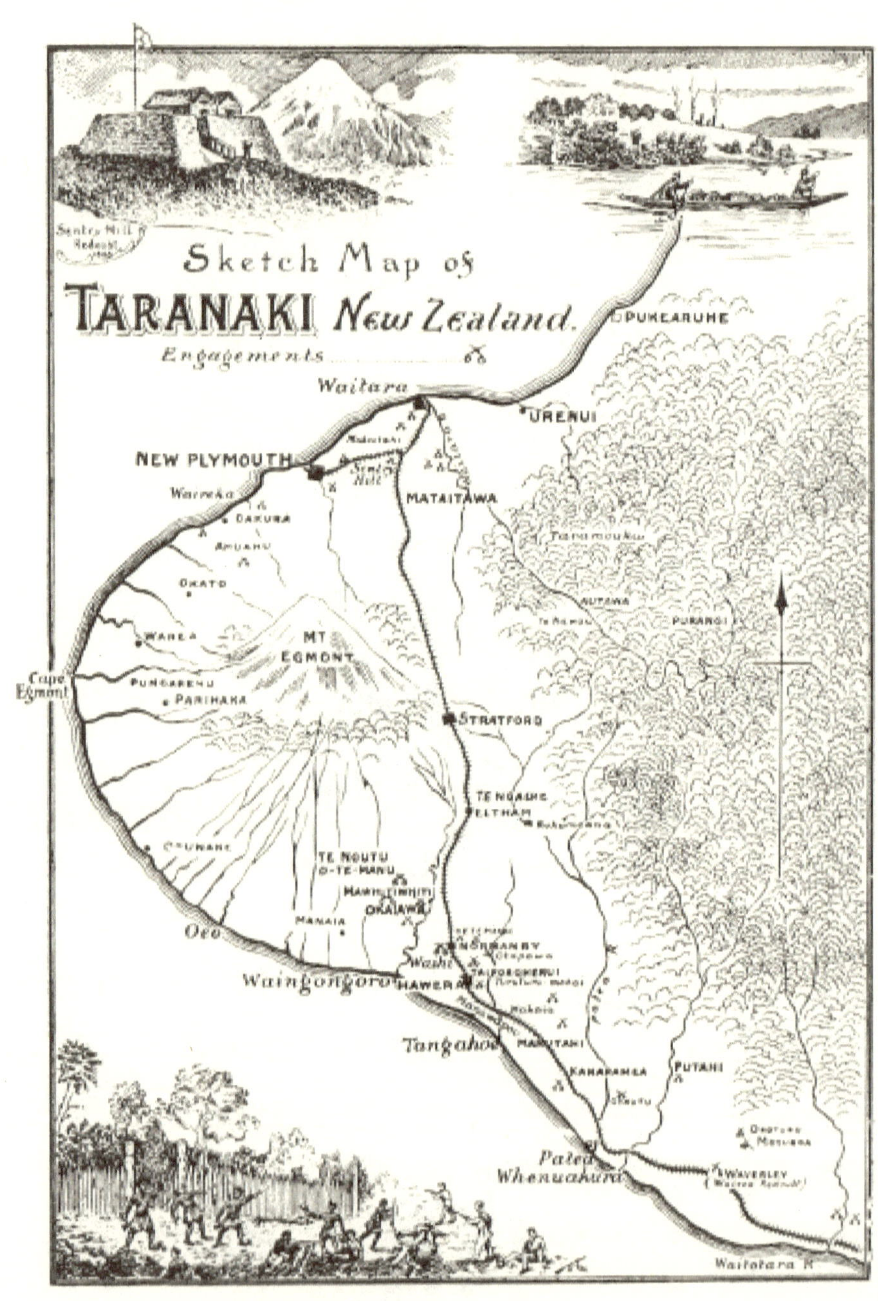

MAP OF TARANAKI, NEW ZEALAND.

(Showing engagements in the Maori War)

THE ADVENTURES OF KIMBLE BENT

A STORY OF WILD LIFE IN THE NEW ZEALAND BUSH

BY

JAMES COWAN

WITH ILLUSTRATIONS

1911

PREFACE

THIS book is not a work of fiction. It is a plain narrative of real life in the New Zealand bush, a true story of adventure in a day not yet remote, when adventure in abundance was still to be had in the land of the Maori. Every name used is a real one, every character who appears in these pages had existence in those war days of forty years ago. Every incident described here is a faithful record of actual happenings; some of them may convince the reader that truth can be stranger than fiction.

Numerous instances are recorded of white deserters from civilisation who have allied themselves with savages, adopting barbarous practices, and forgetting even their mother-tongue. In the old convict days of New South Wales escapees from the fetters of a more than rigorous "system" now and again cast in their lot with the blacks. Renegades of every European nationality have been found living with and fighting for native tribes in Africa and America and the Islands of Polynesia. But none of them had a wilder story to tell than has the man whose narrative is here presented—Kimble Bent, the *pakeha*-Maori. Ever since 1865—when he first "took to the blanket"—he has lived with the New Zealand Maoris. For thirteen years he was completely estranged from his fellow-whites; he had deserted from a British regiment and a price was on his head. British troops and Colonial irregulars alike hunted him and his fanatical Hauhau companions. His hairbreadth escapes were many; he had to risk death not only from British bullet and bayonet, but from the savage brown men of the forest with whom he lived. When at last he came out of hiding, and dared once more to face those of his own colour, he had almost forgotten the English language, and could speak it but with difficulty and hesitation. He has been out of his bush exile many years, but is still living with his Maori friends, and is still known by the Maori name, "Tu-nui-a-moa," which his chief Titokowaru gave him in 1868. When he writes to me, he usually writes in Maori, and he is practically a Maori himself, for he has lived the greater part of his life as a Maori, and he has assimilated the peculiar modes of thought and some of the ancient beliefs of the natives, as well as their tongue and customs.

One of the most remarkable portions of Bent's narrative is his account of the revival of cannibalism by the Hauhaus in 1868. Vague stories have been heard concerning the eating of soldiers' bodies by the bushmen of Ngati-Ruanui and Nga-Rauru and of rites of human sacrifices performed in the woods of Taranaki, but this account of Bent's is the first detailed description from an eye-witness of the man-eating practices in Titokowaru's camps. Many of Tito's Hauhaus are still alive; but they are very reticent on the subject of "long-pig."

I first met Kimble Bent in 1903. In that year Mr. T. E. Donne, now the New Zealand Government Trade Commissioner in London, had induced the old man to come to Wellington for the purpose of being interviewed and photographed; and it is these interviews, very considerably expanded during a seven years' acquaintance with Bent, and carefully checked by independent Maori testimony, that are now embodied in this book. In confirmation and extension of Bent's story, I have gathered data at first-hand both from Taranaki Maoris who fought under Titokowaru, and from soldiers and settlers who fought against him, and these particulars are incorporated with the old *pakeha*-Maori's narrative.

The 1868-9 portion of the book is, therefore, practically a history of the Titokowaru war in Taranaki; and it embraces a great deal of matter not hitherto recorded.

Many of the settler-soldiers who survive from those wild forest days now farm their peaceful lands within sight of the battle-fields of Te Ngutu-o-te-Manu, and Pungarehu, and Moturoa, and Otapawa. With them the recollections of bush-marches and ambuscades and storming of Hauhau stockades are still fresh and vivid. But the younger generation know little of the dangers and troubles through which the pioneers passed. The available histories deal very meagrely and often very inaccurately with the story of the Ten-Years' Maori War, even from the white side, while the Maori view-point is absolutely unknown to all but a few colonists. Therefore it is fortunate, perhaps, that one has been enabled to gather before it is too late from the old Hauhau warriors themselves the tale of their ferociously patriotic past, and to place on record this true story of wild forest life from the lips of one of the last of that nearly extinct type of decivilised outlander, the *pakeha*-Maori.

For information and assistance in regard to various engagements in Titokowaru's war I am indebted to Colonel W. E. Gudgeon, C.M.G., Colonel T. Porter, C.B., and other old Colonial soldiers. Tutangé Waionui, of Patea, who was one of Titokowaru's most active scouts and warriors, has given me many details concerning the campaign from the Maori side; and the Rev. T. G. Hammond, Wesleyan Missionary to the Taranaki Maoris, has also furnished assistance on the same subject. To Mrs. Kettle, of Napier, daughter of Major von Tempsky, I owe my thanks for permission to reproduce three of the illustrations in this book, copies of water-colour sketches by her celebrated father, representing scenes in the Taranaki campaign of 1865-6. The picture of the fight at Moturoa in 1868 is from a black-and-white sketch by a soldier-artist who took part in the engagement; the original was in the possession of the late Dr. T. M. Hocken, of Dunedin, who allowed me to have it photographed for this book.

J. C.

WELLINGTON, N.Z.,
Feb. 1, 1911.

CONTENTS

CHAPTER V

TE UA, PRIEST AND PROPHET

CHAPTER VI

THE STORMING OF OTAPAWA

CHAPTER VII

BUSH LIFE WITH THE HAUHAUS

CHAPTER VIII

THE HAUHAU COUNCIL-TOWN

CHAPTER IX

A FOREST ADVENTURE

CHAPTER X

THE WAR-CHIEF AND HIS GODS

CHAPTER XI

"THE BEAK-OF-THE-BIRD"

CHAPTER XII

THE ATTACK ON TURUTURU-MOKAI REDOUBT

CHAPTER XIII

THE KILLING OF KANE

CHAPTER XIV

ADVENTURES AT TE NGUTU-O-TE-MANU

CHAPTER XV

A BATTLE IN THE FOREST; AND THE DEATH OF VON TEMPSKY

CHAPTER XVI

THE CANNIBALS OF THE BUSH

CHAPTER XXII

THE FOREST FORAGERS

CHAPTER XXIII

A BATTLE IN THE FOG

CHAPTER XXIV

THE HEAD-HUNTERS

CHAPTER XXV

THE LAND OF REFUGE

CHAPTER XXVI

BUSH LIFE ON THE PATEA

CHAPTER XXVII

HIROKI: THE STORY OF A FUGITIVE

CHAPTER XXVIII

OUT OF EXILE

LIST OF ILLUSTRATIONS

THE ADVENTURES OF KIMBLE BENT

CHAPTER I

THE DESERTER

On the banks of the Tangahoé—The runaway soldier—A Maori
scout—Off to the rebel camp.

ON the banks of one of the many swift rivers that roll down to the Tasman Sea
through the Taranaki Plains a young man in the blue undress uniform of a private
soldier sat smoking his pipe. He was dripping with water, and a little pool had
collected where he crouched in the fern, a few feet from the bank of the stream. He
had plainly just emerged from the river. His clothes were torn, and he was capless.
He was a man of about the middle size, spare of build, with sharp dark eyes and a
bronzed complexion that told of past life under a tropic sun.

Less than an hour previously he had left his comrades' camp, the tented lines
of Her Majesty's 57th Regiment, on the ferny flats of Manawapou. Left unofficially,
and without his arms, strolling down towards the Tangahoé River as if for a bathe.
A "shut-eye" sentry was on duty that morning; and the deserter's tent-mates, too,
were sympathetically blind to his departure. The Tangahoé was the border-line
between the country covered by the British rifles and the unconquerable bush of
the Maori rebels. Towards this rubicon he made his way through the thick, high
fern, which soon concealed him from view. He attempted to ford the rapid, muddy river, but it was up to his waist, and almost swept him off his feet. Struggling
ashore again, he took to the fern and travelled slowly and with great toil through
it, keeping parallel with the course of the Tangahoé, and heading down stream.
He forced his way through the thick fern "like a wild pig," to use his own simile.
In this way he travelled something over a mile down the river, and then once
more attempted to ford across, but it was too deep and swift. He crawled back up
the bank again, and quite exhausted, with scratched hands and face and gaping
half-buttonless clothes, he sat down to recover his breath and strength. His heart
was thumping fearfully with his frantic exertions in the closely matted, entangling
fern, and it was some minutes before he could command his trembling fingers to
fill and light his pipe.

After the soldier had sat and smoked a while he rose, and making his way to a
slight elevation on the banks where he could see over the top of the coarse *rarauhe*

fern, in some places ten feet high, he looked around him. Directly across the river the bush began, the seemingly impenetrable forest solemn and dark, pregnant with danger and mystery. Turning in the other direction, and facing the north-west, he could just discern in the distance the tops of a number of bell-tents — the camp he had left behind him. And as he looked his last on the tents of his comrades and his tyrants, he heard the sweet notes of a bugle sounding a call. The midwinter air was very clear and still. It was the midday mess call — "Come-to-the-cookhouse-door."

"No more cookhouse-door now, that's a moral," said the soldier aloud. "Pork and potatoes for you, me boy — or else a crack on the head with a tomahawk."

Beyond the tents, another tent-shaped object took the soldier's eye. It was a lofty snowy mountain, glittering in the midday sun. It was far away in the nor'-west, so far that its base was hidden by the intervening bush, and only the white symmetrical upper part of the vast cone, a wedge of white culminating in as perfect an apex as any bell-tent, was visible to the eye from this part of the great plains. It was the peak of Taranaki mountain, which the white man calls Mount Egmont.

Satisfying himself that there was no one in sight and that he was not followed, the soldier squatted down again and smoked his pipe meditatively.

Suddenly he started up and listened intently. He heard something, and any noise meant danger. The sound was the trotting of a horse.

Scrambling through the fern a little space back from the bank, he found that a narrow track wound through the tangle of tall brown bracken. Peering out from his shelter place he saw — first, the glitter of the muzzle of a long rifle above the fern; then, next moment round a turn in the path came a mounted man, a Maori. He was a tall, black-bearded fellow, wearing a European shirt and trousers, but bare as to feet. Each stirrup-iron was thrust between the big toe and the next one, as was the universal Maori mode when riding bare-footed. In his right hand he held an Enfield rifle, of the pattern used by the white troops in those days; the butt rested on his thigh, cavalryman fashion. Round his shoulders hung a leather cartouche-box; there was another buckled round his waist, from which there hung also a revolver in its case. A Hauhau scout, evidently, venturing rather daringly close to the British camp.

The white man hesitated only a moment. Then he boldly stepped out on to the track, directly in front of the startled Maori, who pulled his shaggy pony up sharp, and instantly presented his gun at the white man.

Seeing the next moment, however, that the white man was unarmed and alone, the Maori brought his rifle-butt down on his leg again, and stared with wonder at the forlorn-looking white soldier before him.

"Here, you *pakeha*!" he cried, in mixed English and Maori; "go back, quick! *Haere atu, haere atu!* Go 'way back to t'e soldiers. I shoot you suppose you no go! *Hoki atu!*"

"Shoot away!" returned the white man. "I won't go back. I'm running away from the soldiers. I want to go to the Maoris. Take me with you!"

"*You tangata kuwaré!*" the Maori said. "You *pakeha* fool, go back! T'e Maori kill you, my word! You look out."

"I don't care if they do," replied the soldier. "I tell you, I want to live with the Hauhaus."

"*E pai ana!*" ("It is well"), said the scout. "All right, you come along. But you look out for my tribe—they kill you."

"I'm not frightened of your tribe," said the soldier.

"What your name, *pakeha*?" was the next question.

"Kimble Bent," answered the *pakeha*.

The Maori attempted the pronunciation of the name, but the nearest he could get to it was "Kimara Peneti."

"Too hard a name for t'e Maori," he said. "*Taihoa*; we give you more better name—good Maori name. If"—he qualified it—"my tribe don't kill you."

Then the swarthy warrior dismounted and ordered the *pakeha* to get into the saddle; he saw that his prisoner was dead-tired. He turned the horse's head back towards the Maori country, and the strangely-met pair struck down along the banks of the Tangahoé, the Maori striding in front.

For about three miles the track wound down through the fern and flax, parallel with the course of the river. Then the travellers came to a ford. They crossed safely, and clambering up the steep muddy bank on the other side, they marched on towards the blue hills of the rebel country.

CHAPTER II

KIMBLE BENT, SAILOR AND SOLDIER

Kimble Bent's early life—An Indian mother—Service in the American Navy—Departure for England—"Taking the Shilling"—British Army life—The flight to America—A sinking ship—Rescue, and landing in Glasgow—Back to the Army again—Soldiering in India—The 57th ordered to New Zealand—The Taranaki Campaign—A court-martial—At the triangles.

WHILE the runaway soldier is riding on to the camp of the brown warriors of the bush—a journey which is to be the beginning of a wild and savage life leading him for many a day, like Thoreau's Indian fighter, on dim forest trails "with an uneasy scalp"—there is time to learn something of his previous history and adventures.

Perhaps the impulse that led to his passionate revolt against civilisation and rigid army discipline came from his American Indian blood.

Kimble Bent's mother was a half-caste Red Indian girl, of the Musqua tribe, whose villages stood on the banks of the St. Croix River, State of Maine, U.S.A. Her English name before marriage was Eliza Senter. She became the wife of a ship-builder in the town of Eastport, Maine; his name was Waterman Bent; he worked at first for Caleb Houston, shipbuilder, but afterwards had a yard of his own. This couple had seven children, two sons and five daughters; one of these sons was Kimble Bent. He was born in Eastport on August 24, 1837.

The roving wayward element in young Kimble Bent's blood soon made itself manifest. When he was about seventeen, he ran away from home and went to sea. He shipped on a United States man-of-war, the training frigate *Martin*, and spent three years aboard her, cruising along the Atlantic Coast. He quickly became a smart young sailor and gunner, and from the rank of seaman he graduated to deckman, a sort of quartermaster. It was part of his duty during the last year of his service to instruct the boys who came aboard as recruits in the working of the muzzle-loading 6-pounder and 8-pounder guns.

Paid off from his frigate at the end of his three years, Bent returned to his people as unexpectedly as he had left them. But he didn't stay in Eastport long. The prosaic life of the old town was no more to his liking than when first he had run away to follow a sailor's life; so he soon took to the seas again. He gathered together what money he could—a considerable sum, he says, for his father was indulgent—and took ship across the Atlantic, in his head some such unexpressed sentiment as Robert Louis Stevenson long afterwards put into verse in his "Songs of Travel":

> "The untented Kosmos my abode
> I go, a wilful stranger,
> My mistress still the open road
> And the bright eyes of Danger."

But no man-of-war life for him. He booked his passage in a barque sailing for Liverpool, resolved to see something of life in the Old World.

When he landed in the big city he "made himself flash," to use his own expression, and went the pace with a few like-minded young fellows, and one way and another his stock of cash soon vanished, and he found himself stranded, friendless, and alone—his companions of the "flush" times had no more use for him. One day, as he wandered disconsolate along the streets, his eye was taken by the scarlet tunic and lively bearing of a smart recruiting-sergeant, and on the impulse of the moment he took the Queen's shilling and was enlisted in Her Majesty's 57th Regiment of Foot. This was in the year 1859.

The young Eastport sailor soon bitterly regretted the day that his eye was dazzled by the Queen's scarlet. The British Army was less to his taste than life in Uncle Sam's Navy. He was sent to Cork with a draft of two hundred other recruits, and the interminable drill soon gave him an intense disgust for the routine of barrack-yard instruction. Four months of recruit-drill—then one day Private Bent took a stroll down the Cork wharves and cast his eyes round for a likely craft in which to give the army, drill-sergeants, and all the slip.

A Boston barque, the *Maria*, happened to be lying at one of the tees, and her skipper, one Captain Cann, Bent, to his joy, found to be an old acquaintance. He unfolded his dejected tale, and the sailor at once offered his assistance in rescuing a fellow-countryman from John Bull's grip. That evening Bent stole away quietly from the barracks, boarded the barque, and was stowed away safely below in the dunnage-hole. He did not show his nose above hatches for two days; the barque by that time had left the harbour on her return voyage to Boston, and the deserter was able to appear on deck, a free man.

But not for long. Bent's misfortunes were only beginning. When about three hundred miles off the land a furious easterly gale began to blow, and the old barkey sprang a leak. Hove-to in the storm, all the crew could do was to stand to the pumps. The huge Atlantic seas came thundering on deck, and more than once washed the men away from the pumps. For six days and six nights they wallowed in the deep, all hands, sailors and passengers, taking turns at the pumps, working for their lives.

All those terrible days of storm and fear the *Maria's* hands had nothing to eat but hard biscuits soaked with salt water. There was no place to cook and no means of cooking, for the galley with all its contents had been washed overboard. While the crew laboured at the pumps, the captain tried to cheer them up and put a little life into their weary bodies and despairing hearts by playing lively airs on his concertina and singing sailors' chanteys.

"One day," says Bent, "a German brig hove in sight and spoke us. Seeing our signal of distress she asked the name of our barque and the number of the crew. We signalled our reply, and she answered that she could not help us, there was too much sea. Then she squared away and left us. All this time we were labouring at the pumps to keep the old barque afloat. Next day another brig, a Boston vessel deep-loaded, from the West Indies, hailed us and stood by, signalling to us to launch our boats. This we did, after hard and dangerous work, and managed to reach the brig's side, where all the sixteen of us were hauled on board safely. About two hours after we left our ship we saw her go down."

To Bent's intense disappointment he found that the brig that had rescued him was bound for the wrong side of the Atlantic. She landed the shipwrecked mariners at Glasgow. Bent was walking about the streets one day, wondering however he was going to get a passage home, for he had no money, when he was arrested as a deserter—recognised by the description which had been posted in every barrack-room and every police-station. He was taken to the military barracks, and then sent under guard to Ireland and down to Cork, where he was tried by court-martial, and sentenced to eighty-four days in prison. When he had served his term he was shipped off to India with his regiment, landing at Bombay, and for some time did garrison duty at Poona.

The 57th spent two years in India, only just recovering from the terrible throes of the Mutiny. Then news came of a serious war with a wild native race in a distant country called New Zealand, far away down in the Southern Ocean, and the regiment was ordered to hold itself in readiness to go route-marching to Bombay, thence to sea. Marching orders soon followed, and the headquarters of the regiment sailed for Auckland; the company in which Bent was a private (No. 8 Company) was one of those left behind to look after the women and children of the regiment. Orders for them also quickly came, and they took the road for Bombay.

The journey from Poona to Bombay took four days, or rather nights, for all the marching was done by night. Part of the way was through a dense jungle in which man-eating tigers swarmed. The troops marched through this jungle by torchlight, winding along a narrow track through the densely-matted vegetation. The growling of the tigers was heard all round at night, but the blazing torches kept them away.

Embarked in a troopship at Bombay, Bent and his fellow-soldiers sailed not unwillingly for a land spoken of by report as a country which, though wild and new, was a pleasanter place to live in than scorching sun-baked India.

After a voyage of eighty-nine days, the troopship anchored in Auckland Harbour, and her soldiers spent their first week on New Zealand soil in the old Albert Barracks, where the bright flower-gardens and tree-groves of a beautiful park now crown the hill that in those troubled days was girt with a massive crenellated wall, and was alive with all the martial turmoil of campaigning-time. Then the new arrivals were sent down to Taranaki by sea to join the headquarters of the 57th, and went into new barrack life on Marsland Hill, New Plymouth.

Kimble Bent's longing for a free independent life became stronger than ever in this new country. He would gladly have exchanged camp-life for even the perilous occupation of a frontier settler, so that he were free. The parade ground was a purgatory, and the restraint of discipline and the ramrod-and-pipeclay system of soldiering were irksome beyond words. He was sick to death of being ordered about by sergeants and corporals. Fighting would have been a relief, but there was none yet. He endeavoured to get his discharge from the regiment, but without success; and his impatience of discipline led him into various more or less serious conflicts with the regimental authorities.

So opened Kimble Bent's life in the new land, the land in which he was to roam the forests an outlaw for more than a decade.

In those war-days of 1860-70 dense forests covered the wide plains of this Taranaki province, where now most of the dark old woods have been hewn away, and have given place to the pastures and homesteads of dairy farmers. It was a wild but beautiful land. The coast curved out and round in a great sweeping semicircle from Waitara in the north to Wanganui in the south; the intervening region of forest, hill, and plain was the theatre of war. High and central, Taranaki's great mountain-cone, which the *pakeha* calls Egmont, swelled to a height of over 8,000 feet, its base hidden in the forests, its snowy peak glittering far above the broad soft swathes of clouds, the sailor's landmark a hundred miles out at sea. Remote from all other high mountains it soared aloft—"lonely as God and white as a winter morn," as Joaquin Miller wrote of his beloved Mount Shasta. On all sides Taranaki—the holy mountain of the Maoris—sloped evenly and gently to the plains, and from its recesses sprang the head waters of many a beautiful river. The mountain, huge yet exquisitely symmetrical, was revered by the old-school Taranaki Maori as the mighty symbol of his nationality, and regarded as being in some mystic fashion the source of his tribal *mana*. Under the shadow of Taranaki began the Ten Years' War; here the Hauhau fanaticism took its mad rise in 1864. From Taranaki's foot set out the Hauhau apostles, preaching a strange jumble of Scriptural expressions and pagan Maori concepts, promising their converts that no *pakeha* bullet should harm them if they but repeated their magic incantations; and brandishing before the ranks of their devotees the dried and smoked heads of slain white soldiers. The relapse into barbarism was more marked in Taranaki than anywhere else, and even to this day the hatred of the white man lingers there, amongst the remnants of the old Hauhau stock. Te Whiti, the Prophet of Parihaka, until his death in 1907, held his court under the shadow of lofty Taranaki, and preached his old mysticism fortified by the towering presence of his mountain-god, cold and immutable, and all unmindful of the *pakeha's* march through the plains below.

MOUNT EGMONT, TARANAKI.

In March, 1864, the 57th were ordered from New Plymouth to Manawapou (not far from the present town of Hawera), near the Tangahoé River. The fanatic Hauhau faith had just been born amongst the Maoris, whose palisaded *pas* dotted the outskirts of the great forests on the farther side of the Tangahoé, and whose war-songs could sometimes be heard from the white soldiers' camp. At Manawapou the regiment went under canvas, and now began the regular round of sentry-go and outpost duty, and all the preparations for an advance on the rebel positions.

A TARANAKI FRONTIER FORT.

(*Sketch by Mr. S. Percy Smith, 1865.*)

Meantime there was fighting in the northern and western parts of the Taranaki province, between the 57th camp and New Plymouth. There was the disastrous affair at Te Ahuahu, where Captain Lloyd and several soldiers were killed; their heads were cut off and smoke-dried by the Hauhau savages, and were carried away to distant tribes by Kereopa, Patara, and other rebel emissaries, the Hauhau recruiting officers. Another momentous affair which happened soon after the 57th took post at Manawapou was the desperate assault on the British redoubt at Sentry Hill (Te Morere). A large force of Hauhau warriors, deluded by their prophet Hepanaia into believing that his incantations rendered them invulnerable to the white man's bullets, rushed against the redoubt in open daylight one morning, but were beaten off, leaving some fifty of their number lying dead in front of the fort. It was in this engagement that Titokowaru—who was afterwards Kimble Bent's chief and master—lost one of his eyes through a bullet wound.

Kimble Bent's final revolt against constituted authority came one wet, cold day in the Manawapou camp in April 1864. It was pouring with rain, but a corporal, one who took a vindictive sort of pleasure in asserting his authority over those privates whom he happened to dislike, ordered Bent to go out and cut some firewood in the bush. Irritated by the manner in which the order was given, the young "Down-Easter" was foolish enough to argue with his enemy the corporal.

"Look here," he said, "this is no day to send a man out cutting wood. The officers can stay in their tents laughing at us fellows out in the rain. We're treated like a set of blessed dogs."

"Oh, you won't go, won't you?" sneered the corporal, rejoicing at having irritated the soldier into insubordination.

"No, I won't go," said Bent defiantly; "so you can do what you like about it."

The corporal reported Bent to his immediate superiors, and the soldier was arrested and lodged in the guard-tent. Next morning he was brought before a court-martial and tried for disobedience of orders. Major Haszard was the president of the court. With him sat Captain Clark, Lieutenant Brown, and Ensign Parker. Bent knew it was useless to attempt a defence, for his offence was an inexcusable breach of discipline. He was found guilty, and the sentence of the court was that he should receive fifty lashes, and serve two years in gaol.

The triangles were then a familiar institution in every military camp in the Waikato and in Taranaki; for those were flogging days, when even slight breaches of military rules brought down the lash upon the soldier's back.

One of the regimental surgeons, Dr. Andrews, examined Bent, as was the practice before flogging was inflicted, and he reported that in his opinion the young soldier was not constitutionally fit to endure the fifty lashes ordered.

Soon after Bent had been taken to his tent under guard, one of the officers of the court-martial came in to see him. This was Captain Clark, a fine jovial young Canadian-born soldier, who had rather a liking for the unfortunate man from his end of the world.

"Cheer up, Bent," he said; "you'll only get twenty-five—the sentence is reduced. And put that in your mouth when you go to the triangles," and he threw down a sixpence. Then, when the guard-tent corporal was not looking, the kindly officer took a flask of rum from his breast-pocket, laid it on the tent floor, and walked away to his quarters.

When Bent was called out for punishment, he quickly drank off the rum, and put the sixpence in his mouth. He knew the old soldier's recipe for a "stiff upper lip" in the agony of flogging—"bite on the bullet." The sixpence would serve him as well. It would keep his teeth from biting through his tongue in the throes of that horrible punishment.

A bugle sounded the "Fall in." No. 8 Company was paraded in review order on the drill ground to "witness punishment." Bent was marched down to the square; he was stripped to the waist and tied to the triangles. The big drummer of the Company stepped to the front; he was the flagellant. Bent bit on his substitute for a bullet as the cat swished through the air and fell like a red-hot knife on his quivering back. Again and again came the frightful cuts, criss-cross upon his back and shoulders, till the tale of twenty-five was complete. Then the prisoner was cast loose, swearing in his pain and passion to have the drummer's life. A blanket was thrown across his raw and bleeding shoulders, and he was marched back to the guard-tent, where the surgeon prescribed for him in rough-and-ready fashion; then to prison—he refused to go into the camp hospital.

Bent served some months in Wellington Prison, doing cook-house work, in expiation of his offence against military discipline. Then he was sent back to his hated regiment. The shame of that morning at the triangles, with his comrades paraded to witness his disgrace and agony, was burned into him for ever. He grew morose and desperate. At last he resolved to desert to the enemy. He confided his resolve to his tent-mates, and they, knowing that other soldiers had deserted to the Maoris and had not been killed, did not attempt to dissuade him. "I can't be worse off with the Maoris than I am here," he told them; "if they do tomahawk me, it will end all my troubles. I don't very much care."

So he bided his time for a favourable opportunity to steal from the camp; and soon his chance came. It was on June 12, 1865, that he broke camp and fell in with the Hauhau scout on the banks of the Tangahoé.

CHAPTER III

THE CAMP OF THE HAUHAUS

In the Maori country — Arrival at a Hauhau *Pa* — Maori village scenes —
The ceremonies round the sacred flagstaff — "*Riré, riré, hau!*" — The
man with the tomahawk — A white slave — The painted warriors
of Keteonetea — The blazing oven.

THE saturnine Hauhau spoke little to the white man during that journey to
the rebel camp. He stalked silently on in front, his rifle over his shoulder, turning
quickly now and again to assure himself that the soldier was still following him.
Presently they forded another stream, which Bent afterwards came to know as
the Ingahape, and passed through a deserted settlement, with its tumble-down
dwellings of *raupo* reeds, and its old potato-gardens. A few minutes later they
came in sight of their destination, the Ohangai *pa*. A high stockade of tree-trunks
sunk in the ground, some of the upper ends hewn into sharp points, others with
round knobby tops that suggested impaled human heads, surrounded a populous
village of thatched huts. Just beyond it was the bush, stretching away as far as the
eye could carry. It was a secluded, pretty scene, that village with its neat enclosure,
its rows of snug *wharés* which could be seen through the gateway and the openings
in the palisade, and its squares of maize and potato cultivations, sheltered by the
friendly belt of dark green forest.

Some little, nearly naked children were playing about on the open space in
front of the palisades. When they suddenly beheld a white man riding along towards them, with a Maori walking by his stirrup, they stared wide-eyed and open-
mouthed, and then rushed helter-skelter into the *pa*, calling out at the top of their
voices, "*He pakeha, he pakeha!*"

What a commotion that cry of "*Pakeha*" aroused in the slumbering *pa*! Men
leaped from the flax *whariki* (mats), where they had been drowsing away the afternoon awaiting the opening of the steam ovens, and poured out of the narrow
gateway armed with their guns and tomahawks. When they saw that the European was a harmless, unarmed individual, and that he was apparently the prisoner
of one of their own people, the clamour died away, and they escorted the soldier
and his captor into the *pa*. Bent quickly perceived that his companion was a man
of some importance, from the peremptory orders he issued and the alacrity with
which they were obeyed. The scout was, in fact, the chief Tito te Hanataua, a *rangatira* of high standing in the Ngati-Ruanui tribe, and one of the Hauhaus' best
fighting-leaders.

It was a wild scene that met the young soldier's gaze when he entered the stockade, and his heart sank before the savagely hostile gaze of a crowd of armed, half-stripped warriors, the black-bearded and shaggy-headed men of the bush, and their scarcely less savage-looking women.

A strange ceremony began.

In the centre of the village square or *marae* stood a rough-hewn pole or flag-staff, about fifteen feet high, on which flew one or two coloured flags. This was the *Niu*, the sacred staff which the Hauhau prophet Te Ua had commanded his followers to erect as a pole of worship in each of their villages. [The *Niu* was in more ancient times the name of a peculiar ceremony of divination often resorted to by the *tohungas* or priests; it is perhaps worth noting, too, that in the Islands of Polynesia, the traditional Maori Hawaiki, it is the general name for the coco-nut-tree.] All the inhabitants of the village—men, women, and children—formed up, and began to march round and round the *Niu*, with a priest in their midst, rushing frantically to and fro, and brandishing a Maori weapon as he yelled a ferocious-sounding chant. The people, too, lifted up their voices as they marched, and, after listening a while, Bent found to his astonishment that part of what they were chanting in a singular wild cadence were these words in "pidgin" English: "Big river, long river, big mountain, long mountain, bush, big bush, long bush," and so on, ending with a loudly chanted cry, "*Riré, riré, hau!*" This meaningless gibberish formed part of the incantations solemnly taught to the Hauhaus by Te Ua, who professed to have the "gift of tongues" of which the *pakeha's* New Testament spoke; his disciples fondly believed that they were endowed by their prophet's "angel" with wonderful linguistic powers.

The singular march suddenly ceased, at an order from the shawl-kilted *tohunga* in the centre, and then the people filed into the village meeting-house, a large *raupo*-reed-built structure, taking Bent with them. He was motioned to a seat beside a Maori, whose name, he afterwards found, was Hori Kerei (George Grey), and who could speak English fairly well.

Sitting opposite Bent was a white-bearded old fighting-man, a dour-faced savage, his brown face deeply scored with the marks of blue-black tattoo; his sole attire was a blanket; in his right hand, and partly concealed by the blanket, he held a tomahawk. His hand twitched now and then, as if he were about to flash out the tomahawk and use it on the *pakeha*, from whose face he never withdrew his fierce old eyes. He was the chief, Te Rangi-tutaki.

A long talk began. Hori Kerei interpreted. The Maoris asked Bent why he had come to them, why had he run away from his own people. The deserter frankly told them that he was tired of being a soldier, that he had been ill-treated and imprisoned, and that he came to them for protection.

"*Pakeha*," said Kerei, "they want to know if you will ever leave the Maori and go back to the soldiers."

"No," said Bent; "tell them I'll never run away from the Hauhaus. I want to live with them always; I don't ever want to see a white man again!"

"Kapai!" said Grey good-humouredly. "That the talk! All right, I tell them true."

When Kerei had interpreted the white man's reply, the old man with the tomahawk leaned over and said, very earnestly, tapping the blade of the weapon with his left hand as he spoke:

"Whakarongo mai! Listen, *pakeha!* You see this *patiti* in my hand? Yes. If you had not at once replied that you would never return to the white soldiers I would have killed you. I would have sunk this into your skull!"

After this brief speech, delivered with a fierceness of mien and glitter of eye that made the refugee tremble in spite of his efforts to appear calm, the old barbarian shook hands with him.

Then Tito te Hanataua—the man who had brought the soldier to the *pa*—rose and said:

"O my tribe, listen to me! Take good care of the *pakeha*, and harm him not, because our prophet has told us that if any white men come to us as this man has done, and leave their own tribe for ours, we must not injure them, but must keep them with us and protect them."

Tito's word assured Bent's safety, and the tone of the people changed to one of friendliness; many of them shook hands with the lonely white man. The women cooked some pork and potatoes for him in an earth-oven, and he was given to eat, and received into the tribe. Henceforth he was as a Maori.

Now began for the runaway an even harder life than that which he had endured in the army. He found that he was virtually a slave amongst the Maoris. He had had fond imaginings of the easy time he would enjoy in the heart of Maoridom, but to quote from his own lips, "they made me work like a blessed dog." Soon after his arrival in the *pa* a party of men was sent off to Taiporohenui—a celebrated old village and meeting-place near the present town of Hawera—and he was ordered to go with them, and was set to work felling bush, clearing and digging, gathering firewood, and hauling water for the camp. Tito was his master—not only his master, but in hard fact his owner, with power of life and death over him. Bent divined the Maori nature too well to refuse "fatigue duty," as he had done in the Manawapou camp. There would have been no court-martial in Taiporohenui—just a crack on the head with a tomahawk. So he bent his back to the burdens with what cheerfulness he might, and was thankful for the good things Tito provided, though they took no more elaborate form than a blanket and a flax mat for a bed, and two square meals a day of pork and potatoes.

Tito was, says Bent, a man of about forty-five years of age, a stern, but not unkindly owner, with a pretty young wife of seventeen or eighteen, whose big, dark eyes were often turned with an expression of pity on the unfortunate renegade *pakeha*.

The people watched the white man closely, thinking no doubt that as he was being worked so hard he might be tempted to run away if he got the chance. And whenever he went out of doors the old man who had sat opposite him in the meeting-house on the day of his first arrival followed him about, never speaking a word, with his tomahawk in his hand.

The news that a white soldier had run away to the Hauhaus soon spread amongst the Ngati-Ruanui. One day a messenger from the large village of Keteonetea came to Taiporohenui and announced that he had been sent to fetch the strange *pakeha* to that settlement.

"What do they want with me?" asked Bent, when Tito told him that the envoy was waiting for him.

"They want to see the colour of your skin," replied Tito.

Bent, in alarm, begged Tito not to send him to Keteonetea, for he greatly feared that he would be killed.

Tito reassured his white man, telling him that the Keteonetea people were his relatives, and that he was not to be alarmed at their demeanour, because they would not harm him.

The messenger and his white charge tramped away through the bush to the village, a lonely little spot hemmed in by the dense forests—long since hewn away and replaced by grassy fields and dairy farms. A palisade surrounded the *kainga*; within were clusters of large well-built reed *wharés*, and the inevitable *Niu* pole stood in the middle of the *marae*.

Bent found a large number of Maoris, about three hundred, assembled on the *marae*, the village parade ground. The scene still lives vividly in his memory—an even wilder, more savage spectacle than that of his first day at Tito's *pa*. The men's faces were painted red, in token of war—red smudges of ochre on their cheeks and red lines drawn across their brows; they wore feathers in their hair, their only clothes were flax mats. The lone *pakeha* might well have imagined himself back in the days of ancient Maoridom, before missionaries or traders had changed the barbaric simplicity of the aboriginal life. The only modern note was the firearms of the warriors; all the men carried guns (most of them double-barrelled shot-guns, and a few rifles and carbines), and wore tomahawks stuck in their broad-plaited flax belts. Most of the women were as primitive in their garb as the men; their clothing consisted chiefly of flaxen cloaks; a few wore shawls and blankets.

"The people looked at me very fiercely as I came into the *marae*," says Bent, "and I felt my heart sinking low, in spite of Tito's assurance." They put him into a *raupo* hut by himself, and fastened the door—a proceeding that did not at all tend to elevate his spirits.

The ex-soldier was left to himself in the dark *wharé* for quite a couple of hours. He could hear the people gathered on the village square discussing him excitedly; one orator after another declaiming with frantic energy. At length a Maori unfastened the door of the *wharé*, and, taking Bent by the hand, led him out on to the *marae*. The native could speak English; Bent afterwards found that he had been an old whaler, and had lived amongst white people for many years; his name was Kere (Kelly). He told the *pakeha*, with some show of kindness, that he must not be frightened, that no one would harm him, but he must go to the sacred *Niu* and promise that he would never return to the *pakehas*.

The first thing that met Bent's eyes on stepping out through the low doorway of the *whare* was a great fire blazing in the centre of the *marae*, surrounded by a ring of short stakes. Accustomed as he was by this time to sights of terror, this struck a fresh note of alarm.

"Good Lord!" he said to himself, "are they going to burn me alive?"

"Friend," he said to Kere, "tell me, what's that fire for?"

The Maori explained that it was an *ahi tapu*, a sacred fire, used in the Hauhau war-rites.

Bent was very doubtful. "I'm afraid," said he to his companion, "that it's for me! Are they going to throw me into it? I've heard they do such things."

"No, no, *pakeha*! It's all right. You'll be safe. But remember, do as the *tohunga* tells you, and promise him you'll never go back to the *pakeha* soldiers, or you'll die!"

The Maori led the white man up to the foot of the *Niu* pole, a tall ricker, with rough crosstrees and with flag halliards of flax rope. Bent was told to sit down at the foot of the pole. The people all gathered around in a ring.

A tall old warrior stood in the middle of the ring, facing Bent—the prophet of the *Niu*. He was naked from the waist up; his face was completely covered with tattooing. He was a *tohunga*, or priest, Bent afterwards discovered; by name Tu-ahi-pa, or Tautahi-ariki, a man held in much awe by the people as a worker of *makutu* (witchcraft).

For a long time the old wizard closely eyed the pale-faced stranger before him. Then he said, through the interpreter, Kere:

"You behold this ring of people, the people of Keteonetea?"

"Yes," said Bent.

"I ask you this, will you return to your people or remain with us?"

"I will never return to the *pakehas*," Bent replied; "I want to live with the Maoris and to make them my people."

"Good!" exclaimed the Hauhau priest. "Now, turn your eyes upon yon fire, burning there upon the *marae*. Well, if you had not promised to become a Maori and live with us, the tribe would have thrown you into that blazing oven. It is well that you have spoken as you have."

This, to Bent's great relief, ended the ordeal. The Hauhaus, at a cry from the priest, began their mad march round the *Niu*—men, women, and children—chanting as they went their savage psalms, rolling their eyes and lifting their arms high in the air as every now and again they cried their wild refrain, *"Riré, riré, hau!"*— the last word literally barked out from the hundreds of throats.

When the Hauhau ceremony was at an end, a young woman who had joined in the march round the *Niu* came to Bent, took him away to a hut and gave him a meal of pork and potatoes, and then led him to her father's house. The father was the principal chief of the *kainga*, and, as it turned out, cousin to Bent's *rangatira* Tito.

Here the white man spent the night, the chief's daughter lying across the entrance just inside the doorway, for fear—as the chief told him—that some young desperado might take it into his head to earn a little notoriety by tomahawking the pale-face. Outside, the Maoris were gathered on the *marae*, by the light of great fires, the chiefs making speeches and *taki*-ing up and down in excited fashion, weapon in hand; now and again the fanatic crowd would burst into a loud Hauhau chant that echoed long amidst the black encircling forest. So the wild *korero* went on, far into the night.

CHAPTER IV

IN THE OTAPAWA STOCKADE

The return from Keteonetea—The hill-fort at Otapawa—A *korero* with
the Hauhaus—Bent's one-eyed wife—"The wooing o' 't"—Bent is
christened "Ringiringi."

Morning came at last, but the solitary white man in this nest of savages had
hardly closed his eyes. More than once he fancied some one was trying the low
door of the *wharé*, and he looked round the dimly-lighted hut—a small fire was
kept burning in the centre of the floor—in search of a weapon, but found none.
Bent lay there, listening intently, and longing with an inexpressibly bitter longing
for the old camp-life, hard though it was, and for the sound of a white comrade's
voice. It had not always been "pack-drill and C.B." in his army life, in spite of the
tyrant sergeants. But now it was the bush and the *wharé* for the rest of his days—or,
in other words, for just so long a period as he might be able to save his head from
the tomahawk.

Daybreak—and no sooner was it light than the Hauhaus began to gather round the *pakeha's* hut, while the women were lighting the *hangis*—the earth
steam-ovens—for the first meal of the day. "Come out to us!" they yelled; "come
out, *pakeha*!" They ran to and fro in front of the *wharé*, and raised barking cries that
sounded fearfully menacing to the *pakeha* sitting on his low mat-bed, and feeling
not in the least disposed to respond to the invitation to come outside and be killed.

But the old chief speedily ended the uproar by opening the sliding door and
shouting angrily:

"*Haere atu! Haere atu!*" an imperative phrase that the deserter had already
learned to recognise as one that could be exactly translated "Clear out!"

Thereafter there was comparative peace. The white man was under the protection of the chief, and was allowed to wander round the village pretty much as
he chose; but he was warned not to go far, or some warrior might take a fancy to
his head.

Four or five days passed without incident, and then a horse was brought up
for Bent, and he returned to Tito's *kainga*, escorted by the chief's daughter and ten
armed men, all mounted. Tito seemed relieved to have his *pakeha* back again in
safety, and after feasting the Maori guard on the best the village women could lay
on the dinner-mats, he sent them back to Keteonetea loaded with new clothes and
baskets of *kumara* (sweet potato) and *taro*—another tropic root-food brought from

Polynesia by the ancestors of the Maori, but now no longer grown by the Taranaki people.

Soon Bent was on the tramp again. His chief, Tito, set off one morning, taking his white man with him, for a fortified village called Otapawa, where the Hauhaus were preparing to offer a strong resistance to the British troops. Otapawa was about four miles away by a narrow and winding forest track. A small river, the Mangemange, had to be forded on the way, and here Bent had a taste of some of the minor adventures of the bush. Bent being a rather small man and Tito a big, powerful fellow, the Maori good-naturedly took his *pakeha* on his back to *pikau* him across the stream. Bent was rather heavier than Tito had imagined, and after balancing to and fro precariously on a slippery place in the deepest part of the ford, the Maori's feet suddenly went from under him, and he and his protégé were capsized in the middle of the creek. Tito, however, kept a tight grip of the white man, and, though the stream was running swiftly, they managed to struggle out to the opposite bank in safety, and after drying their clothes as well as they could continued their bush journey.

About midday the Hauhau chief and his companion emerged from the solitudes of the forest to find themselves in the Otapawa clearing. A hill about three hundred feet high rose like an island from the great *rimu* and *rata* woods that compassed it on every side; at the back ran the Tangahoé River. At the foot of the hill there was some cultivation; a steep winding path led to the top; here were a ditch and a bristling double stockade of tall tree-trunks set solidly in the ground, connected by cross-rails lashed with forest vines; within was the Hauhau village. The only access to the interior of the stockade was through a low and narrow gateway, painted red.

A shawl-clad figure with a gun rose from a squatting position just outside the *pa* gate as the two travellers walked out from the shade of the forest and began the ascent of the mound. A loud cry of astonishment and warning brought out the villagers, one after the other, bobbing their heads as they ran through the gateway. Then the shout was raised, as they recognised Bent's companion:

"*Aue!* Here comes Tito with a *pakeha*! A *pakeha*!"

Waving shawls and blankets and weapons, the people cried their greetings to the chief, and the white man and his protector walked in between two lines of wondering men and women and children, who pressed in close behind the new-comers as they passed into the palisaded *pa*.

A long, low-eaved, thatched house stood near the middle of the *pa*, somewhat apart from the smaller *wharés*. Into this building Tito and Bent were taken, and finely woven flax mats, patterned in black and white, were spread out for them. Tito rose and addressed the crowd. He explained, with a good deal of pride, as Bent imagined, how he had become possessed of a live white man—a somewhat unusual acquisition amongst the Maoris in that unrestful period, for the impatient Hauhau was, as a rule, too fond of trying his new tomahawk on a *pakeha* skull to keep a prisoner long. The *korero* over, food was brought in in freshly plaited baskets of green flax—boiled pork, dried shark (a present from a seaside tribe), boiled *taro* and *kumara*—quite a bountiful meal for a war-time bush camp.

Up to this time the deserter's adventures had been, if not exactly tragic, at least of a severely unpleasant turn. Now, however, they took a humorous twist—humorous from an onlooker's view, though to the white man himself it seemed rather the final pannikinful in the bucket of his misfortunes.

A woman was brought into the *whare*. She walked over and seated herself on the flax *whariki* by Bent's side.

The white man turned and looked at her in some surprise. Her vision still haunts the memory of the old adventurer as that of a particularly ugly woman. She was not old, probably not above twenty-five, but she was blind in one eye, her lips were of negroid thickness—such "blubber" lips as seen here and there among Maori tribes tell their tale of an ancient Melanesian strain in the blood of the Polynesian immigrants. She was tattooed on the chin, and there was a deeply chiselled blue line on the inner cuticle of her lower lip. Her hair hung round her face in a tangled mop. "Well," said Bent to himself, "she is no beauty."

The woman spoke some words of greeting to Bent, but he steadily gazed on the floor and said nothing.

Then a Maori sitting near by, who could speak a little English, said, "This woman wants to marry you!"

"Oh, Lord!" exclaimed Bent. "What for? I don't want to get married."

An old man, whose name was Peneta, and who was draped from shoulder to ankles in a red blanket, walked up to the white man and, halting in front of him, pointed to the one-eyed woman.

"*Pakeha*," he said, with a quiet grimness in his tone, "this is my niece, Te Rawanga. You must marry her (*me moe korua*). If you refuse, you will die! That is all."

This was translated to Bent.

Here was a dilemma, indeed! Bent had nothing to say. He looked at the woman by his side, and she smiled at him as coquettishly as her one good eye allowed. He looked, and the more he looked the less he liked her. Then he glanced at the dour old uncle, and cast his helpless eyes around the crowded meeting-house. The men were glum and scowling; one or two of the young girls seemed to perceive the humour of the situation, for they giggled, and then hid their faces in their shawls.

Bent eyed his prospective uncle-in-law again. The old man was impatient. He said again, "Take my niece as your wife."

"*Ae*," assented the white man, who could see no hope of escape. "I'll take her."

So the young soldier was mated, to the satisfaction of every one but himself. "She wasn't my fancy, to put it mildly," he says. "But I suppose it was her last chance, and the old man would have tomahawked me if I hadn't taken her."

Mrs. Bent's wedding-furnishings, which she bundled a little later, with determined air, into the corner of the communal house assigned to the white man, were spartan and primitive in the extreme.

They consisted solely of a large plaited *whariki* (sleeping-mat) and a wooden pillow, which, to the white man, seemed alarmingly like some weapon of chastisement.

Matrimony amongst the Hauhaus was simplicity itself.

Bent, now fully received into the tribe, had a Maori name given to him. It was "Ringiringi," a name he bore for two or three years, until the war-chief Titokowaru rechristened him "Tu-nui-a-moa."

The origin of this name "Ringiringi" may be explained, as an example of the way in which the Maoris so frequently acquire new names often from very trivial incidents. It was a contraction of "Te Wai-ringiringi," which was one of Tito te Hanataua's nicknames, bestowed upon the chief about two years previously. A party of Ngati-Maniapoto Maoris from the King Country were at that time on a visit to Taiporohenui, where a large war-council of the rebel tribes was held. Tito te Hanataua was one of the Taranaki orators, and as he *taki*'d up and down, spear in hand, in the usual energetic manner of the Maori speech-maker, he spoke so rapidly and fluently that the Kingites dubbed him "Te Wai-ringiringi," meaning "The Pouring Water," because his words poured from his lips like water. Tito was rather proud of this nickname, and his bestowal of it upon Bent was in a sense a mark of favour.

Bent at this time was a thin, rather weak-looking man, and his slimness was made the subject of a *haka* chorus amongst the people, a little song for which his one-eyed wife was responsible. These were the words:

> *"Ki te kai, e Ringi,*
> *Kai poroporo te manawa,*
> *Te iti to hopé,*
> *Whakapai Angoré,"*

("Eat away, O Ringi,
Eat your fill of poroporo berries
To make you strong again;
Lest your waist be small and weak,
Eat to become a fine Englishman!")

The *poroporo* is a forest shrub which bears an abundance of large red berries, a favourite food of the *tui* and pigeons, which become very fat on this rich bird-fare.

The white man, however, as he told his *wahiné*, preferred to leave the *poroporo* to the *tuis*, and to fill out his attenuated waist, which the people looked upon with some amusement, with good Maori pork and potatoes.

CHAPTER V

TE UA, PRIEST AND PROPHET

Te Ua and his gods—The *Pai mariré* faith—"Charming" the British bullets—Bent's interview with the prophet—His life *tapu'd*—Preparing for battle—Life in the forest *pa*.

ABOUT this time Kimble Bent became acquainted with a man whose name has passed into New Zealand history. This was Te Ua Haumene, the founder and high-priest and prophet of the Hauhau religion, or, more correctly speaking, fanaticism. Te Ua came riding into the Otapawa village one day with a bodyguard of armed men. Bent describes him as a stoutly built man of between forty and fifty, attired in European clothing, and carrying a carved *taiaha*—a chief's halbert or broadsword of hardwood, flattened at one end in a blunt blade, and sharpened at the other into a tongue-shaped point, and decorated with tufts of red *kaka* feathers; in a plaited flax belt round his waist was thrust a greenstone *mere*.

Te Ua was the man who taught the Taranaki rebels the *karakia*, or incantations—some of them a curious medley of Maori and English—which they chanted in their wild marches round the sacred *Niu* in their village squares. These incantations and chants he professed to have heard from supernatural visitants, the spirits who came on the four winds, and from the angel Gabriel, who spoke in his ear as he lay asleep in his *raupo* hut and bade him go abroad and spread a new religion, which should band together the tribes of the Maori nation. Many strange tales Bent had heard about the prophet and his wondrous *mana*. Te Ua had succeeded in imbuing his fanatic disciples with an unquestioning Moslem-like faith in the potency of the Hauhau cult and its accompanying charms and magic formulæ. He was the Mahomet of the Taranaki people, and exercised an influence over the bush-fighters of Ngati-Ruanui and allied tribes almost as great as that which Te Kooti, the Chatham Islands escapee, commanded a few years later amongst the warriors of the East Coast.

The absolute faith the Hauhaus reposed in Te Ua's precepts and his pretences to supernatural power has parallels in the records of the Mahdi's wars in the Soudan, and in other campaigns waged under the banner of Islam, and more recently still in the Zulu rebellion in Natal. He assured his followers that when they went into battle the bullets of the white soldiers would be turned aside in their flight if they but raised their right hands as if warding the ball off, at the same time repeating the words "*Hapa! Pai mariré!*" ("Pass over me! Righteousness and peace!") The expression "*Pai mariré*" was adopted as one of the designations of the Hauhau religion; and the sign of the upraised hand became the outward sign and symbol of the warrior faith. To-day, should you visit the large European-built house of the late Te Whiti, the Prophet of the Mountain, at Parihaka, you will see a picture of Te Ua on the wall of the speech-hall, his right hand raised to his shoulder, palm outwards, as if in the act of invoking his gods to turn the *pakeha* bullets aside—"*Hapa! Pai mariré!*" And many a deluded Hauhau fell to the rifles of the white men before the Maori confidence in the efficacy of the charm was shaken. But Te Ua had a very good explanation to offer for any casualties—that if the *pakeha* bullet refused to be waved aside and insisted on entering the body of a "righteous and peaceful" son of the faith, it was because the stricken man had lost faith in the *karakia*—the ritual—and, very properly, suffered for his unbelief.

A sublimely simple explanation, and one that was perfectly satisfactory to the prophet and every one concerned, except perhaps the Hauhau who had happened to stop the bullet.

Even when the glacis of the Sentry Hill redoubt was strewn with the dead bodies of Hepanaia and fifty of his red-painted braves, the best manhood of Ngati-Ruanui and Nga-Ruahiné—who fell in a mad attack upon the walled fort in open daylight chanting their "*Hapa! Pai mariré! Hau!*"—the faith in Te Ua and his charms was but little abated. And, unlike the Moslem warrior, who fought to the death in the certain hope of a speedy translation to Paradise, the Maori fanatic expected no heavenly reward for his faith and his death-despising ferocity. No *houris* with welcoming arms; no eternity of fleshly bliss. No, it was just utter blind bravery, a sheer trust in a mad creed of Death-to-the-Whites and Maori Land for the Maori Race.

So the visit of the high-priest of Hauhauism was a great event in the bush *pa*. The prophet was received with a *powhiri*, or chant and dance of welcome, by the people of the village; then the *tangi* and the doleful hum of weeping for the dead. The *tangi* over, the prophet addressed his disciples in the meeting-house; and hearing that there was a white runaway soldier in the *pa*, he sent for Bent.

It was a curious interview. The white man no longer appeared in the soldier's uniform, which he had worn for some time after deserting, but had taken to the garb of the savage. He was bare-headed and bare-footed. His sole garments were a shirt made of pieces of blanket and a flax mat tied round his waist. He entered the crowded council-house and stood before the prophet.

PATARA, A HAUHAU PROPHET.

"*E noho ki raro*" ("Sit down"), said Te Ua, pointing to the floor-mat in front of him.

By the prophet's side was a flax basket containing some potatoes and pork, with which he had been breaking his fast after his journey. This food being appropriated to his use was, of course, *tapu* in the eyes of the assemblage. Te Ua took a potato from the basket, broke it into two pieces, and gave one piece to Bent and told him to eat it; the other half he ate himself.

"Now," said the prophet, "you are *tapu*—your life is safe; no man may harm you now that you have eaten of my sacred food. Men of Tangahoé! This *pakeha* is my *pakeha*; and if any other white men should come to us as this man has done, fleeing from their people and forsaking the *pakeha* camps for our *pas*, you must protect them, for the gods have sent them to us."

"You are a Maori now," added Te Ua to Bent, "and you must have a woman to cook your food for you."

Bent, in his imperfect Maori, informed the prophet that he had already been supplied with a wife by the Maoris, but, like a prudent man, made no comment on her imperfections.

"That's all right then," said the prophet. And he gave Bent a large cloak of dressed flax, called a *tatara*. "Wear this," he said; "it is a *tapu* garment and sacred to you; no other man may wear it."

During the next few days, before Te Ua returned to his home at Opunake, on the coast, Bent had further interviews with the prophet, who treated him with kindness, and gave him what was to the runaway a very welcome present—some *pakeha* tobacco. Though something of a madman, like most Maori prophets, Te Ua was of more benevolent spirit than his acolytes, Kereopa and Patara, and their kin, who had been sent to preach the gospel of *Pai mariré* to the outer tribes. Had Kereopa, for instance, come to Otapawa, Bent would, in all probability, have fallen under the tomahawk as a sacrifice for the savage ritual of the *Niu*, and his head would have been smoke-dried and carried over forest-trails from distant tribe to tribe, or stuck up like a scarecrow on a palisade-pole.

Bent learnt a good deal of the personal history of the prophet, and of his peculiar delusions. Te Ua had fought the white soldiers at Nukumaru about a year before this, when a force of Hauhaus made a desperate attack on the camp of two thousand British troops, under General Cameron, and killed and wounded nearly fifty soldiers before they were driven off with the loss of about thirty killed.

The outward and visible sign or incarnation (*aria*) of Te Ua's deity was a *ruru*, or owl. This bird is sacred amongst Taranaki Natives; they will not kill or harm one; they say it is an *atua*, a god, and has a hundred eyes.

An incident which Bent relates as occurring in another bush settlement where he and Te Ua both happened to be staying is illustrative of the prophet's peculiar respect for his owl-god. Just at dusk, when the evening meal was over, and the night creatures began their roamings, an owl flew softly from the trees and settled above the window of the house in which Te Ua was sitting. "Ha!" said the prophet, when he saw it; "there is my *atua*." He recited an incantation, calling the *ruru* by name, and when the *karakia* was ended the bird as noiselessly flew back to the forest. Te Ua said nothing more till the next morning, when he announced that he would leave the place at once, because his owl-god had appeared to him as a warning to return to his home.

Soon after the wandering prophet rode out of Otapawa, word reached the *pa* by a spy who had been in the British camp that the troops under General Chute were preparing for an advance against the Hauhaus, and that it was probable the hill stronghold, being so close to the white men's base of operations, would shortly be attacked.

All was excitement in the *pa* when this became known. The palisading of the *pa* was strengthened with stout timbers from the forest; trenches and rifle-pits were dug within the walls. The natives worked away like mad, and Bent with them. He had caught the fever of the moment, and in all but skin was a Maori. He was not at all happy, however, at the news that his old regiment, the 57th, was expected to march on Otapawa, and he heartily wished himself far away from these scenes of constant commotion and terror. But for the present he was safer with the Hauhaus than with the men of his own colour and tongue.

Day after day passed, and the Maoris lay behind their strong stockade waiting for the attack. The underground food-stores were well supplied; water was carried in in *taha*, or calabashes, made by scooping out the soft inside of the *hué* gourd; bullets were cast and cartridges were made. Then, as no troops appeared, and the scouts who kept constant watch on the forest outskirts reported that there was no sign of immediate action on the part of the enemy, the tension of garrison life relaxed, and the ordinary avocations of the *kainga* were resumed.

In a clearing hewn and burnt from the heart of the woods were the cultivation grounds. Here all the able-bodied men of the fort were set to work, turning up the rich black soil and planting potatoes, *kumara*, and *taro*. Planting over, the lengthening days were spent in hunting wild pigs, and in gathering wild honey, which was plentiful in hollow trees in the forests; or in strolling, pipe in mouth, about the *pa*; playing draughts (*kaimu*) on the *marae* in Maori fashion; singing songs and narrating old stories and legends. Night and morning there were long Hauhau prayers, led by the priest of the *pa*, old Tukino, who was one of Te Ua's apostles.

Life in this bush-fort presented to the lonely *pakeha* a picture of barbaric simplicity. Few of the people had European clothing; the men's working garb was just a rough flax mat hanging from the waist to the knees. They lived on the wild foods of the forest until their crops were ready for digging; snared *kaka* (parrots) and the sweet-tongued *korimako*, or bell-birds; *tui*, or parson-birds, and the swarming wood-pigeons, and shot or speared the pigs that abounded in the dense woods. They lived to a large extent, too, on *aruhe*, or fern-root, which they dug up in the open patches of fern-land; and in the bush they gathered the berries of the *hinau*-tree, steeped them in water to rid them of their astringency, dried them in the sun, and then pounded them into cakes, which made a sustaining if not very palatable food. Another food-staple was *kaanga-pirau*, or maize steeped in water until if was quite decayed. "The smell of this Indian corn," says Bent, with an emphasis begotten of unpleasant memories, "was enough to kill a dog. Nevertheless, I had to eat it, and in time I got used to it."

"I had at this time," continues the deserter, recounting his wild days in Otapawa, "no boots, no trousers, no shirt—just Maori flax mats to cover me, and a mat and blanket for my bed. I had managed to procure some needles and thread, together with paper and pencil (I kept up a sort of diary now and then), and one or two other little things which I kept in a kit, thinking that, though I had nothing to sew with the needles and thread, and very little to do with the other belongings, they might come in useful before very long. One of my greatest troubles was the want of salt; as for bread, I had not tasted any for many months."

CHAPTER VI

THE STORMING OF OTAPAWA

British forces attack the stockade—The bayonet charge—Flight of
the Hauhaus—Through the forest by torchlight—Doctoring the
wounded—The *Tangi* by the river.

SUMMER was on the forest. The beautiful midsummer of Maori Land, with
its soft airs and brilliant sunshine, its blaze of crimson blossom on the grand old
rata-trees, and its showering of scented, white, peach-like flowers on the thickets of ribbon-wood. Birds flooded the outskirts of the bush with song; the early
morning chantings and pipings and chimings of the *tui* and the *korimako* made
a feast of melody to which the brown forest men were in no way deaf, for they
delighted as much as any *pakeha* in the sights and sounds of the free, wild places,
and the call of the creatures of the bush. "*Te Waha-o-Tané*," literally "The Voice of
the Tree-God"—the Song of Nature—they called these morning concerts of the
birds; it was their poetic expression in the classic tongue of old Polynesia for the
sounds that betokened the daily awakening to light and life of the deep and solemn forests of Tane-Mahuta. Pigeons, *ku-ku*-ing to each other, with blue necks and
white breasts gleaming in the sun, went sweeping across the clearing on softly
winnowing wings, and flapped from tree to tree and shrub to shrub in search of
the tenderest leaves, for it was not yet the season of the choicest bush fruits, the big
blue *tawa* berry, the sweet yellow *koroi*, and the aromatic *miro*.

Life went easily in the *pa* when the early harvesting was over. There was little
to do but eat and sleep and lie about in the sun, or join in the daily prayers and
the procession round the *Niu* pole, where the brightly coloured war-flags hung.[1]
There was abundance of food in the camp—potatoes, maize, potted birds, pork,
and dried fish sent as presents from the coast tribes. Early morning, and again
in the warm, golden evenings, long, straight columns of pale blue smoke arose
from the cooking-ovens of the village, and mingled with the thin vapours that
crept about the tree-tops; then little clouds of steam curled up as the women, with
lively chatter, uncovered the *hangis* and arranged the well-cooked food in little

---

[1] Those flags, displayed on the war-poles in the Hauhau villages in 1865-70, carried
many a strange device. The ground was white calico, on which red patterns and lettering
were sewn or painted. Favourite designs were a red half-moon, like the crescent of Islam, a
five-pointed star representing Tawera, "the bright and morning star," and what was called
a Kororia, in shape like the half of a méré-pounamu, or greenstone club, cut longitudinally.
These colours had been made in the Waikato during the war, and had been sent round after
the manner of the Highlanders' fiery crossto the various tribes in the Island.

round flax baskets, which they presently carried off, women and girls in a double line, keeping time with a merry old dance-song—the lilt of the *"tuku-kai"* the *"food-bringing"*—as they marched on to the green *marae* and laid the steaming meal before their lounging lords.

It was all very pleasant and idyllic from the point of view of the brown bushmen. But "Ringiringi," the *pakeha*-Maori, though he led by no means a hard life now that the heaviest work of the year was over, had an uneasy mind. He was—or had been—a civilised man, and he could not forget; moreover, he often woke from unpleasant dreams. One was a vision of a British regiment charging him with fixed bayonets and pinning him against the palisades of his *pa*. Fervently he hoped that he would not be in the fort when the troops marched to the assault, and that the Hauhaus would not compel him to level a *tupara* against his one-time comrades, the old "Die-Hards."

This peaceful state of things did not endure for long. In a few days—it was early in the year 1866—the long-expected attack on Otapawa was delivered. Before the troops came, however, the prophet of the *pa* ordered all the old people and most of the women and children to retire to the forest in rear of the fort, and told "Ringiringi" to accompany them. News had just been brought in that the scouts out in the fern country had noticed signs of an impending movement in the British camp. The white man and the tribal encumbrances pushed back into the bush for about three miles, and camped in a quiet little nook by a creek-side, with high, forested hills towering around. The weather now became cold and bleak, and there was little food to sustain the refugees, for the principal stores of *kai* had been left in the *pa*.

Early one morning the sound of cannon was heard in the distance, then heavy rifle-volleying, followed by desultory firing.

The Queen's soldiers were storming the fort.

Here I may give a more detailed description of the defences of Otapawa than has appeared in the preceding pages, to enable the reader to realise the sort of place the white general was attacking. Curving round under the rear of the *pa* and partly protecting it on the flanks, flowed the Tangahoé River. The hill-top where the *pa* stood was flat, and the rear dropped precipitously to the Tangahoé. The only access to the interior of the stockade was through a low and narrow gateway. Just within, the entrance was blinded by a short fence, so that an enemy could not charge straight, even if the gate were open, but would have to turn first to the left for a short distance and then to the right, exposed to a fire from between the palisades, before the open *marae* was reached. The *pa* was defended by two rows of palisading, with a ditch between, and another shallow trench inside the inner stockade. The outer stockade, the *pekerangi*, was about eight feet high, and was the lighter fence of the two. The principal timbers were six or eight inches thick, but the stakes between were smaller and did not quite reach the ground; they were fastened with bush-vines and supplejack to the sapling rails that ran along the stockade. The open spaces at the bottom of the fence were for the defenders in the outer trench to fire through. The inner fence, the *tuwatawata*, was a stouter structure, of strong, green tree-trunks set solidly in the ground, and with openings here and there for rifle-fire. And finally—an important thing in Maori eyes—there was the "luck-stone" of the fort, the greenstone *whatu*. This was buried under the foot of a large stockade post, close to the right-hand corner nearest the river, as one approached from the *pa* gate.

It was soon after daylight that the *pa* was attacked. The assailing British force was assisted by some Colonial troops and a contingent of "friendly" Maoris, or *Kupapas*, chiefly men from the Wanganui district, under the afterwards celebrated bush-fighter, Kepa te Rangihiwinui (Major Kemp). General Chute commanded the operations. An Armstrong gun was brought to within a short distance of the hill-fort, and several shells were fired into the stockade. Then the general gave the order for the assault.

As the storming party of Imperial soldiers, with bayonets fixed, doubled eagerly up the hill face to the front stockade, the Hauhau chiefs, Tukino and Tu-ahi-pa, cried to their men, crouching in the outer trench with levelled guns:

"Sons! Be steady, and wait till they come close up, then let them have it!"

As the first files of the soldiers dashed up to the stockade, "*Puhia!*"—"Fire!"—shouted the chiefs, and under the thundering volley many whites fell. Another volley, and then the soldiers were at the stockade, firing through the gaps in the obstruction, and slashing at the ties of the fence. Hand-grenades were carried by some of the stormers, and one of these bursting in the outer trench wounded fierce old Tu-ahi-pa, who had just killed a soldier in the act of cutting away at the *pe-kerangi* in an endeavour to force an entrance.

The Maoris did not wait for the bayonet. The wild rush of the maddened troops was irresistible. Leaving seven of their men killed in the trenches and about the palisades, the defenders gathered their wounded and fled. The trenches led to the steep bank overlooking the Tangahoé River. Down the trenches they ran, and sliding down the bank, they took to the bush, scrambling up along the river-side as hard as they could go. Kepa, with his Whanganui friendlies, pursued the flying Hauhaus and shot two or three.

As Bent had expected, it was his old regiment, the 57th, that stormed the *pa*. The 57th were led by Lieutenant-Colonels Butler and Haszard, and were supported by the 14th regiment, who were very jealous of the famous old "Die-Hards." Eleven whites fell and twenty were wounded. One of those who received his death-wound was Lieutenant-Colonel Haszard. It was generally reported afterwards that he was shot by Kimble Bent, but this was mere camp gossip. Gudgeon's "Reminiscences of the War in New Zealand," gives currency to the report, but it is strongly denied, and with every appearance of truth, by Bent. When the *pa* was attacked he was at least three miles away, on the northern side of the Mangemange stream. "It is false to say that I killed my old officer," says he, "or that I ever even fired at him. I never fired a shot against the whites all the time I was with the Hauhaus." This is confirmed by the Maoris, who say that Bent was not allowed to handle a gun in an engagement for fear he might use it against the Hauhaus themselves.

The refugees in the bush-camp with Bent waited anxiously for news of the fight. Was it a victory or a defeat? Soon, the first of the defenders of the *pa* dropped into camp, blood-stained and angry. And then, as the afternoon went on, the rest straggled in. Many were wounded, and seven dead bodies were carried in on hastily made litters of supplejack vines lashed to poles. Then the full story of the battle was told.

It was a sad and angry camp, that remote pocket between the hills. Most of the Hauhaus came in nearly naked, just as they had jumped up when the first shot was fired in the grey dawn. They were desperately sullen and grief-stricken over their dead and the loss of their stronghold, which to them had seemed almost impregnable, for it was the strongest stockaded position they had yet built. Many a dark look was bent upon the white man as he sat by one of the fires, not daring to speak a word.

That night the camp was suddenly abandoned by order of the Hauhau leader, who feared pursuit, not by the Imperial soldiers, who had no relish for "bush-whacking" at night—or, indeed, at any other time—but by Kepa's Government warriors, hereditary enemies of the Taranaki men. Hurriedly packing on their shoulders what few belongings they had managed to save from the *pa*, they set off in single file through the thick forest, making for the banks of the Tangahoé River, which they reached before daylight, and there halted. The wounded who were unable to walk were carried with difficulty through the tangled bush, where it was often necessary to cut away at the supplejacks and *aka* vines, so intricately interlaced and festooned across their path, before a passage could be made for the litter-bearers. There was no moon; it was an intensely dark night, rendered more Cimmerian still by the unbroken roof of foliage overhead. The Hauhaus made torches of pieces of dry pinewood, bound together with scraps of flax torn from their scanty mat garments, and with these they managed to dimly light their way through the forest—a wild and savage band; the warriors in front and rear, their cartouche-belts over their naked shoulders, and guns slung across their backs, or carried in their left hands; in their right they gripped their tomahawks and slashed away at the twining impediments of the jungle.

A camp was made near the banks of the Tangahoé,[2] and here, as soon as it was light, the Hauhaus mustered and reckoned up their losses. There were about three hundred and fifty of them now in camp—men, women and children. With

---

[2]   There is an interesting Maori proverb concerning this rapid Tangahoé stream and the Tangahoé tribe who lived on its banks. This is the proverb, or pepeha:

> "Tangahoé tangata, e haere;
> Tangahoé ia, e kore e haere."

This, being interpreted, is:

> "Men of Tangahoé depart;
> But the current of Tangahoé remains."

A pepeha which recalls Tennyson's "Brook":

> "Men may come and men may go,
> But I go on for ever."

wonderful celerity the forest-men cut a little clearing, and built *wharau*, or rough huts, of saplings, thatched with the long fronds of the *nikau* palm and the *mamaku* tree-fern. Here the wounded men were attended to as well as the primitive methods of the bush allowed. Women were sent out to search the river-banks for flax-plants; the flax-roots were dug up, boiled, and the resultant mucilaginous juice poured over the gunshot and bayonet wounds. This was the Maoris' most favoured method of treating injuries of this character, and it generally bore good results.

"Ringiringi" himself took a hand in the bush-surgery, for he had watched army surgeons at their work, and the Hauhau wounded, though most of them preferred their own people's doctoring, were grateful to the white man for his efforts to ease their sufferings.

A picked band of the fugitives scouted back through the forest and cautiously reconnoitred their captured fort, which had been set on fire by the troops, and was now a heap of blackened ruins. The Government force had by this time passed on to the attack of other *pas*, and the scouts re-entered their destroyed fortress and searched for their dead.

The scene in the camp by the Tangahoé waters when the war-party returned from Otapawa was one that "Ringiringi" never forgot. It was the first great *tangihanga*, or wailing over the dead, that he had witnessed. The people gathered in the middle of the little clearing, and for hours the sound of lamentation rang through the forest, often rising into a wild, heart-breaking shriek as some blanket-draped or mat-kilted woman, her long hair unbound, and her cheeks streaming with tears, cried her keening song for her slain. The chiefs *taki'd* up and down, weapon in hand, and told of the deeds of those who had fallen; each ended his mournful speech with a chanted dirge. When the song was a well-known one, the whole tribe would join in and sing the lament with an intensity of feeling that made their very bodies quiver. It was the full and unrestrained outpouring of the soul of the savage.

CHAPTER VII

BUSH LIFE WITH THE HAUHAUS

Wild days in the forest—The Hauhau hunters—Maori wood-craft—
Bird-snaring and bird-spearing—The fowlers at Te Ngaere—The
slayer of Broughton—Another runaway soldier, and his fate—
The tomahawking of Humphrey Murphy.

For some weeks the fugitives remained in their well-hidden camp by the Tangahoé's stream. When the wounded were able to travel, "Ringiringi" and his Maori companions took them a few miles through the bush to a place called Rimatoto, the overgrown site of an olden village. All the able-bodied men of the tribe now set to work to build a new settlement. Thatched *nikau*-palm houses were quickly run up, and the forest rang day after day with the axes of the bush-fellers, clearing the ground for potato-planting.

As it was intended to make this a permanent *kainga*—always providing Kepa's dusky forest-rangers did not find their way to it in their scouting expeditions—a large clearing was made. The felled trees were allowed to lie for about three months until they were dry enough to be fired; then the potatoes were set in amongst the half-burned stumps and logs. In the meantime the forest was scoured for food, and foraging parties were sent out to Turangaréré and other villages on the outskirts of the forest and returned laden with pork and potatoes, strapped across their shoulders in the usual Maori *pikau* fashion.

Four miles away by a rough bush track, a track hardly discernible to any but a Maori, was the Maha village. There the white man was taken by his *rangatira* Tito, after the bush-felling work was over, and three or four peaceful months were passed, varied only by occasional armed scouting expeditions to the forest edge, and by long fishing, birding, and pig-hunting trips into the great wilderness of jungle-matted timber that hemmed in the lonely village on every side.

Bent had now been a year with the Maoris, and had thoroughly settled into the native life. He had quickly picked up the language of his adopted people, and there was nothing of the *pakeha* about him but the colour of his skin, and that was browning with constant exposure and outdoor labour. A waist-shawl or a flax kilt was his single article of everyday clothing; in cold weather a shoulder-mat or a blanket was added. In this village of the woods there were few emblems of civilisation except the weapons of the warriors. Stories of battle and skirmish now and again reached the bushmen by messengers from the plains; and the white general's great march through the forest from Ketemarae by the Whakaahurangi track around the eastern side of Mount Egmont to Mataitawa and New Plymouth—when the soldiers fell so short of food that they had to shoot and eat their pack-horses—was discussed many a night in the village *wharepuni*, the communal council-room and sleeping-house.

Bent's half-Indian temperament soon adapted itself to this wild life in the forest. No drill day after day, no parades, no sentry-go, no buttons to polish, and no uniform to mend—surely this savage life had its compensations. When the Maoris had urgent and laborious work on hand they worked like fury, and compelled—with the spur of a tomahawk—the white man to toil with equal industry, if not willingness. Fort-building, trench-digging and timber-felling were undertakings in which the whole strength of the community laboured from dawn till dark, and the chiefs as hard as the common men and slaves. It was warrior's work. But there were periods of halcyon, lazy days in Maoridom, when "Ringiringi" and his ragged comrades of the bush, their work over, could just "lie around" and smoke and eat, and take no thought for the morrow so long as they could procure a pipe-full of strong *torori* (tobacco) and a square meal of potatoes and pork. Tito proved a not unkind master, when he found that his white man neither attempted to escape from the tribe nor shirked the often heavy tasks imposed upon him.

A BRITISH COLUMN ON THE MARCH.

(*From a water-colour sketch by Major Von Tempsky, 1866.*)

The *paheka* soon became an adept in the wood-craft of the Maoris. He accompanied the young men of the tribe on their forest expeditions, bird-snaring and bird-spearing; these camping-out trips sometimes lasted for a week or more. Far into the solitudes of the great woods the little hunting-parties penetrated, always armed, for they never knew when or where the Government Maori scouts might be encountered. The days were spent in birding and pig-hunting, and the long nights by the blazing camp-fire, when the white man learned from his Hauhau comrades many a wild legend and folk-story, hair-raising tales of witchcraft, and mournful *tangi*-songs and love-ditties without end.

Powder and shot were too valuable to waste on the birds of the forest in those days. One of the Maori snaring methods, as practised by "Ringiringi" and his companions, was to cut out wooden *waka*, or miniature canoes or troughs, fill them with water, and place them in some dry spot in the forest where pigeons and *tui* were plentiful. Just over these troughs flax-snares were arranged, so that when the birds, thirsting for water after feasting on the bush-berries, flew down to drink, and stretched their heads through the running loops, they were tightly noosed. Other snares were set on the *miro*-trees, of whose sweet berries the pigeons and *tui* were particularly fond. "Ringiringi" quickly learned the art of setting snares of flax or cabbage-tree leaf with cunning slip-loops in the branches of the fruit-laden *miro*; in a clump of these pines he sometimes caught in a single day as many as three hundred or four hundred birds—*kaka* parrots, *tui*, and pigeon—for the forests were alive with feathered creatures, and in the autumn time, when the wild fruits were ripe and abundant, they were to be taken with little trouble; the noisy *kaka* parrot was the most easily lured of all. The only forest bird that was not welcomed by the hunters was the owl, or *ruru*; should one happen to be killed it was never eaten, because in Maori eyes it was an *atua*, a spirit or the incarnation of a tribal deity.

Bird-spearing was another forest art widely practised in those times. Long slender limber spears of *tawa* wood, twelve feet long and more, were used.

In making the bird-spears, the pole from which each was cut was scorched with fire till very dry, then it was scraped and scraped down with *pawa*-shells and scorched again, and once more scraped and shaped with great care and industry, until it had been reduced to the size desired and was perfectly smooth. These spears were armed with barbed tips, often of bone, sometimes of iron. The villagers trailed the weapons after them as they travelled through the forest, until they came to some tree where *tui* and pigeon perched in numbers; then the spear was slowly and cautiously pushed upwards until close to the unsuspecting bird, and a sudden, sharp thrust impaled it on the barbed point.

The *pakeha* was carefully schooled in the art of using the spear, and was enjoined, above all, never to strike the pigeon full in the breast, because the bone would often snap the barb-tip off; it must be speared in the side. In the late autumn the pigeons were "rolling fat"; and many hundreds of them were preserved or potted in Maori fashion by the birding-parties in *taha*, or calabashes (the *hué* gourd), which were hermetically sealed with the fat of the cooked birds.

One foraging expedition which Bent accompanied was farther afield than usual, up northwards to the great Ngaere swamp, a huge morass near where the present township of Eltham stands, and where dairy cattle now graze on fields that in those days of '66 were seemingly irreclaimable bogs and wildernesses; lagoons, where millions of eels crawled, snake-like, in the ooze, and where countless thousands of wild fowl and water-birds fished and screamed and squabbled all day long. To the edge of the great swamp came the food-hunters; they waded across to the two islets which rose from the middle of the bog—ancient refuge-places of fugitive tribes—and camped there, catching and smoke-drying huge quantities of eels for winter food in the home *kainga*, and snaring many ducks and other birds. In this primeval spot the beautiful *kotuku*, the white heron so famous in Maori song and proverb—now never seen in the North Island—then abounded; the white man often admired this graceful bird as he stood on silent watch on the marge of some sedgy pool, then, like lightning-flash, darted his long spear-bill on his prey. The birds were tame, and easily caught, and many were snared and eaten by the foragers. "Ringiringi" captured some on the shores of the lagoon by the simple expedient of a bent supplejack and an arrangement of flax loops, set near the *kotuku's* daily haunts; a day seldom passed without a heron being found flapping and choking tightly noosed in the snares of the fowlers.

One day in the spring of 1866, when Tito and his *hapu*, their bird-hunting expeditions over for the season, were gathered in their bush-village Rimatoto, three strange Maoris, fully armed, entered the settlement. They had travelled overland from the King Country, far to the north, on a mission from Tawhiao, the Waikato King, who, after the conquest of the Waikato Valley by the white troops, had taken refuge with the Ngati-Maniapoto tribe. The envoys had been sent down to recover some Waikato war-flags which were in the possession of the Taranaki Hauhaus.

In the crowded *wharepuni* that night, when the Waikato warriors made their errand known, one of them caught sight of the white man, sitting silently in his corner, and asked who he was. When Tito explained, the visitor asked,

"Why don't you kill him?"

"He is my *pakeha*," said Tito, "and I will protect him, because our prophet Te Ua has *tapu'd* him, and ordered us not to harm him."

"That is indeed a soft and foolish way to deal with *pakehas*" exclaimed a fierce-looking young warrior, one of the Waikato trio. "We don't take any white prisoners in our country. You ought to have his head stuck on the fence of your *pa.*"

Tito laughed. "Ringiringi is going to be useful to us," he said. "Besides, he is a Maori now."

Next morning Tito despatched the white man and an old Maori named Te Waka-tapa-ruru through the forest to Te Putahi, a stockaded village some ten miles away, on the banks of the Whenuakura River, with a message to the people of that *pa* requesting them to return the colours for which the king had sent. This mission accomplished, Bent stayed a while in Te Putahi, where he was treated with much kindness, because of his association with Tito.

On the morning after his arrival a man came to his sleeping-hut and, without saying a word, placed on the mat before him a couple of blankets and a watch.

The history of the watch was afterwards explained to him by Te Waka-tapa-ru-ru. This warrior was a typical old bush-fighter. He had a very big head; he was tattooed on the cheeks; he was wiry and wonderfully quick on his legs. He told Bent, with a devilish grin on his corrugated face, that the watch had belonged to a white man, called Paratene, whom he—Te Waka—had shot the previous year at Otoia, on the Patea River. This *pakeha* was Mr. C. Broughton, a native interpreter who had been sent on a special Government mission to the Hauhaus, and was barbarously murdered while in the act of lighting his pipe in the village *marae*.

Broughton's slayer, despite his repulsive antecedents, became a friend of Bent's, and they were close comrades until 1869, when the old man was killed in the act of charging furiously on the Armed Constabulary at the attack on the Papa-tihakehake stockade.

At Te Putahi "Ringiringi" was astonished to find another white man, clothed like himself in a blanket. This man walked up and greeted him, and the *pakeha*-Maori recognised the long-haired, rough-bearded fellow as an old fellow-soldier. His name was Humphrey Murphy; he, too, had been a private in the 57th, and had become as dissatisfied with the life as Bent had done, and deserted to the Hauhaus. Bent sums him up as "a bad lot." Murphy was an evil-tempered Irishman, faithful to neither white man nor Maori. He belonged to two chiefs, Te Onekura and Wharé-matangi, who lived in the *pa* at Te Putahi.

Murphy, it appeared from his own story, had been taken over as a *taurekareka*, a slave, by one of the Hauhau chiefs when he deserted, and had been sent as a food-carrier to Te Putahi by his owner, who treated his "white trash" with scant consideration. At Te Putahi he had been taken over by the two local chiefs. The deserter bragged to Bent, as they sat side by side on the village *marae*, that he would shortly return to his old Maori "boss," as he called him, and kill him, and take what money he could find as payment for his enforced labour.

While Murphy was speaking, a young Maori girl sat by quietly listening.

When the runaway soldier rose and walked off to his hut, the girl said:

"Ringi, I heard what that *taurekareka* white man was saying. I have learned enough of the *pakeha's* tongue to know that he is going to kill his *rangatira* and steal his money."

"*Kaati!* Don't say a word about it," cautioned Bent.

But the girl rose up in the meeting-house one night after "Ringiringi" had departed to his home at Rimatoto, and repeated the threat she had overheard from Murphy's lips.

That settled the *taurekareka's* fate. Bent, some time later, inquiring after Murphy from one of Tito's men who had been on a visit to Te Putahi, was told that he had been killed. The Hauhaus had a short way with such as he. He was quietly tomahawked one night as he lay asleep, and his despised remains dragged out and cast into the Whenuakura River that ran below the village.

At this time there were at least four white men living with the Hauhaus in South Taranaki. One came to Rimatoto to see "Ringiringi," and remained with him for a week. His name was Jack Hennessy, and he had, like Bent, deserted from the 57th Regiment. He was in fact the "shut-eye sentry" who had seen Bent steal off from the Manawapou camp in 1865. He gave himself up to the white forces some time later, tired of life with the Hauhaus, and was court-martialled and sent to prison.

CHAPTER VIII

THE HAUHAU COUNCIL-TOWN

Life in Taiporohenui — A great praying-house — The ritual of the *Niu* —
Singular Hauhau chants — *"Matua Pai-mariré"* — Bent's new owner, and his new wife — The tattooers — Another white renegade

ANOTHER summer came, and the crops were gathered in, and the men of Tito's
hapu, after nearly a year of comparative peace, wearied for the war-path again.
Rimatoto and other small bush-hamlets were deserted, and the tribes gathered in,
bearing their food supplies to the Hauhau council-village of Taiporohenui — close
to where the town of Hawera now stands. Taiporohenui was a famous name — a
word of *mana*, as the Maori would say — amongst all the tribes from Whanganui
to Waikato. The name, say the wise men of Taranaki, goes back far beyond the
days of the later Maori migration to New Zealand, in the canoes Aotea, Tokomaru,
Tainui, and other Polynesian Viking ships. It was that of a great temple in Tahiti,
in the tropic isles of the Hawaiikian seas, countless generations ago. And in this
latter-day Taiporohenui the Maoris, mindful of their ancient traditions, built another temple.

This Hauhau praying-house and council-hall, constructed of hewn timber with
raupo-reed walls and *nikau*-thatch roof, is described by Bent as the largest building
of native construction that he had seen. It was about one hundred and twenty feet
in length, and was of such exceptional size that the ridge-pole was supported by
four *poutoko-manawa*, or pillars, instead of one or two, as in the ordinary Maori
meeting-house; there were five fires burning in it at night, in the stone fireplaces
down its long central aisle; on either side were the mat-covered resting-places of
the people. The timbers of the house were of the durable *totara* pine. The inside
was lined with beautiful *tukutuku* work, of *kakaho* reeds and thin wooden lathes
artfully fastened with *kiekie* fibre, arranged in many handsome geometrical patterns. Beneath the first large *poutoko-manawa* in the house was buried a large piece
of greenstone in the rough, the *whatu*, or "luck-stone," of the sacred house. It was
the Maori custom when the centre-pole of a large meeting-house or the first big
palisade-post of a fort was set in position, to place a piece of greenstone, often in
the form of an ornament, such as an ear-drop or a carved *tiki*, at its foot.[3]

[3]   We have survivals of this widespread ancient custom amongst ourselves, in the
practice of placing coins, etc., under the foot of a mast of a new ship, and under the founda-
tion-stone of a church or other important building. The cult is found amongst many savage
nations in its primitive form. Here is an instance narrated by Mr. T. C. Hodson in an article
in Folk-Lore (Vol. XX., No. 2, 1909) on "Head-hunting amongst the Hill-tribes of Assam":

In front of the great house on the *marae*, or village square, stood the sacred *Niu*-pole, a *totara* pine flagstaff, nearly fifty feet in height, with a yard about fourteen feet long; the staff was stayed like the mast of a ship. The war-flags of the Hauhaus were flown from the *Niu*, and the people daily marched around its foot in their "*Pai-mariré*" procession, intoning the chants their prophet had taught them. This *Niu* was one of the first worship-poles planted in Taranaki by the Hauhau prophet's command, and it was the centre of many a wild fanatic gathering. At its foot there was planted a large piece of unworked greenstone—as was done when the first house-pillar was set up—as the *whatu* of the sacred pole; this block of *pounamu* is still there, says Bent.

Round this staff of worship, where the bright war-flags hung, the people marched daily in their strange procession, chanting their wild psalms. Tito te Hanataua was one of the priests of the *Niu*, and he led his tribe in the services after the Hauhau religion.

Some of the chants were amazing mixtures of English and Maori; some were all pidgin-English, softened by the melodious Maori tongue. Here is a specimen of the daily chants, intoned by all the people as they marched round and round the holy pole. The priest shouted, "*Porini, hoia!*" ("Fall in, soldiers!"); then "*Teihana!*" ("Attention!"), and they stood waiting. Then they chanted, as they got the order to march:

	Translation.
Kira	Kill
Wana	One
Tu	Two
Tiri	Three
Wha—	Four—
Teihana!	Attention!

Round the sacred flagstaff they went—men, women, and children—chanting:

Rewa	River
Piki rewa	Big river
Rongo rewa	Long river
Tone	Stone
Piki tone—	Big stone—
Teihana!	Attention!

"The head-man of a large and powerful village (on the frontier of the State of Manipur) was engaged in building himself a new house, and to strengthen it had seized this man (a Naga) and forcibly cut off a lock of his hair, which had been buried underneath the main post of the house. In olden days the head would have been put there, but by a refinement of some native theologian a lock of hair was held as good as the whole head."

It was the olden Maori custom to place a human head beneath the central pillar of a sacred building, and to have a human sacrifice at the opening of a new house.

Rori	Road
Piki rori	Big road
Rongo rori	Long road
Puihi	Bush
Piki puihi —	Big bush —
Teihana!	Attention!
Rongo puihi	Long bush
Rongo tone	Long stone
Hira	Hill
Piki hira	Big hill
Rongo hira —	Long hill —
Teihana!	Attention!
Mauteni	Mountain
Piki mauteni	Big maountain
Rongo mauteni	Long mountain
Piki niu	Big staff
Rongo niu —	Long staff —
Teihana!	Attention!
Nota	North
No te pihi	North by East
No te hihi	N. Nor'-east
Norito mino	N.E. by North
Noriti	North-east
Koroni —	Colony —
Teihana!	Attention!
Hai!	Hi!
Kamu te ti	Come to tea
Oro te mene	All the men
Rauna	Round
Te Niu —	The *Niu* —
Teihana!	Attention!

Hema	Shem
Rurawini	Rule the wind
Tu mate wini	Too much wind
Kamu te ti—	Come to tea—
Teihana!	Attention!

And so on, a marvellous farrago of Maorified English words and phrases. It was Te Ua's "gift of tongues," they imagined, that had descended upon them.

Night and morning, too, the sound of Hauhau prayers rose from the great camp. Here is one, the "Morning Song" ("*Waiata mo te Ata*"), in imitation of the English Prayer-book:

	Translation.
Koti te Pata, mai mariré;	God the Father, have mercy on me;
Koti te Pata, mai mariré;	God the Father, have mercy on me;
Koti te Pata, mai mariré;	God the Father, have mercy on me;
To riré, riré!	Have mercy, mercy (or peace, peace)!
Koti te Tana, mai mariré;	God the Son, have mercy on me;
Koti te Tana, mai mariré;	God the Son, have mercy on me;
Koti te Tana, mai mariré;	God the Son, have mercy on me;
To riré, riré!	Have mercy, mercy!
Koti te Orikoti, mai mariré;	God the Holy Ghost, have mercy on me;
Koti te Orikoti, mai mariré;	God the Holy Ghost, have mercy on me;
Koti te Orikoti, mai mariré;	God the Holy Ghost, have mercy on me;
To riré, riré!	Have mercy, mercy!
To mai Niu Kororia, mai mariré;	My glorious *Niu*, have mercy on me;
To mai Niu Kororia, mai mariré;	My glorious *Niu*, have mercy on me;
To mai Niu Kororia, mai mariré;	My glorious *Niu*, have mercy on me;
To riré, riré!	Have mercy, mercy!

The more warlike chants ended in a loudly barked "*Hau!*" the watchword and holy war-cry of the rebel bushmen. Very wild they were, these savage hymns, haunting in rhythm, and stirring the people to a frenzy of fanatic fire.

Kimble Bent joined in these Hauhau war-rites like any Maori, and marched, chanting with his wild comrades, round and round the *Niu*.

Several skirmishes between the whites and Maoris occurred in the winter and early spring of 1866, and one of these had some concern for the exile. About three miles away from Taiporohenui was a village called Pokaikai, to which "Ringiringi" was sent awhile by his chief. While he was there the prophet Te Ua arrived. He dreamed a dream, one of bad omen, and he straightway counselled "Ringiringi" to return at once to Taiporohenui. "Ringi" obeyed. Three days, or, rather, three nights afterwards, a force of colonial soldiers under Colonel McDonnell unexpectedly attacked Pokaikai and rushed the village, killing several Hauhaus. In some way the Forest Rangers under McDonnell had heard that the deserter Kimble Bent was in Pokaikai, and they were eager to capture or shoot him. Some of them surrounded one of the *wharés* in which they imagined Bent was sleeping. A young volunteer named Spain had just previously, unnoticed by them, gone into the *wharé* to bring out a dead Hauhau, and while he was there the Rangers—hearing some one say there was a white man within—fired a volley into the hut, which unfortunately mortally wounded Spain. This young soldier was the only *pakeha* killed in the fight.

THE SCOUT

Tu-Mahuki, a friendly Maori of the Whanganui tribe who served on the British side in the Maori War, with his wife Takiora.
(*From a sketch by Major von Tempsky, 1866.*)

When "Ringiringi" heard of the Pokaikai affair from the fugitives who fled through the bush to Taiporohenui, he felt that the Hauhau prophet had indeed been his good angel, for it was only Te Ua's injunction to return to the main Hauhau camp that had saved him from the vengeful bullets of his fellow-whites. And thenceforward the white man was a dreamer of many a strange dream, and he came to believe almost as implicitly as the forest-men themselves in the omens that lay in the visions of the night, and in warning voices from the spirit-world.

About this time "Ringiringi" changed hands, much as if he were a fat porker or a keg of powder or any other article of Maori barter. Rupé ("Wood-pigeon"), a chief of Taiporohenui, made request of Tito—to whom he was related—for his *pakeha mokai*, his tame white man. He had never owned a *pakeha*, he explained, and would like one all to himself, and he knew that "Ringiringi" would be a handy man to have around, to keep his armoury of guns, of miscellaneous makes and dates, in repair, and to make cartridges for him. So "Ringiringi" was passed over to his new owner, whom he served, with the exception of some short intervals in the war-time and in the period of exile on the Upper Waitara, until 1878.

Soon after "Ringiringi" had become one of Rupé's household, his chief's son, a young lad named Kuku (another name for the wood-pigeon), fell seriously ill. The white man doctored and carefully nursed the boy, and under his treatment he recovered. Rupé's gratitude to his *mokai* took a chieftain-like form. As payment, or *utu*, for curing his son, he led up his daughter, a young girl of fifteen or sixteen, and presented her to "Ringiringi" as his wife.

"Indeed, she was a pretty girl," says the old *pakeha*-Maori, recalling the dead past. "I'll never forget her. She had handsome features, almost European, though she was of pure Maori blood. Her lips were small, her hair was wavy and curly, instead of hanging in a straight, black mat, and she had what was very strange in a Maori, blue eyes—the first blue-eyed native I have ever seen. She was a very gentle girl—she never *kanga*'d or said unpleasant things about others, never quarrelled with the other women. She did not smoke either, which was unusual. Her chin was tattooed, but not too thickly or deeply. She had, too, the *rapé* and *tiki-hopé* patterns engraved on her body, the hip, and thigh, tattooing which was in fashion in those days, and which the girls and women were proud of displaying when they went out to bathe."

With this agreeable young wife, whose name was Rihi, or Te Hau-roroi-ua, Bent lived for nearly three years. She bore one child, which died, and soon after she, too, died, to the *pakeha*-Maori's great sorrow. His one-eyed wife, the lady of Otapawa, had left her unwilling husband some months before he took Rihi in Maori marriage.

Amongst the primitive arts of the Maori with which "Ringiringi" became familiar about this time was that of *moko*, or tattooing. The *kauae* tattooing—on chin and lips—was still universal amongst the native women, though few of the men now submitted their faces to the chisel or the needle of the tattooing artist. A popular form of tattooing amongst both sexes was that technically known as *tiki-hopé*, the scroll-patterns on the thighs and other parts of the body usually concealed by the waist-shawl. The white man saw numbers of women as well as men decorated in this fantastic fashion. In fact, he was so thoroughly Maori by this time that he was about to undergo the operation himself, in the winter of 1867, when living at the village Te Paka, near the old fort Otapawa. He had the *ngarahu*, or *kapara*, the blue-black pigment, ready for the dusky engraver, and would shortly have been made pretty for life in Maori eyes had not the tattooing been peremptorily forbidden.

"I wanted my face tattooed," says Bent, "for I was as wild as any Maori then. I intended to have the curves called *tiwhana*, or arches, tattooed on my forehead, over the eyes, and the *kawekawe* lines on the cheeks, extending to the corners of the mouth. What a curiosity I would have been, though, when I came out of the bush! I would have been able to earn my living in my old age, going on exhibition, like the bearded lady in the circus!"

It was Te Ua the prophet who forbade the tattooing. He happened to be in residence at Te Paka just then, and he reminded "Ringiringi" that he had *tapu*'d him, and explained that to *moko* his skin would be a violation of that particular brand of *tapu*. To the white man this was not quite clear; nevertheless, he agreed to obey the prophet's Mosaic command "to make no cuttings" in his flesh, and remained a plain, undecorated *pakeha*.

However, he acquired some skill himself with the tattooing instruments, and exercised it in printing names and sundry devices on the persons of the villagers. He learned, too, how to manufacture the indelible *ngarahu*, or *kapara*, pigment. In making this tattooing-ink the soot from fires of white-pine (*kahikatea*) wood was used. A cave-like hole was dug in the side of a bank, with an opening resembling a chimney in the top. A large fire was kindled in the cave, or *rua*, and for several days was constantly fed with the resinous timber of the *kahikatea*. Above the earth-chimney were arranged a number of twigs of the *karamu* shrub (a coprosma), with the bark stripped off, set up in the shape of a tent, and covered with a layer of leaves. The dense smoke from the fire deposited a thick soot on the *karamu* sticks. For some days the fire was kept up; then the twigs were removed, and the soot scraped off into wooden receptacles. It was mixed with water, and worked into little round balls. The soot-balls were then placed on a layer of *poroporo* leaves in an *umu*, or earth-oven, and steamed for about three hours, when they were taken out and set to dry. In later times, after the war, Bent often employed himself in the manufacture of this tattoo-dye; and was, he says, accustomed to receive ten shillings for a ball of *ngarahu* the size of a peach.

To Te Paka village there came one day another renegade white man, an Irish soldier named Charles Kane, or King. He had been a private in the second battalion of the 18th Royal Irish Regiment, and had, like Bent, revolted against army discipline, and deserted to the Hauhaus. The Maoris had christened him "Kingi." He lived in Bent's *wharé* in Te Paka for some time. He was exceedingly bitter against his old officers, and, in fact, against his fellow-whites in general; so much so, that he boasted of his intention to fight against them, and, as will be seen later, actually did so in the attack on the Turuturu-mokai redoubt. Like most of the soldiers who traitorously deserted their colours in those war-days, he fell at last a victim to the tomahawks of his Hauhau companions.

CHAPTER IX

A FOREST ADVENTURE

The two eel-fishers—Bivouac in the bush—A murderous attack—The
Waikato's tomahawk—"Ringiringi's" escape.

FAR away to the east and north of the great Hauhau council-camp stretched
the forest, clothing hill and valley with one endless wavy garment of unvarying
green. For weeks one might tramp through these vast, jungly woods and not see or
hear sign of man, or of any living thing but the twittering birds in the tree-tops and
a stray wild pig rooting in the soft, fern-matted earth or scampering away through
the thickets. The free, unspoiled wilderness of Tane-Mahuta.

Climbing to the wooded crest of some of the steep little hills that rose from the
gently undulating plain, one might here and there, through the gaps between the
towering tiers of foliage, catch narrow glimpses of the surrounding country; and
perhaps far away to the nor'-west see between the branches, set like a picture in its
forest-frame, the pure white snow-cone of tent-shaped Taranaki.

Deep in these bush solitudes one day, when the spring had come, the voice
of man broke upon the silences. The wild boar stopped his root-foraging to listen, and then turned and crashed off through the supplejacks. A band of brown
men, some clad in nondescript articles of European clothing, some wearing only
a shoulder-cape of flax and a shawl or blanket-kilt, wound in single file through
the bush, striking due east. There were fourteen or fifteen of them. Most of them
carried weapons—double-barrelled guns and short-handled tomahawks, stuck in
the waist-belt of flax; all had large flax baskets, some containing gourd-calabashes,
strapped across their backs. Some sang little lilts of Maori song, and some called
now and then to the others, or mimicked the *tui* and the *kaka* parrot that cried
above them in the trees.

Mid-line in the file was a fairer-skinned young forester, bare-footed like the
rest, clad only in a "home-made" shirt that seemed to have been cut out of a blanket and a coloured shawl strapped round his waist. He had a thick beard, and his
hair was so long that it would have fallen down over his shoulders had it not been
caught at the back of his neck and tied with a piece of flax. This was "Ringiringi,"
the *pakeha*-Maori, wearing as little clothing as his Hauhau companions, and to all
appearance as seasoned a bushman as they, as he bent along the jungly way with
the easy, noiseless jog of the Maori scout.

This party had been despatched from Taiporohenui by Rupé, to work inland through the bush to the upper waters of the Patea River, and scour the country for food supplies for the assembled tribes. They were ordered to bring home wild pork and wild honey, and to catch as many eels as they could carry. They travelled far into the heart of the bush, and then divided into small parties of twos and threes for eel-catching in the creeks.

The white man's companion on the eel-fishing excursion was an old Maori from the "King" Country, a Ngati-Maniapoto man, who had joined the Taranaki Hauhaus; he was a short but strongly built fellow, with a big head and of dark and sullen visage, made more forbidding still by the blue-black tattoo with which cheeks and brow and nose were scrolled and lined. The couple, leaving the others after arranging a general rendezvous for the following day, selected a small creek, winding in a slow, brown current beneath the roof of verdure which the outstretching branches of the *rata* and the pines nearly everywhere held over it. It was a tributary of the Upper Patea above Rukumoana. They fished with short rods and flax lines, with worms for bait, and by the evening had caught between them about sixty good-sized eels.

The eel-fishers bivouacked where the twilight found them, in a tiny nook near Orangimura, where there was just room to build their camp-fire and spread their bush-couches of fresh-pulled tree-fern fronds, between the buttressed *ratas* and the creek-side.

"Ringiringi" had a little cold food in his *pikau* kit, potatoes and *kopaki* corn; that is, maize in the sheath. He was about to grill some of the fat eels on the fire when his Maori companion stopped him.

"*E tama!*" he said. "Don't you know it is unlucky to cook the *tuna* in the night-time? Do not touch those eels until the morning; should you disobey, it will surely bring heavy rain."

The superstitious old warrior was so insistent that "Ringiringi," to please him, agreed to his wishes; he contented himself with the little he had in his kit, and then, filling his pipe with *torori* tobacco, lit it, and smoked as he lay beside the camp-fire. His Maori mate squatted smoking on the other side.

The warmth of the fire, and the low, murmurous singing of the little river—the *wawara-wai*, the babble of the waters, in the musical Maori tongue—pleasantly lulled the tired *pakeha*. He lay there, with his scanty bush-ranging garments wrapped about him, listening, half-asleep, to the lazy run of the creek, and to the songs that his savage old companion recited to himself in a monotonous chant. War-songs of Waikato, songs that he and his Kingite comrades had shouted in many an armed camp before the white man drove them out beyond the *Aukati* line, the frontier of the Waikato. In one of these chants the eel-fisher's voice was lifted in a quick burst of passionate remembrance—a defiant *haka*-song the Hauhaus of Taranaki, too, had adopted as a composition exactly expressing their opinion of *pakehas* in general, and of the *pakeha* Governor in particular. It likened Governor Grey to a bush-bullock devouring the tender leaves of the *raurekau* shrub—a Maori simile for the land-hunger of the whites:

"*A he kau ra.*

He kau ra!
U— —u!
He kau kawana koe
Kia miti mai
Te raurekau.
A he kau ra,
He kau ra!
A— —u— —u!"

("Ha! A beast art thou,
A beast that bellows—
Ooh— —ooh!
A beast art thou, O Governor,
That lickest in
The leaves of the raurekau.
Ho! A beast, indeed,
A beast art thou!
Oo— —oo— —ooh!")

The old Hauhau, warming to the *haka*, almost yelled the virulent words. The chant broke the white man's drowsing, and he sat up and listened as his companion repeated the vigorous dance-song.

"Well, *pakeha*!" he said; "that is our Waikato *ngeri*, our war-cry. That is what we think of the Governor—and of all *pakehas*! I hate all white men! They are thieves and pigs. I could cook and eat them all! All, every one! I would not leave a white-skin alive in this island! They are slaves, *taurekarekas*—like you! Now go to sleep, for we must rise when the *kaka* cries."

And the old man curled up by the fire, while "Ringiringi" found uncomfortable reflection in the fact that he was here alone, far in the heart of the forest, with a murderous old savage who was armed with a war-tomahawk, while he, the weaker man, though the younger, had nothing with which to defend himself. But by this time he was familiar with the face of danger, and worked and slept in the midst of alarms; so simply remarking to the Maori, "Friend, I am sleepy," and throwing some fresh fuel on the fire, he lay down again on his ferny *whariki*.

However, he had his suspicions of the old savage, and presently he glimpsed the Maori eyeing him dangerously through his narrowed lids and handling his tomahawk restlessly. When he lay down to rest, the white man had drawn his blanket partly over his face, as if he were asleep, but he kept one eye lifting. Once the Maori half rose and looked cunningly over at his companion, with his hand on his war-axe, then he sank down again.

The little dark brook went singing on beneath the forest; the fire gradually burned lower and lower as the night wore on; the morepork now and then cried his sharp complaint of "*Kou-kou!*" from the shadows. The two fishers lay silent; to all appearance both were asleep. But in the Maori's heart was black, treacherous murder.

Utu—payment, satisfaction, revenge—summed up in a word the darker side of the Maori character.

The lone *pakeha's* head would be indeed a trophy to bear back through the wilderness to his tribe. He would be a hero; he could brag to the end of his days how he slew a white soldier in single combat, and none could contradict him. He saw himself already *taki*-ing and prancing up and down the home *marae* before his admiring clan, the *pakeha's* head in his hand, his tomahawk—the victor's tomahawk!—flashing in air. Ah! That, indeed, would be *utu*—though long-deferred *utu*—for his kinsmen who fell to the *pakeha* bullets at Rangiriri and Orakau!

It must have been nearly midnight, and "Ringiringi" was half-asleep with fatigue, in spite of his fears, when suddenly all his senses were awakened. Through his half closed eyelids he saw the Maori rise, tomahawk in hand; he rose from his blanket noiselessly, then cautiously stretched one foot across a *tawa* log that lay on the fire, with its end projecting. His eyes blazed, his face was frightful, with intent to murder plain upon it in the firelight.

He was just in the act of stepping over the log, with his little axe upraised, when the white man suddenly threw off his blanket and leaped for the savage.

The old fellow flew at him with his upraised tomahawk glittering in the little light that the bivouac-fire yet threw out.

But "Ringiringi" was too quick for him. He ducked dexterously, and caught the Maori by the ankle, and, with a lightning twist that he had learned from his Taranaki people, threw him to the ground.

The murderer-in-intent fell on his back and almost on the fire, and the tomahawk dropped from his hand.

"Ringiringi" pounced on the furious old savage as he fell, and with a knee on his bare chest, and one hand on his throat, reached out with the free hand for the tomahawk, which lay just within his grasp.

The Maori would have continued the struggle, and in the rough-and-tumble would probably have got the better of the white man, had not "Ringiringi," now roused to murderous mood himself, threatened to split his head in two if he moved, and emphasised his words by bringing the weapon down until the blade was within an inch of the old fellow's ugly, tattooed nose.

The Maori sulkily promising to lie quietly in his sleeping-place for the rest of the night, the *pakeha* relinquished his grip of the old man and backed to his own side of the bivouac. He fed the fire with dry branches of pine, and presently the little glade was a blaze of light again, and the black tree-shadows danced like forest-ghosts to the rising and falling of the flames.

The old Maori pulled his blanket over his face and pretended to go to sleep, but "Ringiringi" did not take his eyes off him the rest of that night. He sat by the fire till daylight, the captured tomahawk between his knees.

In the morning the two enemies silently packed their takes of eels in their kits, and slung them on their backs by flax-leaf straps, for the home-journey.

The little river had to be forded. It was about knee-deep. The Maori hung back, waiting for Bent to cross first; but the white man knew that if he did so his enemy would spring upon him or trip him up and try to drown him in the creek.

"Now, you go first," ordered Bent, when he had settled his *pikau* on his shoulders and stood, tomahawk in hand, facing the Maori, "and walk in front of me all the way home, or I'll kill you!"

So the old fellow sulkily stepped into the stream and waded across, Bent following him, and in this order they travelled.

So they made their way homewards, striking west through the pathless forest, wading watercourses and climbing and descending hills, until they emerged on the fern country. "Ringiringi," immensely relieved, and weary beyond words, reported himself to his chief.

Rupé was furiously angry when he heard the story of the Waikato's attack on his *pakeha*.

"The *kohuru*!" he cried, as he leaped to his feet. "The murderer! I shall slay him this instant, on the *marae*, though all Waikato come down to avenge him!" And seizing an axe from the wall, he ran out in chase of "Ringiringi's" night antagonist.

The old fellow, when the chief rushed out at him like a madman, turned and fled from the village, and ran for his life until he disappeared in the shelter of the bush. Rupé did not pursue him far; his fit of anger was soon spent, and he returned to his *wharé*, and made his white man relate again, with Maori wealth of detail, the story of the eel-fishing bivouac.

"Ringiringi's" would-be slayer was never heard of again; at any rate, he did not venture back to the camp of the Hauhaus; and whether he ever succeeded in taking a *pakeha* head in settlement of his *utu* bill no man knows.

CHAPTER X

THE WAR-CHIEF AND HIS GODS

The war-chief Titokowaru—Ancient ceremonies and religion revived—Uenuku, the god of battle—Titokowaru's *mana-tapu*—
Bent makes cartridges for the Hauhaus—A novel weapon.

THE year 1867 was one of little activity amongst the Hauhaus with whom "Ringiringi" lived, except in respect of their interminable meetings and *Niu*-parades
and prophesyings. Hostilities had been suspended by both sides for the time, but
the temporary peace was only the prelude to the fiercest fighting of the Ten-Years'
War.

The white man worked for his master Rupé all that year, digging and planting,
carrying wood and water, and performing, in fact, the duties of a household slave.
But it was a slavery that had its privileges and its compensations, and there were
long days of abundant food and little work, in the intervals between the seasons
of communal labour in the potato-fields and the periodical birding and eeling and
pig-hunting expeditions.

It was while living at Te Paka that "Ringiringi" became well acquainted with
the celebrated Titokowaru, the great war-chief of the Hauhaus. Titoko, as his
name was usually abbreviated, came riding into the little bush-village one day
at the head of an armed band of Ngati-Ruanui and Nga-Ruahiné men, and held
a meeting in the *marae*, urging the people to renew the war. He was travelling
from village to village, haranguing the Hauhaus, and explaining his new plan of
campaign, which briefly was to make surprise attacks on small isolated redoubts
garrisoned by the white soldiers, and to lay ambuscades. He declared, too, that
his tactics would be, not to build any more stockaded forts in positions where the
Europeans could easily reach them, but to entice the troops into the midst of the
forest, where the Maori warrior would have the advantage. This scheme met with
general approval, and the tribespeople signified their intention of joining Titoko
and fighting his battles for him whenever he gave the word to begin.

Titokowaru was the most brainy, as well as the most ferocious, of the Taranaki
chiefs who led the Hauhaus against the whites. It was his strategy that was responsible for the most serious defeats inflicted on the Government forces in the
war of 1868-9. In appearance he was a stern, commanding man, with a counte-
nance disfigured by the loss of an eye—reminder of the Battle of Sentry Hill. He
was not tattooed. "When roused," says Bent, "he had a voice like a roaring lion."
In his attire he was often quaintly *pakeha*, for he frequently appeared in a black

"hard-hitter" hat and a full suit of European clothing. He carried no weapon but his sacred *taiaha*, his tongue-pointed staff of hardwood, ornamented with a plume of red *kaka* feathers.

The war-chief revived many a half-forgotten savage practice in the campaign that followed. Besides being a Hauhau "prophet," he was a *tohunga*, or priest, of the ancient Maori religion.

Before despatching a war-party he invariably recited the customary spells (*karakia*) to ensure their success, and the worship, or rather placation and invocation of Uenuku, the war-god, was resuscitated in every armed camp and on every battle-field.

Titoko possessed, in a strong degree, what the Maoris termed *mana-tapu*—personal *tapu*, or sacred prestige, heritage from his priestly forefathers of Ariki rank. His body was sacred in Maori eyes, and he was accredited with many a singular supernatural attribute: "Even the winds of heaven are his," said the Hauhaus. When the *whakarua*, the north-east breeze, blew, it was a fitting time for the war-parties to set out, for the *whakarua* was the breath of Uenuku, Titoko's deity, and his familiar spirit, and it was an omen of success in battle.

Bent gives some curious instances of Titokowaru's *mana-tapu*. Once, when the white man was travelling through the forest with Titoko and his band of Hauhaus, the chief's shoulder accidentally struck against a flax kit containing some cooked potatoes which an old man was carrying on his back. Titoko immediately ordered the man to throw the potatoes and basket away, for the food had become infected, through contact with the priest, with the mysterious and deadly microbe of the *tapu*, and consequently unfit to be eaten. So the old fellow had to cast his day's rations into the bushes and go fasting.

Titokowaru would suffer no rivals in the *pa*. Now and then it happened during the war-days that some budding *tohunga* would arise and prophesy things, in bold opposition to the chief, and announce that his familiar spirit, or his ancestral gods, had conferred priestly powers upon him. Titoko had "a short way with dissenters." His usual and most effective method of silencing the pretender was to take a basket of potatoes in his hand and seek out his rival.

"What," he would say, "have you then an *atua*, a god of your own?" Should the Hauhau be so imprudent as to answer "Yes," Titoko would lift his potato-kit and set it on his rival's head. "That for your *atua*!" It was enough. The other's *tapu*—if he ever had any—would be immediately destroyed by such an act, for the head of man must not be touched by food, and any self-respecting *atua* would desert a *tapu*-less Maori without delay. But no man dared, by way of retaliation, to try the potato-basket trick on Titokowaru.

"Ringiringi" had now been nearly three years with the Maoris, and spoke their language well. "I lived exactly like a Maori," he says; "worked like a nigger, and always went about bare-footed. They would not give me a gun, nor did they make me fight—for Titokowaru made me *tapu*, and would not permit me to go out on the war-path—but I had to make cartridges for them. They managed to get plenty of gunpowder; I have often seen it brought in in casks and in 25 lb. weights. They got a good deal of it from the neutral and so-called 'friendly' tribes, who procured it from the *pakehas*. The Puketapu tribe, and some of the Whanganuis, helped us in this way. I know there was a white man, Moffatt, living on the Upper Wanganui River, who made a coarse powder for the Hauhaus there, but I don't think any of it came our way. I had a wooden cartridge-filler, and we always had plenty of old newspapers to make the cartridge-cases. Bullets were plentiful, too, as a rule; but sometimes in the bush, when the Hauhaus ran short, they would use old iron, stones, and even pieces of hard wood. I have sometimes loaded my cartridges with bits of supplejack, cut to size, when I had no lead bullets."

In those bush-whacking days the Hauhaus made use of some remarkable devices against their enemies. One of these Maori engines of war was called a *tawhiti*, or trap. It was a sapling of some tough and elastic timber, *matipo* for choice. When a suitable one, about ten feet long or so, was found growing in a likely position outside a *pa* or alongside a bush-track by which the enemy were expected, it would be stripped of its branches, and bent down and back without breaking it, until it was lying in as near as possible a horizontal position, so that it would sweep the road. The end was fastened with flax in such a way that any unsuspecting person marching along the track or approaching the village and touching the trap, would cause the flax to slip, and release the *tawhiti*. The tree in its rebound could inflict a terrible blow.

In 1866 Bent saw ten or twelve of these *tawhiti* set on the tracks just outside Te Popoia, a small *pa* near Keteonetea. The place was attacked by the Government forces in the night, and in the darkness several of the *Kupapas*, or Government Maoris, who formed the advance guard, were injured by the unexpected release and rebound of these savage traps.[4]

---

[4]   Compare this with the ingenious form of "spring-gun" which an English exploring expedition found in use in 1910 amongst the Negrito pigmies on the slopes of the Snow Mountains, in New Guinea. This spring-gun is made by setting a flattened bamboo spear against a bent sapling, fastened to a trigger in such a way that it is released by the passer-by stumbling against an invisible string stretched across a game-track. These hardened bamboo spears inflict serious wounds, as they are launched with considerable force.

CHAPTER XI

"THE BEAK-OF-THE-BIRD"

The stockade at Te Ngutu-o-te-Manu—In the *Wharé-kura*—Singular
Hauhau war-rites—The "Twelve Apostles"—The enchanted *taiaha*—The heart of the *pakeha*: a human burnt-offering—An ambuscade and a cannibal feast.

EARLY in 1868 "Ringiringi" and his Hauhau comrades took up their quarters in
the stockaded village of Te Ngutu-o-te-Manu ("The Beak-of-the-Bird"), soon to be
the scene of the sharpest action of the war. This settlement was deep in the *rata* forest, about ten miles from where the town of Hawera now stands, in the direction of
Mount Egmont. Out on the fern-lands on the edge of the bush were the European
redoubts of Waihi and Turuturu-Mokai; the smaller of these, Turuturu, was sin-
gled out by Titokowaru as a position which could apparently be easily stormed;
he therefore laid his plans to attack it, and gathered in his best fighting-men in the
forest-fort.

Te Ngutu-o-te-Manu was now the headquarters of the Ngati-Ruanui and
Nga-Ruahiné belligerents, and all hands were set to work to fortify the village and
to gather in food-supplies for the *hapus* who crowded the "Bird's-Beak" *pa*. The
front of the village faced a cleared stretch of fern-land, but the forest surrounded it on the other sides; at the rear ran a little creek. There were no trenches or
earth-parapets; the principal defences were stout palisades, solid tree-trunks and
split timber, eight to ten feet high, sunk firmly in the ground, and connected by
cross-ties of saplings, fastened to the posts with forest vines. Close to the palisades
were some great *rata*-trees, very ancient and hollow; several of these the Hauhaus converted into miniature redoubts. Some of the hollow trees were cunningly
loopholed for rifle-fire, and within them stagings were made for the musketeers;
rough stages, too, were constructed up among the *rata* branches, where the dense
foliage and the interlacing boughs formed a perfect shelter for the brown-skinned
snipers. One of the tree-platforms, just inside the *pa* walls, was used as a *taumaihi*,
or look-out tower.

At one end of the village was the large Hauhau meeting-hall and praying-house
called *Wharé-kura* ("House of Learning," or "Red-painted House"), after the olden
Maori sacred lodges of priestly instruction. This building, built of sawn timber in
semi-European style, was about seventy feet in length. It was erected by Titokowaru's working-party in six days—in obedience to the Scriptural command "Six
days shalt thou labour"; they finished it on the sixth day, and religiously rested

on the seventh—and for many days thereafter. The *Wharé-kura* was consecrated by Titokowaru in the ancient heathen fashion; it was the temple of the Hauhau ritual, and here the high chief assembled his men when he wished to select war-parties for assaults and ambuscades. At the rear end of the great house was his sacred seat and sleeping-place, laid with finely woven flax mats and hedged by the invisible but potent barriers of *tapu*.

As often happened in Maori warfare, the first intimation the Hauhaus gave of their intention to renew the fighting was the murder of two or three incautious *pakehas* on the frontier.

Titokowaru's war-parties despatched on special missions usually numbered sixty men. Though consisting of this number they were termed the *Tekau-ma-rua,* or "The Twelve."

This term, though applied to the whole war-party, really belonged to the first twelve men, the advance-guard, who were usually the most daring and active warriors of all, but who had been selected in a peculiar manner which will be described. These twelve were *tapu*, and were all *tino toa*—tried and practised fighting-men. They numbered twelve because of the mystic force or prestige supposed to attach to that number. Titokowaru and all his Hauhaus were students of the *pakeha* Scriptures—Titokowaru when a young man had been a pupil in a mission school—and "The Twelve" were so named and numbered for several reasons: one was that there were twelve Apostles in the Bible; and another that there were the twelve sons of Jacob; then, also, there were twelve months in the year. Clearly to the Maori mind there was much virtue in twelve. In Maori belief none of the *Tekau-ma-rua* proper could be touched by a bullet in a fight if they but obeyed the instructions of Titokowaru.

Singular heathen ceremonies were practised in the selection of these war-parties. The spirit of ancient Maoridom was but slightly leavened by *pakeha* innovations and missionary teachings; and the savage gods of old New Zealand took fresh grip on the hearts of these never-tamed forest-men.

"Ringiringi" on several occasions witnessed the rites of the *Wharé-kura* what time the one-eyed general picked out the soldiers of the *Tekau-ma-rua.*

On the day before an armed expedition was to set forth from "The Beak-of-the-Bird," Titokowaru summoned the people by walking up and down outside his great *wharé* chanting a song which began:

> *"Tenei hoki au*
> *Ki te Ngutu-o-te-Manu."*

> ("Here am I
> In the Beak of the Bird.")

Then the people would all file into the sacred house and seat themselves on the mat-covered floor, the fighting-men of the *pa* in front. The war-chief took his seat cross-legged on his sacred mat that was spread on an elevated stage at the rear of the *Wharé-kura*, with a short rail in front; this dais was *tapu* to him. The men all chanted together a wild *haka* song, and then sat silent as death, waiting the will of

Titoko's war-god and the divination-by-*taiaha*.

The chief stood, grim and stern, facing his people, his sacred carved hardwood *taiaha*, called "Te Porohanga," in his hand. His wild eyes glittered as he recited in quick, sharp tones his invocation of the war-god Uenuku and the battle-spirit breathed on the wings of the *whakarua* breeze. Then, balancing his long plumed weapon in a horizontal position on his thumb and forefinger, the tongue-shaped point directed at the warriors, he stood stiff and motionless as in a trance. He was awaiting the message of his *atua*, the guiding-breath of Uenuku.

Suddenly, apparently of its own volition, and without any visible movement or effort on the part of the chief, the weapon would move. It would slowly, slowly turn—watched with intense, breathless earnestness by hundreds of fanatic eyes—until its tongue pointed so as to indicate some particular man. Ha! 'Twas the breath of Uenuku, deity of blood and fire, that gave it its impulse; Titoko was but the medium of the gods!

THE AMBUSCADE.

From a sketch by Major von Tempsky in Taranaki, 1866.

The warrior indicated would be questioned by the war-chief, and asked whether his "heart was strong" within him. If his answer were deemed satisfactory, he would be told off as one of the *Tekau-ma-rua*, the sanctified advance-guard.

Again and again this strange method of divination was repeated, the balanced weapon indicating—to the perfect satisfaction of the superstitious Hauhaus—the men whom the Maori war-god desired as the instruments of vengeance on the whites. Name after name the priest and chief pronounced, as his *taiaha* pointed along the squatting ranks, until the tale of bare-legged warriors was complete.

Then, when the *taua*, or war-party, had filled their cartridge-belts and seen to their weapons, there was a ceremony of a livelier sort. The women and girls of the *pa* attired themselves in their waist *piupiu* of coloured flax, decked their hair with feathers, dabbed ochre-paint on their cheeks, and lined up on the *marae* for the *poi*-dance, to send the warriors off "in good heart," as the Maori has it. *Hakas*, too, were danced by the men and boys of the village, and the merry *poi*-songs and the loudly yelled war-chants put a brisker jig into the feet of the brown soldiers as they marched out of the settlement and struck into the forest, hunting for *pakehas*.

As the men of the *Tekau-ma-rua* left the stockade, Titokowaru himself would loudly farewell them, shouting in his terrible gruff voice the ferocious injunction:

"Patua, kainga! Patua, kainga! E kai mau! Kaua e tukua kia haere! Kia mau ki tou ringa." ("Kill them! Eat them! Kill them! Eat them! Let them not escape! Hold them fast in your hands.")

Should the *Tekau-ma-rua* meet with success in their murderous raids, it was usual for the leader of the party to chant in a loud voice, as the home-palisades were neared, a song beginning, *"Tenei te mea kei te mou ki toku ringa,"* meaning that he had in his hand a portion of the flesh of a slain *pakeha*. This was called the *mawé*; it was an offering to the god of war. The *mawé* was almost invariably a human heart, torn from the body of the first man of the enemy killed in the fight.

On two or three occasions Kimble Bent witnessed the ceremony of the offering of the *mawé*, the ancient rite of the *Whangai-hau*. The heart (*manawa*) or other piece of human flesh, was brought into the *marae* and given to a man named Tihirua, who was the priest of the burnt sacrifice. He was a young man about twenty-five years of age, belonging to the Ngati-Maru tribe, of the Upper Waitara. "He would take the heart in his hand," says Bent, "and strike a match, or take a firestick and singe the flesh. When it was slightly scorched he would throw it away; it was *tapu* to Uenuku. This was an ancient war-custom of the Maoris; Titokowaru adopted it because he believed it would cause the *pakehas* to lose strength and courage, and become unnerved in time of battle. After the fight at Papa-tihakehake, in 1868, I saw this man Tihirua cut a white man's body open outside the *marae*, tear out the bleeding heart, hold lighted matches underneath it until it was singed, and then throw it away."[5]

A more frightful scene still that the sun looked down upon in that forest den was a cannibal feast. On June 12, 1868, a party of about fifteen Hauhaus from the *pa*, prowling out in the direction of the Waihi redoubt, cut off and shot and tom-ahawked a trooper of the Armed Constabulary, a man named Smith, who had incautiously ventured out to look for his horse beyond rifle-range of the redoubt. An Armed Constabulary officer, who happened to be walking across the parade ground at the time, heard and saw the firing, and with his field-glasses distinctly saw the flashing of the tomahawks as the Hauhaus cut the man to pieces. An armed party was immediately sent out at the double, but all they found when they reached the spot was half the body! The legs and hips were lying on the trampled and blood-drenched ground amongst the fern; the head and the upper part of the body down to the waist had been carried off by the savages, who had vanished into the forest as quickly as they had come. The remains of the poor trooper were

---

[5]   Tihirua died at Ohangai, near Hawera, in 1907.

cooked and eaten by the people in Te Ngutu-o-te-Manu, after the heart had been offered to Titokowaru's god of war by the young priest Tihirua.

Titokowaru, according to Bent, did not eat human flesh himself, but a boastful letter sent by him a few days later to a philo-*pakeha* chief at Mawhitiwhiti, seems to indicate that he was a cannibal of the most ferocious sort, unless, as is quite possible, he was speaking of his people generally when he used the first person singular. In this letter, addressed to Puano, and dated "Wharé-kura, June 25, 1868," he wrote this emphatic warning:

"Cease travelling on the roads, cease entirely travelling on the roads that lead to Mangamanga (Camp Waihi), lest ye be left upon the roads as food for the birds of the air and for the beasts of the field, or for me. Because I have eaten the white man; he was cooked like a piece of beef in the pot. I have begun to eat human flesh, and my throat is continually open for the flesh of man. *Kua hamama tonu toku korokoro ki te kai i te tangata.* I shall not die, I shall not die. When death itself shall be dead, I shall be alive (*Ka mate ano te mate, ka ora ano ahau*).—From Tιτοκο."

CHAPTER XII

THE ATTACK ON TURUTURU-MOKAI REDOUBT

Hauwhenua's war-party — A night march — Attack on Turuturu-Mokai
Redoubt — A heroic defence — The heart of the captain — Touch-
and-go — Relief at last.

ONE biting cold evening in July, 1868, the whole population of the "Bird's-
Beak" *pa* gathered on the *marae* to watch the departure of a fighting-column
launched by Titokowaru against the whites. It was a night fitter for the snug *wharé*
than for the war-path, but the omens were propitious for the expedition, and the
war-god's sacred breeze, the *whakarua*, breathed of Uenuku, blew across the forest.

The sixty warriors of the *Tekau-ma-rua* took the trail with the lilt of the dance-
girls' *poi*-chant in their ears, and the war-choruses yelled by their comrades in
the village gritted their battle-spirit. They were fittingly and thickly *tapu*'d for the
night's work, *karakia*'d over with many hardening and bullet-averting *karakias*,
and thoroughly Hauhau-bedevilled for the fight. Some of the warriors, belted and
painted, carried long Enfield muzzle-loaders, some double-barrelled guns, some
stolen or captured carbines, and a variety of other firearms. Each rifleman's equip-
ment included a short tomahawk thrust through his flax girdle; a few — the storm-
ing-party — were armed with long-handled tomahawks, murderously effective
weapons in a hand-to-hand combat. Though a winter's night, most of them were
scantily clad, as befitted a war-party. Some wore shirts and other part-European
dress; some only flax mats and waist-shawls.

Up and down the village square, as the Hauhau captain, Hauwhenua, led his
band out into the forest, strode Titokowaru, in a blaze of fanatic exaltation, crying
his commands to the warriors. Waving his plumed *taiaha*, he shouted, "Kill them!
Eat them! Let them not escape you!" And as they disappeared in the darkness he
returned to his place in the great council-house, where on his sacred mat he spent
the night in commune with his ancestral spirits and in reciting incantations for the
success of his men-at-arms.

In single file the Hauhau soldiers struck into the black woods. As they entered
the deeper thicknesses of the forest, where not a star could be seen for the density
and unbroken continuity of the roof of foliage above them, they chanted this brief
karakia, a charm invoking supernatural aid to clear their forest-path of obstructions
and smooth their way:

"Wahi taratara e i

Me tuku ki te Ariki
Kia taoro atu e—i,
Nga puke puke i noa."

Away through the bush they tramped, lightening the march with Hauhau chants, until their objective was neared—the little redoubt of Turuturu-Mokai.

One word of warning Titokowaru had given the *Tekau-ma-rua* when he chose them for this expedition. Kimble Bent, squatting with his fellows in the big house, had watched the divination-by-*taiaha* and the demon-like red tongue of the high priest's sacred weapon turning now to one silent warrior, now to another. He heard Titokowaru's injunction to the chosen of the war-god:

"Kaua e haere ki te kuwaha o te pa; kei reira te raiana e tu ana! Ka pokanoa koutou, ka ngaua te raiana ia koutou!" ("Do not charge at the gate way of the fort; there stands the lion! Should you disregard this command, the lion will devour you!")

This caution was designed to restrain the more impetuous of the young warriors, for Titokowaru was a crafty general, and did not believe in wasting good fighting-men. He had learned by dear experience at Sentry Hill in 1864 that to dash straight and blindly at the foe, though valiant enough, was not always sound tactics.

The leader of the *taua*, old Hauwhenua, must have been nearly seventy, but he was as active and agile and keen-witted as any young man of his fighting band. He was a product of the ferocious old cannibal times when every tribe's hand was against its neighbour's, and when year after year Waikato armies besieged the stockaded holds of Taranaki. In person he was not the ideal of a Maori warrior, for he was short of stature, a stoutly built man, with short grey beard and no tattoo-marks on his face. But he had fought against Maoris and against whites for many years of his life, and no war-captain surpassed him in the many stratagems of bush-warfare, and particularly in the artful laying of ambuscades.

Marching with the savages of the *Tekau-ma-rua* was the white man—Charles Kane, or King, called by the Maoris "Kingi," the deserter from the 18th Royal Irish. He was armed with a gun, intending to assist his Hauhau friends in their attack on his fellow-whites. Kimble Bent, it was reported afterwards in the *pakeha* camps, also accompanied the warriors, but he denies this, asserting that he did not stir from the *pa* all night; this is confirmed by the Maoris. "Kingi," he says, was a fiercely vindictive man, and swore to have a shot at the white men from whom he had cut himself off for ever.

Emerging from the forest, the warriors stole quietly down over the fern-slopes, and crossing the Tawhiti creek, which wound down through a valley close to the present town of Hawera, they worked round to the front of the little parapeted fort that stood in a singularly unstrategic position on a gently rising hillside, close to the celebrated ancient *pa*, Turuturu-Mokai. Hauwhenua passed round the word to hide in the fern and remain in cover there as close up to the redoubt as possible, until he yelled the *"Kokiri!"* cry—the signal for the charge.

The Turuturu-Mokai redoubt was but a tiny work, so small that the officer in charge, Captain Ross, had to live in a *raupo* hut built outside the walls. The entrenchment, consisting of earth-parapet and a surrounding trench, was being strengthened by its garrison of twenty-five Armed Constabulary, and the work was not quite finished when the Maori attack was delivered.

The night dragged on too slowly for the impatient and shivering warriors. Some wished to rush the white men's *pa* at once, but Hauwhenua and his sub-chiefs forbade it till there was a little more light. Several of the younger men began to crawl up through the fern towards the wall of the little fort. The form of a solitary sentry was seen, pacing up and down outside the walls. He could easily have been shot, but the Hauhaus waited.

The sentry was relieved at five o'clock in the morning. The new sentinel was not left in peace very long. Five minutes after he went on duty, while he was walking smartly up and down to keep warm, he heard a suspicious rustle in the fern. He stopped and peered into the dimness. Yes, he couldn't be wrong; those dark forms crawling towards him through the fern were Maoris! He raised his carbine and fired, then turned and raced for the redoubt, shouting out, "Stand to your arms, boys!"

The darkness—it was not yet dawn—was instantly lit up by the blaze of a return volley, and, with a fearful yell, the host of half-naked Maoris leaped from the fern and rushed for the redoubt.

The white soldiers, roused by the firing, rushed from their tents and manned the parapets and angles of the work, so furiously assailed by the swarming forest-men.

Captain Ross had leaped from his sleeping-place at the first alarm. He ran out from his *wharé*, armed with his sword and revolver, and clothed only in his shirt. He just managed to cross the ditch by the narrow plank-bridge ahead of the enemy, who missed the plank in the darkness.

The captain quickly called for volunteers to defend the gate.

"I'll make one, sir!" cried Michael Gill, an old Imperial soldier.

"All right, Gill," said the captain; it was pitch dark, but he knew Gill's voice. "Any more?"

Yes; they rushed for the gate—Henry McLean, George Tuffin, Swords, Gaynor, and Gill. The others manned the two flanking angles.

Private George Tuffin, one of the garrison—who is still alive, in Wanganui—was up with the others at the first alarm. He fired his revolver into the mass of Maoris outside the gateway; then, dropping the revolver, he got to work with his carbine. He had fired one shot out of his carbine, and stooped under the shelter of the parapet to slip in another cartridge. Just as he was rising to fire again he was struck in the head by a Maori bullet, and fell to the ground unconscious. He could not have been in that condition very long, for when he came to, Captain Ross was still alive and fighting to keep the Maoris out of the gateway.

"Hello, old man!" cried the captain; "are you hit?"

Young Tuffin lay there, unable to reply.

"Where's your rifle?" asked the captain; he was reloading his revolver while he spoke.

Tuffin pointed to where his gun was lying on the muddy ground beside him.

"Come on, boys!" yelled the captain; "they're coming in at the gate!"

Those were the last words Tuffin heard his commanding officer utter. A few moments later, in that fearful confusion of attack and defence in the darkness, the gallant Ross was struck down, defending the gateway to the end with his sword.

A Hauhau charged right into the redoubt, and killed the captain with his long-handled tomahawk. Making a clean cut in his breast, he tore out the heart, a trophy for the terrible ceremony of the *mawé* offering. Then he darted back as quickly as he had come, yelling a frightful cry of triumph. And another heart was torn from a white man's body even before it had ceased to beat. This was the corpse of Lennon, the keeper of the store and canteen. He had been killed alongside his little hut, just outside the redoubt, when the fight began. He was tomahawked almost to pieces and his heart cut out.

And in the very midst of that battle in the dark the pagan ceremony of the *whangai-hau* was performed, the oblation to the god of war. The priest of the war-party offered up one of the *pakeha* hearts—some Maoris say it was Captain Ross's, although Lennon's would really be the heart of the *mata-ika*, the "first-fish" slain, which was usually the one offered to the gods. The savage *tohunga* lit a match (he carried *pakeha* matches for this dreadful purpose), and held the bleeding heart over the flame. Immediately it began to sizzle and smoke, he cried in an exultant voice, "*Kei au a Tu!*" ("I have *Tu!*"), meaning that Tu, the supreme god of war, was with him, or on his side. Then he threw down the burnt sacrifice, and, clutching his long-handled tomahawk, rushed into the fight again. The captain's heart was discovered after the fight was over lying on the blood-stained ground outside the trench.

For two hours it was desperate work. The Hauhaus charged up to the parapets, and many of them jumped into the ditch, whence they attempted to swarm over the walls, but were beaten off again and again by the little garrison. The endeavour to rush in force through the gateway of the redoubt did not succeed. The impulsive young men, however, disregarded Titokowaru's warning about the "lion" in the path, and it was in this tomahawk charge at the fort gate that most of those who were killed fell.

After the captain's death Gill and McLean took up their posts in one of the angles, and fought there till daylight. Their Terry carbines gave them a good deal of trouble. After a few rounds had been fired the breech-blocks jammed, and were difficult to open and close.

Unfortunately, all hands did not show equal bravery. At least four—Michael Gill says five—men bolted for the redoubt, some of them jumping from the parapet, soon after the fight began. Gill called to them to stop and help to protect the wounded. But they fled and left their comrades.

One of the pluckiest men in the redoubt was Cosslett Johnston (now of Hawera), a military settler. Mr. Johnston's intrepid example put fresh courage into his despairing comrades on that terrible morning. Michael Gill was an old Imperial soldier; he had served in the 57th Regiment, the old "Die-Hards"—Kimble Bent's regiment—and his coolness did a lot to steady his fellow-soldiers. Gill was recommended for the Victoria Cross for his bravery, but did not get it. He, like his comrades, certainly deserved that decoration or the New Zealand Cross, but did not get either.

When the Captain fell, Tuffin crawled, more than half-dazed with his wound, to one of the angles. There he received four more bullet wounds. In the angle there were five other men; of these two were killed.

Failing in their first attempt to take the redoubt by assault, some of the Hauhaus took post on the rising ground a little distance off, where they could fire into the work, and one after another the defenders dropped, shot dead or badly wounded. The ditch was full of Maoris. Only the narrow parapet separated them from the whites, and they yelled at the defenders and shouted all the English "swear-words" in their vocabulary. The *pakehas* "talked back" at them, says one of the few survivors of the heroic garrison, and cried "Look out! The cavalry are coming!" but the Hauhaus only laughed and said, "Gammon, *pakeha*—gammon!" Then, finding that any Maori who showed his head above the parapets was quickly shot down, they started to dig away at the wall with their tomahawks, and succeeded in undermining the parapet in several places. By this time half the garrison had been shot down. One of the first killed was Corporal Blake, who fell in one of the angles. Private Shields, the captain's orderly, was killed in one of the angles; Private George Holden was shot dead behind the parapet; Gaynor was killed at the gate. Then Sergeant McFadden fell while bravely helping to hold an angle against the swarming enemy.

Private Alexander Beamish, who fell mortally wounded while helping to defend an angle of the fort, told his brother, John Beamish (now a resident of Patea), who was fighting by his side, just before he died, that he believed it was a white man who shot him. Bent says that the deserter Kane, while taking part in the attack, was wounded in the right cheek by a *pakeha* bullet, and then retired from the fight. John Beamish was struck by an Enfield bullet and severely wounded about the time his brother was shot, but though then unable to shoulder his carbine, he opened packets of ammunition and passed cartridges to Gill, the only unwounded man in his angle of the redoubt, until the end of the combat.

Here is John Beamish's story of the fight, as he told it to me some years back:

"The Maoris surrounded the redoubt and tried again and again to swarm over the wall, and they kept it up till broad daylight. We could not see much at first but the flashing of guns all around us. Presently some of the Maoris set fire to the *wharés* outside the redoubt. They were armed with muzzle-loading Enfields and shot-guns, and we could now and then see the ramrods going up and down as they rammed the charges home. Then sometimes we would see the flash of a tomahawk and catch a glimpse of a black head above the parapets. One of our troubles was that there were no loopholes in the parapets, otherwise we could have shot many of the Maoris in the ditch. We were exposed to the fire of the enemy on the rising ground close by, and this was how so many of the men in our angle were hit.

"Then they started to dig and cut away at the parapets with their tomahawks. We could plainly hear them at this work, and I heard one Maori ask another for a match. I suppose he wanted to try and fire our buildings inside the walls. One after another our men dropped, shot dead or badly wounded. I had very little hope of ever getting out of the place alive. But we well knew what our fate would be if the Maoris once got over the parapets, so we just put our hearts into it and kept blazing away as fast as we could load. We had breech-loading carbines which had to be capped. One incident I remember was a black head just appearing over the parapet in the grey light, then came a body with a bare arm gripping a long-handled tomahawk. Quietly the Hauhau raised himself up, and was just in the act of aiming a blow at one of our men who did not see him when we fired and brought him down.

"My younger brother was fighting not far from me. He fell mortally wounded, and before he died he told us he believed it was a white man who shot him. I was wounded about the same time. An Enfield bullet struck me in the left shoulder. It took me with a tremendous shock, just as I was stooping down across a dead man to get some dry ammunition. The bullet slanted down past my shoulder-blade and came out at the back. This incapacitated me from firing, or, at any rate, from taking aim, so I had to content myself with passing cartridges to Michael Gill—one of the men in my angle—who kept steadily firing away, and with levelling my unloaded carbine as well as I could with my right hand whenever I saw a head bob up above the parapet. When the fight ended Gill was the only unwounded man in our angle of the redoubt; out of the six who manned it when the alarm was given, three were shot dead and two were wounded. One man, George Tuffin, was wounded in five places.

"Daylight came, and those of us who could shoulder a carbine were still firing away and wondering whether help would ever reach us. We knew they must have heard the firing and seen the flashes of the guns at Waihi redoubt, only three miles away. Suddenly the Maoris ceased firing and retired into the bush. Their sentries had given them warning that troops were coming. As they dropped back we rushed out of the redoubt and gave them the last shot, and then Von Tempsky and his A.C.'s arrived at the double, and the fight was over. My wound kept me in the hospital for five months. The only wonder is that any of us ever came out of that redoubt alive."

The sun had risen before the fight was over. A few minutes more and the Hauhaus would have succeeded in undermining the parapets sufficiently to force an entrance, and the defenders would have fallen to the last man, and the whole of their arms and the post-supplies have been carried off to Titokowaru's fort in the forest.

The little redoubt was a frightful sight. Dead and wounded men were lying all over the place in pools of blood; two of them were shockingly mutilated with tomahawks. Out of the twenty-one defenders of the redoubt, ten were killed and five were wounded; only six came through the fight without a wound.

Hauwhenua withdrew his disappointed *Tekau-ma-rua*, carrying those of their wounded who were unable to walk, and marched back to Te Ngutu-o-te-Manu. The "lion" of Titoko's speech, though sore wounded, had in truth closed his mouth on some of their most daring braves. Takitaki, a bold, athletic young Hauhau, who was in the *Tekau-ma-rua*, was one of those who attacked Captain Ross at the gateway. The Captain shattered Takitaki's left arm with a bullet from his revolver before he fell.[6]

---

[6]   Of this Hauhau Colonel W. E. Gudgeon wrote in the Polynesian Society's Journal, No. 59 (Sept. 1906): "Had there been but ten men of the stamp of Takitaki the redoubt must have been taken; but luckily there were not, and therefore a mere handful of men held the redoubt to the end."

CHAPTER XIII

THE KILLING OF KANE

Bent and Kane brought before Titokowaru — Kane's flight — Captured
by the Hauhaus — A traitor's end.

WHEN the renegade Charles Kane, or "Kingi," fled from the Turuturu-Mokai
fight after receiving his bullet-wound, he made his way to the Turangaréré village,
and announced that he would not return to Te Ngutu-o-te-Manu. The Maoris,
however, took him back to Te Ngutu, and he and Kimble Bent were brought before
Titokowaru, who was sitting in the *Wharé-kura*. Bent now appears, from his own
account, to have wearied of his terrible life amongst the Hauhaus.

The war-chief fiercely questioned "Kingi," whom he suspected of an intention
to return to the European camps.

Then turning to "Ringiringi," he said:

"E Ringi, speak! Do you ever think of leaving us and running away to the
pakehas?"

Bent confessed that he now desired to return to the men of his own colour,
adding. "But I will never take arms against you."

Titokowaru glared at his white man, then he went to the door of the council-house and called to the people in the *marae* to enter.

When they were all in the big *wharé*, Titokowaru ordered them to close the
door and the sliding-window.

In the gloom of the praying-house the people sat in terrible silence, and the
white men trembled for their heads.

Titokowaru, fearfully stern and menacing, addressed the *pakehas*.

"*Whakarongo mai!* Listen to me. If you persist in saying that you wish to return
to the white men, it will be your death! I will kill you both with my tomahawk,
now, in this house, unless you promise that you will never leave the Maoris! I will
slay you, and your bodies will be cooked in the *hangi*!"

"Ringiringi," in real fear of his life, made answer that he would remain with
the Hauhaus if Titoko would protect him, for he dreaded some of the chief's fiercer
followers. "Kingi," too, hastened to give the required promise — a promise which
he, unlike his fellow-*pakeha*, broke at the first opportunity.

When the people had left the *Wharé-kura*, Titoko spoke to "Ringiringi" in a more friendly and reassuring tone, saying that he wished the *pakeha* to remain with him in the *pa*, and that, in order to assure his life against the wilder spirits in the tribes gathered under his command, he would *tapu* him, as Te Ua had done two years before. For his *tapu*, he explained, was a far more effective and binding one than that of the Opunake prophet; a spell that no man dared break on pain of death.

Not many days later the Irish traitor "Kingi" deserted from the *pa*, taking with him a watch, a revolver, and some clothing which he had "commandeered" from the natives.

For some little time nothing was heard of him. At length the warriors of the *Tekau-ma-rua*, while out scouting one day in the direction of Turangaréré, discovered on the track leading to the settlement a note addressed to the white soldiers' commander at Waihi, stating that the writer (Kane) and Bent were at Te Ngu-tu-o-te-Manu, awaiting a favourable opportunity to tomahawk Titokowaru, cut off his head, and bring it in to the Government camp. Kane was evidently clearing the way for his return to civilisation, and this note—which he had left in a spot where he hoped the white troops would come across it—was obviously intended to serve as a palliative in some measure of his military offences.

The deserter's letter was brought to the "Bird's-Beak" *pa*, where it was translated by an English-speaking Maori. "Ringiringi," questioned, disclaimed any knowledge of it, and as to the incriminating reference to himself, he assured Titokowaru that "Kingi" was lying.

Titokowaru immediately despatched the white man and four armed Maoris after "Kingi." They found him at Te Paka village; he disappeared that evening, but was later caught by a party of seven Maoris and confined in a *raupo* hut at Te Paka.

They killed him there that night.

Bent was lying half-asleep in a *wharé* in the settlement when the seven Maoris, who had brought "Kingi" in, entered, in an intensely excited state, sat down, and asked him if he had heard of the judgment on his fellow-white. Then one of them said, "Kingi is dead."

Another man, leaning forward until his passionate face almost touched Bent's, exclaimed:

"Ringi, had you done as Kingi has done, we would not have killed you in the ordinary way. Your fate would have been burning alive in the oven on the *marae*!"

Then the seven, after a conversation between themselves in a strange language the white man could not understand, listen as he would—the Maoris sometimes improvise a secret tongue, by eliding certain syllables in words and adding new ones—the executioners rose and left the *wharé*.

It was not until next day that "Ringiringi" learned the details of the deserter's end.

"Kingi," after being given a meal, was left alone in his hut, but was watched through crevices in the wall until he sank to sleep, fatigued with his enforced tramp. He lay with a blanket partly drawn over his head. One of the Hauhaus, a man named Patumutu ("The Finishing Stroke"), stole quietly into the *wharé*, and attempted to deal him a fatal blow with a sharp bill-hook. The blow, however, only gashed his nose, and he leaped up and grappled with his assailant.

The Maoris outside, hearing the noise of the scuffle, rushed in. An old man—Uru-anini of the Puketapu—seized the white man by the leg, brought him down, and dealt him a terrible blow with an axe as he lay on the floor.

The other Hauhaus completed the work with their tomahawks, and the dead body of the renegade Irishman, cut almost to pieces, was dragged out and thrown into a disused potato-pit on the outskirts of the village.

CHAPTER XIV

ADVENTURES AT TE NGUTU-O-TE-MANU

In the midst of dangers—Bent stalked by Hauhaus—Old Jacob to the rescue—"Come on if you dare!"—The white man's new Maori name—Government forces attack and burn Te Ngutu-o-te-Ma-nu—A new use for hand-grenades.

WHEN Bent returned to the "Bird's-Beak" stockade he found himself in a position of extreme peril.

The Hauhaus, excited by the news of Kane's treachery and summary execution, were fiercely hostile in demeanour, and some of the young bloods came dancing about the white man, as he walked into the village, with menacing shouts, emphasised by savage thigh-slapping, *pukana*-ing, and grimacing with out-thrust tongue and rolling eyes, and similar demonstrations of derision and hatred.

A council of the people was held on the *marae*, and the killing of Kane was narrated in minutest and barbaric detail. Then several Hauhaus rose in turn and demanded the death of "Ringiringi," on the principle that all *pakehas* were unreliable, and that it was a foolish policy to keep one in the camp who might sooner or later betray them. "Let us lead him outside the *pa* and shoot him," proposed one truculent young warrior of the *Tekau-ma-rua*.

"*Kaati!*" cried Titokowaru, in his great roaring voice, as he rose with his spear-staff in his hand. "'Ringiringi' is my *pakeha*. I have *tapu*'d him, and I have told him that his life is safe. If you want to shoot him—well, you must kill me first!"

Then, turning to the white man, the war-chief took him by the hand, led him to his own house, and shut the people out. He told "Ringiringi" that in the present temper of the tribesmen he had better remain as much as he could in the *wharé*, and that, at any rate, he must not venture far from the door unless he, Titoko, were with him or in view.

Some days later, "Ringiringi," imagining from the more settled and pacific attitude of the Hauhaus that he no longer ran any risk in taking his walks abroad, wandered a short distance outside the stockade into the forest, and, seating himself on a fallen tree-trunk, filled his pipe for a quiet smoke. Suddenly he heard a cough. He looked about him, but saw no one.

"Who's there?" he called out.

A voice close above him replied, "It is I—Hakopa."

"Ringiringi" looked up quickly, and saw an old tattooed man named Hakopa (Jacob) te Matauawa, perched on the lowest branch of a *rata*-tree, with a double-barrelled gun in his hand. Hakopa was a tall, lean, straight old fellow, a veteran of the ancient fighting type. Bent had a thorough admiration for him as a man of singular courage, without the braggadocio of the young *toas*; Hakopa had for a long time exhibited a kindly leaning towards the white man, and had been a firm friend of his all through the troubled days in the *pa*.

"Quick, quick!" he said, in a low, cautious voice. "Hide yourself, Ringi! When you walked out of the *pa* I heard two men who were watching you say that they would follow you up and kill you as they had killed Kingi. They went to their *wharés* for their weapons, and I followed you quickly to warn you. I saw you standing there, and climbed on this branch to see what those men are doing. *E tama!* Conceal yourself! They are coming."

The white man hastily selected a hiding-place. He lay down behind a big log near by, a fallen *pukatea*-tree; the log and the creepers and ferns that grew about it quite concealed him from the view of any one approaching from the *pa*.

Hardly had he hidden himself than two villainous-visaged young Hauhaus walked quickly along the track from the *pa* gateway. Both swung tomahawks as they came, and one carried at his girdle a revolver—trophy taken from some slain white officer.

Seeing Hakopa descending from his tree-perch, they stopped and asked:

"Where is the *pakeha*? Did you see him pass?"

"Why do you ask?" said the old man.

"We have come to kill him," replied one of the men. "Where is he?"

Hakopa instantly put his cocked *tupara* to his shoulder and levelled it at the foremost of the Hauhaus, the man with the revolver.

"*Haere atu!*" he said sharply. "Go! Leave this spot at once, or I will shoot you. 'Ringiringi' is my friend."

The old fellow's determined air quite overawed the *pakeha*-hunters, and they sulkily and silently returned to the *pa*.

Jacob watched them off, and when the white man had risen from his hiding-place he escorted him back to the *pa*, walking in front of him with his gun cocked, on the alert for any attack on his protégé. He took "Ringiringi" to his house, and then reported the affair to Titokowaru.

The chief showed genuine anger. He assembled the fighting-men, and sternly ordered them to molest the white man no more. "If you harm him," he said, "I shall leave the *pa* and return to my own village. Listen! 'Ringiringi' is henceforth my *moko-puna*—my grandchild—and I now give him another name, the name of one of my ancestors. His name is now Tu-nui-a-moa."

And behind Titokowaru leaped up old Hakopa, a bright tomahawk in his hand. Making sharp, quick cuts in the air with his tomahawk, he cried, as he danced to and fro:

"Yes, and if any one attempts to touch the white man, he will have to kill me too! Kill me and Titokowaru! Who will dare it? Come on, come on!"

Thereafter Bent was not molested. He went by his new name, and "Ringiringi" he was called no more; at any rate, not by Titokowaru's tribe.

The "Bird's-Beak" soon received its baptism of blood and fire. Colonel McDonnell, with a force of about three hundred Armed Constabulary and volunteers, under Majors von Tempsky and Hunter, attacked the *pa* on August 21, 1868. The whites charged right into the village under a heavy fire, and the Maoris fled to the bush, losing several killed.

Bent, fortunately for himself, was not in the *pa*; he had gone over to the Turangaréré settlement, a few miles away, to procure gunpowder and paper for the manufacture of cartridges, and most of the other men were out cattle-shooting in the bush. Titokowaru retired to his praying-house when the firing began, and sat there muttering incantations, and it was only with great difficulty that he was persuaded by his people to leave the *wharé* and retire. The great house was set fire to by Colonel McDonnell when the *pa* was captured, and the sacred *wharé-kura*, where the high-priest had so often exhorted his people and with enchanted *taiaha* told off the warriors of the *Tekau-ma-rua*, was soon a mass of flames. The Government troops lost four men killed and eight wounded in the engagement. Most of these casualties occurred in the march back to Waihi, which became a heavy rear-guard action, for the main body of the Hauhaus came up in time to attack the troops briskly as they retired through the thick bush. Then they drew off and returned to their half-demolished *pa*, to weep over their dead and the ashes of their great *wharé-kura* and rebuild their ruined homes.

The troops had placed a number of hand-grenades, small shells filled with powder, in the thatch of the *wharés* when they fired the village; but some of the houses were not destroyed, and on the return of the Hauhaus, they found some of these grenades unexploded. The dangerous shells were given to Bent to handle. He pulled out the fuses—which the Maoris called *wiki*, or wicks—and emptied the precious powder into flasks. In this way a sufficient quantity of powder to make eighteen gun-cartridges was obtained from each hand-grenade.

CHAPTER XV

A BATTLE IN THE FOREST; AND THE DEATH OF VON TEMPSKY

The second fight at Te Ngutu-o-te-Manu—Titokowaru's prophecy—
Tutangé and his sacred war-mat—Bent's narrow escape—Government forces defeated—How von Tempsky fell—A terrible retreat—Colonial soldiers' gallant rear-guard fight.

EARLY one warm spring afternoon in 1868, when the vast forest lay steeped
in calm and Taranaki's sentry-peak rose like a great ivory tent out of the soft blue
haze that bathed its spreading base, the sharp, cracking sound of rifle-shots broke
the quiet of the wilderness.

The shots came from the mountain side of "The Beak-of-the-Bird," the opposite one to that by which the white troops had advanced the previous month. Te
Ngutu-o-te-Manu was being taken in the rear this time. Colonel McDonnell had
set out from the Waihi Redoubt before daylight in the morning, with a force of
about two hundred and sixty whites, composed of three divisions of Armed Constabulary (many of them ex-Forest Rangers), the newly joined Wellington Rifles
and Rangers, and a few veteran volunteers, besides about a hundred *Kupapas*, the
friendly Maoris from the Whanganui and Ngati-Apa tribes under Kepa te Rangihiwinui. Fording the swift Wai-ngongoro River (the "Waters-of-Snoring"), the Colonel's force, guided by the woman Takiora, marched through the native village
of Mawhitiwhiti, which was found deserted, then turned into the dense forest,
searching for the Hauhau stronghold, which was now reported to be at Te Rua-ru-
ru ("The Owl's Nest"), situated somewhere in the rear of Te Ngutu-o te Manu. A
disastrous search, for it ended under the palisades of the "Bird's-Beak," the savage
beak that closed savagely on many a gallant *pakeha* before the sun went down in
the western sea that day.

McDonnell had hoped by his early start to take the Hauhaus by surprise. But
wary old Titokowaru was seldom caught napping.

On the previous night—as the old warrior Tutangé Waionui tells me—Titokowaru gathered all his men in the big house (*wharé-kura*), which had now been
rebuilt. Then, when the Hauhau prayers and chants were over, the chief arose and
cried:

"E Koro ma, kia tupato! He po kino te po, he ra kino te ra!" ("O friends, be on your
guard! This is an evil night—a night of danger, and the morrow will be a day of

danger!")

This oracular warning seemed to the superstitious people to be a message from the gods, of whom Titokowaru was the living medium. That night was a night of preparation for battle. Armed men slipped out along the trail in front of the stockade, and lay in wait for the expected enemy.

Long the grim old chief sat on his sacred mat that night in the *wharé-kura*, his enchanted tongue-pointed *taiaha* lying in front of him. *Karakia* after *karakia* he recited in a low monotone, incantations and charms, ancient pagan and latter-day Hauhau *karakia*, for success in the conflict that he felt was to envelop his *pa* on the morrow in a ring of smoke and blood.

In his own little thatched *wharé* that day sat Kimble Bent, the *pakeha*-Maori. He, too, was busy, squatting there on an old flax *whariki* mat. By his side were a keg of gunpowder and a bag of bullets, and in front of him a pile of old *pakeha* newspapers and leaves torn from looted books. He was making cartridges for the Hauhaus. Round a wooden cartridge-filler he deftly rolled a scrap of paper, forming a cylinder, which he tied securely with thread or with fine strips of flax; then, withdrawing the filler, he poured in the gunpowder. The cartridges loaded, he slipped them into the cartouche-boxes and holders, a number of which had been brought to the *wharé* by the men of the *Tekau-ma-rua*; when the boxes were full, the remainder of the ammunition he stored carefully in a large flax basket. Most of the receptacles for the ammunition—*hamanu* the Maoris called them—were primitive affairs smacking of the bush. In size and shape they resembled the ordinary military leather cartouche-boxes, but they were simply blocks of light wood, generally *pukatea* timber, slightly curved in shape so as to sit well on the body when strapped, and neatly bored with from ten to eighteen holes, each of which held a cartridge. A flap of leather or skin—in the earlier days it was often a piece of tattooed human skin—covered the cartridges; and straps of leather or of dressed and ornamented flax were attached to the *hamanu*, which were buckled or tied round the waist or over the shoulders. A well-equipped fighting-man usually wore two *hamanu*, by belts over the shoulders; and at his girdle he carried his pouches for bullets and percussion-caps.

Such was the lone white man's occupation in the forest stockade that day before the looming battle.

Next morning, after the first meal of the day had been set before the warriors by their women and had been quickly eaten, the war-chief came out of his house, *taiaha* in hand, and walked out on to the village square in front of the sacred praying-house.

"Friends," he cried, as he stood there on the *marae*, "I salute you! You have eaten and are content; for the proverb says, 'When the stomach is filled, then man is happy and satisfied' ('*Ka ki te puku, ka ora te tangata*'). Now, rise up and grasp your weapons, for I wish to see you dance the *haka* and the *tutu-waewae* of war."

When the men were assembled on the parade ground, in their dancing costume of a scanty waist-mat, Titokowaru cried in a loud voice and prophesied, saying:

"Kaore e tu te ra, kaore e titaha te ra, ka tupono tatou kia to tatou whanaunga" —of which the meaning is, "The sun will not have reached its zenith, the sun will not have declined, before we have joined issue with our relatives" —the white soldiers.

"Then," says Tutangé, "we danced our *haka* with the fire of coming battle in our hearts, and we hardened our nerves for the fight. For we knew that Titoko was a true and powerful prophet (*poropiti whai-mana, tino kaha*), and we believed that that day would see blood shed again around Te Ngutu-o-te-Manu."

Tutangé Waionui, who was now to distinguish himself as a daring young warrior, was but a boy. He was not more than fifteen or sixteen years old, but was a strong, athletic youngster, full of fire and courage, and as agile as a monkey. He was of the *momo rangatira*, or "blue blood" of Taranaki, tracing a direct descent through a line of high chiefs and priests from Turi, the great sailor who navigated his long mat-winged canoe *Aotea* to the black iron-sand beach of Taranaki from the far-distant Hawaiki, the beautiful palm-fringed island of Rangiatea (Raiatea, as its people call it now) in the Society Group. His father, the old warrior, Maruera Whakarewataua, had carefully schooled him in the business of arms, the handling of the spear-tongued *taiaha*, most beautiful of Maori weapons, the quick and fatal use of the tomahawk, both the terrible long-handled one and the short hatchet, or *patiti*, as well as the musket and shot-gun and rifle of the *pakeha*. So here, now, was young Tutangé on his first war-path.

That morning, when the very air seemed full of rumours of battle and death, Tutangé was girded with the sacred war-mat, the *maro-taua*.

TUTANGÉ WAIONUI, A HAUHAU WARRIOR.

This photo, taken in 1908, shows Tutangé—who was one of Titokowaru's best fighting men—stripped and armed for the war-path as he was in 1868.

"My father's sister," says he, "called me to her, together with certain other young men who were of *rangatira* rank, and who had not yet fought the white man. She was a chieftainess, by name Tāngamoko; she was of *ariki* birth in the Ngati-Ruanui tribe, and being possessed of *mana-tapu* and of a knowledge of charms and incantations, she was as a priestess amongst the people. She called us to her, and told us that she was about to make us *tamariki tapu*, that is, sacred children, for the coming battle. She girded us each with a fine waist-garment, the *korowai*, made of soft dressed and closely woven white flax, with short black thrums, or cords, hanging down it. These flax vestures, falling from our waists to our knees, she had made herself. They were the garments of war; she had *karakia*'d over them and charmed them so that the bullets of the enemy should not touch them, and so that we, their wearers, might conquer in the fight. And very proud and confident *tamariki tapu* we were now, parading the *pa* in our bullet-proof *korowai*, and dancing our weapons in the air as we leaped with our elders in the *haka* and roared out the great chorus of the war-song beginning, '*Kia kutia—au—au!*' and that other one which our fathers had chanted when first they set up the Maori Land League, '*E kore Taranaki e makere atu!*' ('Taranaki will not be cast away from us!')

"One of the songs which we chanted as we wildly danced was this:

> "'*Whakarongo ai au*
> *Ki te koroki manu*
> *Whakaorooro ana i te ngahere.*
> *I na-wa e!*'

> ('I'm listening for the voices,
> The singing of the birds,
> Sounding, echoing in the forest!')

The 'singing of the birds' was a figure of speech for the voices of the soldiers on the march.

"That *maro-taua* was all the clothing I wore in the fight. Round my brows I bound a handkerchief, which held in place my *tiparé rangatira*, my chief-like war-feathers. My weapons were a double-barrelled gun (*tupara*), and a short-handled tomahawk, which I carried stuck in my belt. Round me I had strapped a cartridge-holder. *E tama!* Now I was ready for my first battle."

Meanwhile, what of the *pakeha*-Maori in this nest of Hauhaus?

That morning, after he had supplied the men with ammunition, he sat on the *marae* watching the war-dances. The morning went, but there was no sign from the outlying Hauhau piquets. Most of the women and children had been sent away into the bush at the rear of the *pa* in charge of the old chief Te Waka-tākere-nui, in anticipation of the predicted attack. The *pakeha*-Maori was also a non-combatant, but he remained in the *pa* with Titokowaru until the firing began. There were not more than sixty fighting-men in Te Ngutu-o-te-Manu, but nearly all of these were tried and experienced warriors, and even those who, like young Tutangé, were still to be blooded, were more than a match for the average white soldier in bush-warfare.

It was well on in the afternoon before the first shots were heard. The Maoris had expected attack from the seaward or Waihi side, but to their surprise the sound of the firing came from inland, indicating that the troops had worked round to the rear of "The Beak-of-the-Bird." The Maori advance-guard of Colonel McDonnell's column had encountered the Hauhaus in the bush and fired into them.

When the first sharp rifle-cracks echoed through the forest, Titokowaru went up to his *pakeha*, with a flax kit in his hand.

"Friend," said the stern old captain, "take this *kété* of mine in your charge. It contains some of my *tapu* treasures; take great care of it, for I may not see you again; I may fall with my tribe. Take it and leave the *pa*, and join Te Waka-tākere-nui if you can find his camp in the forest."

The white man took the carefully strapped kit and hurried out of the stockade. Te Waka's camp, he knew, was somewhere away in the rear; the firing was in that direction, and he was in danger of falling into the enemy's hands. However, he struck out into the bush from the rear fence, expecting to steal through the thick timber on the flank of the troops, who, he guessed, were advancing by the track which led in from the east.

He managed to elude his fellow-countrymen as it happened, but it was "touch-and-go" with him. Scarcely had he run out from the stockade and entered the hollow, through which a little creek wound through the bush at the rear of the *pa*, than the advance-guard of the white column also reached the creek, and crossed it to attack the *pa*. A heavy fire was at this moment opened on the troops by the Hauhaus, and bullets flew thick around the *pakeha*-Maori.

Two or three of the Armed Constabulary came almost upon him just as he mounted the farther bank of the creek, near where a little burial-ground clearing broke the continuity of the thick undergrowth; it was here that the Hauhaus had interred those of their number killed in the previous attack on the *pa*.

The Colonial soldiers must have mistaken Bent for a Maori, for they immediately fired at him but missed, and next moment he ducked into the jungle, and on all-fours scrambled down into the creek bed, where he followed down the little stream as hard as he could go.

There was small wonder the A.C.'s took Bent for a Maori, for it would have been difficult in the half-light of that bush, at the distance of a few yards, to have detected much resemblance to a white man in the dark, shaggy-headed, bare-footed fellow with an old and dirty blanket strapped around his waist, a ragged jacket about his shoulders, and a red handkerchief tied round his head.

Scrambling along, stooping low to avoid being hit, the *pakeha*-Maori went down the creek until he came to a large hollow *mahoé*-tree standing by the side of the watercourse. He squeezed into the hollow trunk of the tree, and there he remained for a few minutes listening to the cracking of the rifles and the loud reports of the Hauhau smooth-bores and the yells of the combatants. Soon the firing came nearer, and bullets began to zip through the leaves and come plunk into the *mahoé*, in whose hollow heart the white man hid.

"The bullets are finding me out," said Bent to himself. "I'm in a fix still; anyhow, here goes," and he cautiously crept out from his place of concealment and took to the jungle-fringed creek again. Following down the creek, crawling, scrambling, running, he presently began to feel his head more secure on his shoulders, for the sound of the firing grew fainter. He left the creek, and, striking through the bush, found a familiar track which led him to the little nook in the forest where old Te Waka and the anxious women and terrified children were camped. There he remained that night.

From Te Waka's people he heard the account of the morning's work. The Government Maori forces, Kepa's men, came upon the camp of refugees and killed two children; one of these, a boy of about nine years of age, was the son of the Hauhau warrior, Kātené Tu-Whakaruru. The other child, a little girl, they most cruelly slew by throwing her up into the air and spitting her on a bayonet as she fell. Another child, a little boy, was captured, but was saved by a Whanganui Maori, who carried him out of the forest on his back. He was a son of Te Karere-o-Mahuru ("The Messenger of Spring"). This boy became a protégé of Sir William Fox, who had him educated, and he is to-day a well-known and gifted representative Taranaki man; his name is Pokiha (Fox) O-Mahuru. When the camp was surprised a woman ran away into the forest in terror; as she was never again heard of, it is believed that the soldiers shot her.

For the rest of the story of that battle in the bush, from the Maori side, my chief authorities are Tutangé Waionui, who gave me his narrative in 1908, and Whakawhiria, of Taranaki. Of the disaster from the European side there are numerous accounts, no two of which agree. The truth is, it was a lamentably bungled affair, redeemed by numerous acts of personal heroism, and particularly by the gallant rear-guard action fought by a portion of the column under the brave young Captain Roberts during the terrible retreat which followed the repulse of the troops.

The Government force outnumbered the Hauhaus in the *pa* by more than five to one. Of this, however, McDonnell and his officers and men were ignorant, otherwise there might have been a very different story to tell. In the obscurity of the dense bush, where the savage forest-men were in their familiar haunts, everything was strange and terrible to the recruits, and the imagination magnified the numbers of the foe, who poured bullets from their well-masked fastnesses.

Yet many of the whites were old and seasoned bushmen, who had served in the Forest Rangers and other corps; they had carried their carbines on many a dangerous forest trail, and fought the Hauhaus again and again, and they were led by officers of ability, coolness, and bravery. Under McDonnell there was, for one, that soldier of fortune, Major Gustavus von Tempsky, most picturesque of guerilla fighters, the central figure in many stories of daring and adventure, the adored of his bush-whackers and the terror of the Maoris.

MAJOR VON TEMPSKY

(From a photo, 1865.)

"Wawahi-waka," the Waikato Maoris called him—"The Splitter-of-Canoes"—because of his exploits in war. "Manu-rau"—"Hundred Birds"—was the name by which he was known amongst the Taranaki Hauhaus. The name had been given him because of his activity in rushing from place to place, fighting here and fighting there, as swiftly as the forest-birds that flitted from tree to tree. Every Maori knew of "Manu-rau," and many of those in arms had been chased by him at one time or another during the three years of war since he led his Forest Rangers to the assault at Otapawa stockade.

Von Tempsky was of aristocratic Polish blood. He had begun soldiering life as a Prussian chasseur, had served under the unfortunate Emperor Maximilian in Mexico, and fought in several little wars in Central America; had been a gold-digger on the great tented fields of Victoria and the Hauraki; he was a clever artist in water-colours and a good miniature painter, and he had written a book of travels in Mexico, "Mitla," illustrated with his own sketches. In the Waikato War he and Captain William Jackson had led their Forest Rangers in several sharp skirmishes, and in Taranaki he was in the thick of the bush-fighting, and had tramped with his veterans through the forest in General Chute's great march from Ketemarae northwards to Mataitawa and New Plymouth, round the back of the Mountain.[7]

He was a good shot, a finished swordsman, and could throw a bowie-knife with deadly accuracy. It was in Mexico that he learned the use of the knife, and he never tired of impressing on his men its advantages in bush fighting.

Swarthy of visage, with long, black, curling hair, upon which a forage cap was cocked at a defiant angle, his grey flannel shirt carelessly open at the neck, his trousers tucked into long boots that came nearly up to his knees, a bowie-knife in a sheath and a revolver at his belt, a naked sword, long and curved, in his hand — this was von Tempsky on the war-path, a picturesquely brigand-like figure, upon whom the soldiers' eyes rested with wonder and a good deal of admiration.

Of that disastrous attack on "The Beak-of-the-Bird" stockade many accounts have been given, but the many discrepancies in detail that an examination of each account reveals are hardly to be wondered at, considering the confusion and misunderstandings that arose and that largely wrought the defeat of Colonel McDonnell's column. The dense and roadless forest, with its intricacies of undergrowth and interlacings of supplejack, and the inequalities of the ground made it difficult for the Colonial soldiers to keep in touch with each other, and the extraordinary activity and mobility of their savage assailants, who were perfectly at home in their jungly woods, more than compensated for the difference in numbers. The forest trees were the Hauhau redoubts. Amongst these trees, their naked brown skins nearly blending in colour with the trunks, they were almost invisible, and in most cases only the puffs of smoke, or brown arms moving up and down using the ramrods, indicated their lurking places. They darted from one cover to another with the quickness of monkeys, and though their weapons were mostly muzzle-loading smooth-bores, they managed to fire and reload with astonishing celerity. Too many of McDonnell's force were newly joined, raw young fellows, who now for the first time met the Maori warrior in the bush, and the hidden foe, with their merciless fire and their terrible yells of hate and defiance, struck terror to many a recruit's heart.

Some of the large *rata* and *pukatea* trees growing close to the stockade were

---

[7]   See von Tempsky's sketch, showing General Chute's column setting out on this march.

hollow, and in several of these the Maoris had cut loopholes, which they used for musketry fire. Some of the trees, too, spat leaden death. Brown figures flitted like forest-demons from cover to cover. At these and at the naked arms and shaggy heads that showed themselves for a moment the coolest and best shots of the Constabulary sent their bullets, and every now and then a Hauhau came crashing to the ground; but for every Maori that was hit five white men fell.

The forest rang with the sharp cracking of the rifles and the bang-banging of the heavily charged muzzle-loaders, and within the stockade the women that remained encouraged their warriors with shrill yells.

"Kill them! Eat them!" they screamed, as they waved their shawls and mats. "Fight on, fight on! Let not one escape!"

White men dropped quickly, wounded or shot dead. McDonnell evidently over-estimated the strength of the enemy, for he concluded that it would be impossible to rush the *pa* or to hold it if it was successfully rushed, for the enemy were now all round him. Had he only known the real state of affairs, that there were barely sixty armed Hauhaus, of whom only about twenty remained within the stockade, the story of Te Ngutu-o-te-Manu would have been far less saddening, at any rate to the *pakeha*.

McDonnell, considering the position too strong to be carried by assault, determined to strike out to the left through the forest and retire. Von Tempsky and Major Hunter pleaded with him to let them charge the stockade, but the Colonel would not consent, and presently ordered the retreat. Moving off, he sent a message to von Tempsky telling him to collect his men and form a rear-guard. He sent the wounded on with Major Hunter and Captain Newland, and followed with about eighty men, cutting a way through the undergrowth.

Von Tempsky remained, angry and disgusted at being refused permission to storm the *pa*, but too good a soldier to disobey orders. With him were most of the men of his two Armed Constabulary Divisions, No. 2 and No. 5, with Sub-Inspectors (Captains) Brown and J. M. Roberts, a few Patea Rifle Volunteers under Captain Palmer, the Wellington Rangers under Lieutenants Hastings and Hunter, and about twenty-five Taranaki Volunteers under Lieutenant Rowan.

Sword in hand, von Tempsky moved restlessly to and fro, regardless of the bullets that hummed about him. He ordered those nearest him to take cover but himself remained erect, angrily cutting at the undergrowth with his sword. And there he was when a Hauhau bullet found him.

Now I will let the Maoris tell their story of how von Tempsky and his comrades fell. Tutangé Waionui says:

"When the attack on our *pa* began, two or three of us, including Hotu and Tihirua, climbed up on an old partly hollow *rata*-tree that grew in a slanting position near the centre of the stockade, in order to see whether it would be a good place from which to fire at the *pakehas*. A little way up it forked into two large branches, and it was from this fork that we intended to fire. However, we found that it did not suit us, as we could not see anything of the soldiers who were hidden in the thick bush outside the stockade, so we rushed out into the forest, seeking our enemy.

"There were two large *rata*-trees outside the stockade, but the statement made that von Tempsky was shot from a *rata* is incorrect. I have seen a picture which purports to show him being shot down by a Maori perched in a tree. This is altogether contrary to fact, as I will explain to you.

"When we rushed out to the rear of the *pa* the soldiers were rapidly approaching the stockade. We crouched down amongst the undergrowth, close to the little creek, and directed our shots at the thicket which grew between the *pa* and the creek. Some of the soldiers, crossing the creek, were in this part of the bush, and soon I saw Manu-rau (von Tempsky). Heavy firing was going on all this time, and many white men had fallen. Presently many of the soldiers withdrew, carrying their wounded, but Manu-rau remained with his men, his drawn sword in his hand—the long curved sword which had already become famous amongst the Maoris. He came out into clear view of us, within a very short distance of where we were crouching—I should say less than half a chain. I fired with the others. One of our bullets struck him—I have always believed it was mine. One of his fellow-soldiers, who was close by, ran to pick him up, and he too fell, shot by one of my companions. Others ran out to rescue the fallen *pakehas*, and they were shot down by us and by the other Maoris, until soon there were nine white men lying dead or wounded around Manu-rau.

"When the Government forces had fallen back before a *kokiri*, a charge, led by Kātené Tu-Whakaruru, the Hauhau leader and scout, I ran out to where Manu-rau was lying dying on the ground. He seemed to be still living when I reached him. I snatched out my tomahawk from my girdle and dealt him a cut with it on the temple, to make sure of him, and killed him instantly. Then I took from him his uniform cap, his revolver and sword, and a lever watch which he had in his pocket.

"The sword, revolver, watch, and cap which I took from the soldier-chief's body I carried into the *pa* and laid before our war-chief Titokowaru. That was one of the rules observed by Titokowaru's war-parties; the spoils of war must be taken to the chief for division. I was given the revolver, and used it afterwards in the war.

"That is the story of how von Tempsky was killed. I hope you will, when the opportunity comes, tell the *pakehas* that the picture which represents Manu-rau as being shot by a Maori who was perched up in a *rata*-tree is not correct. You *pakehas* will not regard my action in tomahawking Manu-rau as a *kohuru*, a murder? Well, then, as you say, it was in the course of war, and it was quite *tika* and correct. I was but a very young man then, just a boy, and it was my first battle."

By the side of this I will put Whakawhiria's account. Whakawhiria lives at the big native village of Parihaka, the old-time town of the prophets Te Whiti and Tohu. His narrative was given in May, 1909, to the Rev. T. G. Hammond, of Opunake, Wesleyan missionary to the Taranaki Maoris, who has sent it on to me to supplement the other versions of the fight. Whakawhiria's story is generally accepted as authentic by the Taranaki Maoris; most of the survivors of the fight agree that it was his father Te Rangi-hina-kau, as he says, who shot von Tempsky.

Whakawhiria was a young man of eighteen or so at the time of this engagement, but though so young he was already a veteran on the war-path. He had seen the smoke of battle in 1860, at Waireka, when the Taranaki settlers, for the first time met the Maori on the field of war.

His estimate of the strength of the garrison in Te Ngutu-o-te-Manu is even lower than Tutangé's, for he says there were not more than forty-five fighting men in the *pa* when it was attacked.

Te Rangi-hina-kau, Whakawhiria, and a party of others sallied out from the stockade and met their enemy skirmishing in the bush. In the rear of the *pa* ran a little stream, the Mangotahi. On the banks of the creek the eight Hauhaus took cover, Whakawhiria and his nearest companions crouching under a *karaka*-tree, and it was from that point that they shot von Tempsky and his men. The eight warriors were Te Rangi-hina-kau, Whakawhiria, Ika-wharau, Tutangé Waionui, Te Whau, Heheu, Umu-umu and Wairau. They fired at von Tempsky at very close range, not more than twenty paces, just across the little creek.

"It was Te Rangi-hina-kau who shot von Tempsky," said Whakawhiria. "He dropped on one knee, and, taking careful aim, fired and shot von Tempsky. He shot him through the head, and afterwards cut out his heart as an offering to the Maori war-gods." (Kimble Bent's and Tutangé's versions given me contradict this.) "Young Tutangé," continued Whakawhiria, "acted a very brave part, but it was not he who actually shot the major. Tutangé obtained von Tempsky's watch as his share of the loot, and Whakawhiria got his gun and pistol."

During the engagement Titokowaru remained in the *pa*, shouting to his men, urging them to continue firing, and yelling such battle-cries as "*Whakawhiria! Whakawhiria!*" ("Twist them round and round!" or "Encircle them!") It was from this circumstance that the warrior Whakawhiria assumed his present name.[8]

[8]   The following account of Major von Tempsky's death, given in Auckland by Mr. James Shanaghan, who fought at Te-Ngutu-o-te-Manu as an A.C. private, and was wounded while attempting to rescue the major's body, is worth placing beside the Maori story for purposes of comparison. It is the most circumstantial narrative of von Tempsky's end ever given by a European survivor of the bush-battle:

"Our brave old major was walking to and fro with his sword in hand, furious at being caged as he was. I met him and he spoke to me in his kindly, thoughtful way, and asked why I did not take cover. I answered by putting the same question to him. He then said, 'I am disgusted. If I get out of this scrape I will wash my hands clear of the business.' He then sent me to take up a position and keep my eyes open, as the bullets were coming thick. I left him to obey the last order he ever gave. I had not gone far when a man of our Company was shot. The major went to his assistance and was shot, the bullet entering the centre of his forehead. He fell dead on top of the man to whose assistance he was going. That was how von Tempsky died.

"A Frenchman named Jancey and I went to the major and lifted him up and laid him on his back, and just as we did so a bullet struck Jancey on the side and travelled across his breastbone, and another struck the cartridge-box he had on his back. I left von Tempsky and picked up Jancey, carrying him out across the clearing. I then met Lieutenant Hunter (of the Wellington Rangers), and when we were about ten paces from von Tempsky's body Hunter was shot dead. I got hold of him and started to pull him back. Then I said to one of

On von Tempsky's fall, Captain J. M. Roberts, a cool and gallant young Constabulary officer, ordered his bugler to sound the "Halt" and the "Officers' Call," and tried to form the rear-guard into some order. Collecting as many of the wounded as he could, he began his retreat through that terrible death-haunted forest.

All through the fighting Titokowaru remained within the stockade, directing the defence and reciting incantations and chanting sacred *waiatas* to his gods for success in the fight. With him was the priestess Tangamoko, the woman who had that morning garbed the young warrior Tutangé with the sacred war-mat.

When von Tempsky fell and the retreat of the survivors began, Titokowaru ordered a *kokiri*, or charge, in pursuit, which, as Tutangé has mentioned, was led by the warrior Kātené Tu-Whakaruru.

Those of the Hauhaus who were in or near the stockade gathered under Kātené and danced in their ferocious joy a dance of victory, and this is the *ngeri* (war-song) they shouted all together as they leaped in that terrifying *tutu-waewae*:

> *"Kia kutia—*
> *Au—au!*
> *Kia wherahia—*
> *Au—au!*
> *A kia rere atu*
> *Te Kawana ki tawhiti,*
> *Titiro mai ai!*
> *Ae—ae—au!"*

> ("Squeeze close—
> Au—au! (imitating the bark of a dog)
> Spread out—
> Au—au!
> See the Government soldiers flee away,
> And turn and fearfully gaze at me.
> Yes, yes—*au!*")

The puffy clouds of smoke now drew away from the *pa*, as the Hauhaus followed their defeated foes into the dark forest. With appalling yells they rushed at their white enemies, tomahawking those who had fallen to make sure of them, as Tutangé had done with von Tempsky.

---

our men, 'Come along for Major von Tempsky's body.' This man refused, but Captain Buck (Wellington Rifles) came up and asked if I knew where von Tempsky was. I said, 'Yes,' and he said, 'Come along, lad, let's get him out.' When we came to the body I was hit by a bullet on the left thumb, which was shot nearly off. Just as I changed the carbine to my other hand a bullet went through my left hand and struck the carbine-stock, knocking me backwards. Then Buck was shot dead, and as I got up a bullet took my cap off. I got away from the clearing, leaving von Tempsky and Buck dead together. There were four of us who went for von Tempsky's body; Jancey and I were wounded, and Hunter and Buck were killed."

MAJOR VON TEMPSKY.

"Ka horo! Ka horo!" they yelled. "They are beaten!" And thrusting their bloody tomahawks into their belts they recharged their guns, and, leaping from tree to tree, fired heavily and incessantly at the gallant little rear-guard who were struggling through the tangled bush, caps gone, uniforms torn, nearly every man either

wounded or blood-stained from his comrades' wounds.

The sun had just set. The ghostly tree-shadows lengthened, and it was already dark in the deeper thicknesses of the bush.

Just after the retreat commenced one of Captain Roberts' steadiest men, Corporal Russell, dropped his carbine and fell; a big-calibre bullet had smashed his thigh-bone.

"Shoot me, boys—shoot me!" he begged his comrades. "Don't leave me to be tomahawked."

He knew as well as they did that his smashed leg meant death. The rear-guard was already encumbered with wounded and could carry no more.

"No, we can't shoot you, old man," said a big, tall volunteer sergeant, who was a tower of strength to Roberts' little band, shooting with deadly aim from his post in the rear of the retreat. "Take this," and he shoved into the wounded man's hand a loaded revolver.

Then the sergeant (James Livingston) picked up the corporal's empty carbine, and swinging it by the barrel, hot with much firing, smashed it against a tree-butt. "Old Tito'll never use that gun, anyhow," he said.

Bursting from the trees, the brown, nearly naked savages came yelling at the rear-guard. Hastily slipping fresh cartridges into their carbines, the gigantic volunteer and his comrades sent a volley at the enemy. It was taking *utu* for the corporal in anticipation. Then they sorrowfully turned and went on into the dusky forest, leaving their comrade stretched there on the mossy ground, gazing stern-mouthed, unflinchingly down the way of death.

Out from the ferns and supplejack leaped the foremost of the Hauhaus, a tattooed, blanket-girded man, with wild eyes rolling in blood-madness. His double-barrelled gun he had shifted from his right hand to his left, and he drew his shining tomahawk from his flax belt.

With an ear-ripping cry and the bound of a tiger he came on, hatchet in air.

The corporal stiffened his back, levelled his revolver, and fired.

The Maori fell, and lay with his face touching the soldier's boot.

A yell of *"Patua! Patua!"* came from the trees, and more bare figures with crossed cartridge-belts came rushing on, war-axe in hand.

Gripping his revolver hard, his trigger-finger steady, the corporal fired again, and another of his foes fell.

Now they stood off and shot the brave corporal dead, and so, after all, he died like a soldier and not under the frightful tomahawk.

McDonnell's column, the stronger one, was in the meantime fighting its way out through the forest to the Wai-ngongoro, hard beset by the Hauhaus, who had by this time been reinforced by others from the nearest villages. The Maoris followed closely in the rear and kept up a heavy fire, to which McDonnell and his officers and men could only return occasionally; their ammunition was getting very short. With McDonnell marched a French Roman Catholic priest, Father Jean Baptiste Rolland, the *padre* of the forces, who had been described only a few weeks before, in a letter written by von Tempsky, as "a man without fear." Whenever a soldier fell, whether he was Catholic or Protestant, the kind-faced father was by his side in a moment, tending his wounds, and, if dying, soothing his last moments with a prayer. He took his turn, too, at carrying the wounded.

Three holes, drilled by Hauhau bullets, ornamented the *padre's* old wide-brimmed soft felt hat when he reached the Waihi camp that night.

It was just dark when the snoring Wai-ngongoro was reached, and the bridge-less river, running high and swiftly, was forded with some difficulty under fire. At ten o'clock at night the redoubt was reached, and here it was found that a mixed party of fugitives from the battle-field, numbering about eighty Europeans besides the *Kupapas*, had already arrived, and had reported all the officers, McDonnell included, killed or wounded and left on the field.

And how fared Captain Roberts' little rear-guard of sixty men?

Extending his force in skirmishing order, the young officer pushed on as well as he could, carrying his wounded—one in every six. When darkness came on he halted, for it was hopeless to try to force a way through the jungle-matted woods in the blackness of the night. It was a cold frosty night, and the wounded were in agonies of pain, which their distressed comrades were helpless to relieve. There on the damp and freezing ground they crouched till the moon rose at two o'clock in the morning. Now, guided by five brave fellows of the Maori contingent, Whan-ganui and Ngati-Apa men, who stood by Roberts and his wounded to the last, the rear-guard recommenced the retreat. Struggling wearily on through the tangling *kareao* and the densely growing shrubs, stumbling over logs and splashing through little watercourses, they emerged at last thankfully on to the open country, and soon, bearing their wounded and dying comrades across the dark flooded Wai-ngongoro, were greeted by the joyful cheers of their comrades, European and Maori, under Kepa te Rangihiwinui, who had set out from the Waihi Redoubt to their rescue when daylight broke.

Only then was the full story of the repulse pieced together—a story of a fight that in point of numbers was only a skirmish, as battles go, but that was the most serious set-back the white man had yet suffered at the hands of the brown warriors of the Taranaki bush. Of the twenty-four whites killed five were officers, men who could badly be spared in that frontier warfare. The wounded numbered twenty-six, whose rescue from the tomahawks of the Hauhau was carried out in a way truly heroic.

CHAPTER XVI

THE CANNIBALS OF THE BUSH

After the battle—The slain heroes of Te Ngutu-o-te-Manu—A terrible scene on the *marae*—What Bent saw from his prison-hut—The sword of "Manu-rau"—A funeral pyre—Priestly incantations—A soldier's body eaten—Why the Hauhaus became cannibals.

ON the morning after the battle, Kimble Bent and his companions, who had been informed by a messenger the previous night of the result of the forest engagement, hurried back to the stockade.

The news of the repulse of the white troops had spread with incredible swiftness all over the Maori country-side, and the Hauhaus from the neighbouring villages gathered in Te Ngutu-o-te-Manu to hear the story of the fight and to share in the distribution of the loot taken on the battle-field.

The village was crowded with Hauhaus, all in a fearful state of excitement, a delirium of triumphant savagery.

Yelling like furies, shouting ferocious battle-songs, waving their weapons in the air, the victorious warriors were there with their spoils—carbines, swords, revolvers, soldiers' caps and belts.

More frightful still was the sight of which Bent had just a glimpse as he entered the gateway of the *pa*.

Laid out in a low row in the centre of the *marae*, side by side, were bodies of many white soldiers, nearly twenty of them, all stripped naked—the fallen heroes of Te Ngutu-o-te-Manu.

Just a glimpse the white man had as he entered the blood-stained square. The next moment he was surrounded by a howling mob of Hauhaus, grinning, yelling, laughing fiendishly, shaking their weapons in his face, all in sheer hate and contempt of anything with a white skin.

Two or three of the *Tekau-ma-rua* men whom Bent knew came bounding up. One of them said to him:

"Tu-nui, you must come with me. It is Titoko's command." The Maori led Bent to a small thatched hut on one side of the *marae*. Here he shut the white man in, and fastened the low sliding-door on the outside.

For a little while the white man sat in the gloom of the windowless *wharé*, listening to the demoniac shouts of the Hauhaus outside, and wondering what would come next—whether, indeed, his own body would not soon be added to the terrible pile of slain soldiers on the *marae*.

At last, hearing Titokowaru's great voice raised in commanding tones, Bent's mingled curiosity and fear impelled him to search for a loophole from which he could see what was going on.

Discovering a small crack in the reed-thatched walls of the hut, he enlarged it sufficiently to gain a good view of the assemblage on the village square.

There they squatted, men, women, and children, their faces smudged with charcoal or with red ochre, the paint of the war-path. They were seated on the ground in a great half-circle, facing the staring white corpses of the slain *pakehas*. The frightful clamour of the savages had given place with strange suddenness to a dead silence, as they listened to their war-chief's harangue, and watched him pacing quickly to and fro, with his sacred *taiaha* in his hand, now carrying it at the trail in the *taki* attitude, now dandling it high in the air as he intoned a chant to his battle-god Uenuku.

"Bring out my *pakeha* Tu-nui-a-moa!" cried Titokowaru, when he had ended his speech.

A Maori rose, and, unfastening the *wharé* door, led Bent out on to the assembly-ground.

He was taken up to the corpses of the slain soldiers, and one of the Hauhau chiefs asked him if he knew any of them.

Bent walked slowly past the dead, scrutinising each body carefully. He recognised two of them. One was an old soldier who had been a comrade of his in the 57th Regiment, and who had afterwards joined the Colonial forces.

The other dead soldier he identified was von Tempsky. The major's body lay there naked, with a deep tomahawk cut on the right temple, and the long, curly black hair matted with blood. The other bodies were hacked about the head with tomahawks; this was the work of the Maori women, who delighted in mutilating the dead in revenge for those of their relatives who had fallen.

Before announcing his recognition of the white warrior's remains, he turned to the people and asked if any of them had taken from a *pakeha* officer a sword with an unusual curve in it, and a cap bound with a brass band.

A Hauhau jumped up and said, "Yes, I have them."

"Show me which soldier you took them from," said Bent.

The Maori, with von Tempsky's sword in his hand, pointed to the major's corpse.

"Well," said Bent, "that is the body of Manu-rau, whom the *pakehas* called von Tempsky, and that is his sword."

A great "Ah-h" came from the people, and the exultant possessor of Manu-rau's sword of wondrous *mana* went bounding down the *marae*, flashing the weapon above his head, turning his painted face from side to side in the hideous grimaces of the *pukana,* and thrusting out his tongue to an extraordinary length.

The Hauhaus were in a frenzy of excitement when they realised that the renowned Manu-rau was indeed lying dead before them. Some of them proposed to drag the body out and cook it in the *hangi,* so that they might have the satisfaction of devouring their most dreaded enemy, and eating his heart, the heart of a *tino-toa,* a warrior indeed.

But Titokowaru, raising his sacred spear-staff, forbade the handling of the dead for the present.

Bent was now ordered to return to his hut, and the door was again fastened on him. The proposal to cook and eat the bodies of von Tempsky and his comrades was debated in a wild *korero.* Bent, from his eye-hole in the wall of the *wharé,* saw Hauhau after Hauhau, the orators of the tribes, jump up, tomahawk or gun or sword in hand, and furiously declaim as they went leaping and trotting backward and forward in the open space between the ranks of the victors and the dead; and the deeds of the battle-field were told again and again in great boasting words.

Von Tempsky's body, the *pakeha*-Maori had observed while on the *marae,* had not been mutilated, except for that tomahawk cut. His heart had not been cut out, though Bent half expected it would have been. The rite of the *Whangai-hau,* the ceremony of propitiation and burnt sacrifice following a battle, had not, however, been omitted. On the previous night, Tihirua, the young war-priest, had cut open a soldier's body and had torn out the heart, which he had offered in smoke and fire as oblation to Uenuku, the God of War, chanting a *karakia* as he watched the heart of the hated white man smoking in the flames.

"Manu-rau's" famous sword, too, was set apart as a sacred gift to the gods; it was a *parakia,* or *taumahatanga,* a thank-offering for victory. It became a *tapu* relic, and was religiously preserved by the Hauhaus. It is in their possession to this day.

Presently the bodies of the slain—the "Fish-of-Tu"—were ceremoniously apportioned amongst the several tribes represented in the village, as Bent again watched from his eye-hole in the wall.

One of the chiefs paced up and down past the pile of dead, with a stick in his hand. Pointing to a soldier's corpse, he cried:

"This is for Taranaki! Take it away!"

Pointing to the others, he said:

"This is for Ngati-Ruanui—take it away! This is for Nga-Rauru—take it away"—and so on until the whole of the dead men had been portioned out to the Hauhau clans to deal with as they deemed fit—subject always, however, to Titokowaru's approval.

The Nga-Rauru, the wild tribe of the Waitotara River, were the only men who actually took a body from the line of dead.

Two warriors jumped up and, laying their weapons aside, seized a dead soldier by the ankles and dragged the corpse away. One was Wairau, the other was the celebrated scout Kātené Tu-Whakaruru. This Kātené was a strange fellow. He had fought for some time on the Government side against his own countrymen, then he suddenly reverted to Hauhauism and barbarism, and led his warriors against his old friends and commanding officers, McDonnell and Gudgeon, with utter valour and ferocity. Now he was to turn cannibal.

Kātené and his companion dragged the body along the ground across the *marae* to the cooking-ovens in the rear of the dwelling-huts, watched in silence by the people. "I could not say whose body it was," says Bent, "but it was a man in good flesh!"

When the two Hauhaus had hauled their body away to the *hangi* for a terrible feast, the tribes sat in silence for a few moments, gazing intently on their dead enemies lying there before them. It was a calm, windless day, and the midday sun beat hotly down on that ghastly pile in the middle of the crowded *marae*.

Titokowaru rose, *taiaha* in hand. In his great croaking voice he cried:

"E koro ma, e kui ma, tena ra koutou! Tanumia te hunga tapu, e takoto nei; e tahu ki te ahi. Kaore e pai kia takoto ki runga ki te kino. Te mea pai me tahu ki te ahi!" ("Oh, friends, men and women—I salute you! Bury the sacred bodies of the slain, lying before us here. And burn them with fire! It is not well that they should be left to offend. They must be consumed in fire!")

At this command the people dispersed to collect fuel for a funeral pyre. They brought logs and branches of dry *tawa* timber from the surrounding bush and from the firewood piles in the rear of the *wharés*, and a huge pile of wood was built in the centre of the *marae*. Even the little naked children came running up with their little hands full of sticks to cast upon the heap.

All the mutilated bodies of the white soldiers—except the one that had been dragged away—were lifted up and placed on the roughly levelled top of the pyre, which was about four feet high and about fifteen feet long.

Titokowaru ordered his men to place von Tempsky's body on the fire-pile first, and then lay the others on top of it. The chief suspected, perhaps, that some of the Hauhaus wished to cook and eat Manu-rau's body, and he so far respected his gallant foeman even in death that he resolved to spare it that last degradation.

So the major's body went on first, and then around and above it were heaped the other soldiers. On top of the bodies more wood was thrown.

Bent's hut door was now unfastened, and the natives called to him to come out. What he saw he will tell in his own words:

"When I walked out on to the *marae*, I met two Nga-Rauru men I knew from Hukatéré village, on the Patea River. They had come to Te Ngutu-o-te-Manu with a gift of gunpowder to Titokowaru. With them I presently went down to the cooking-quarters to see what had become of the body that had been dragged away. There we found a large earth-oven full of red-hot stones, and there they were engaged in roasting the white man's corpse. They had prepared it for cooking in the usual way, and were turning it over and over on the hot stones, scraping off the outer skin.

"The cannibal cooks looked round and asked me savagely what I wanted there. They threatened that if I did not leave instantly they would throw me into the oven too, and roast me alive.

"I returned to the *marae*, and was sitting amongst the crowd there some time later, perhaps an hour, when I saw a man's hands and ribs, cooked, carried up. The human flesh was placed in front of the two powder-carriers from Hukatéré, who were sitting close to me. The meat was in a flax basket, and a basket of cooked potatoes was set down with it. This present of food was out of compliment to the visitors.

"The two Maoris refused to touch it, saying, 'No, we will not eat man!' So the other natives ate it. The rest of the body was also served round, and the people consumed the whole of it.

"Kātené and Wairau were two of those who ate the cooked soldier. I saw Kātené squatting there, with a basket of this man-meat and some potatoes before him. He took up a cooked hand, and before eating it sucked up the *hinu*, or fat, that was collected in the palm just as if he were drinking water. The hands when cooked curled up with the fingers half-closed, and the hollowed palm was filled with the melted *hinu*.

"Titokowaru did not eat human flesh himself. His reason for abstaining was that if he ate it his *mana tapu*, his personal sacredness, would thereby be destroyed."

The younger people in the *pa* were rather awe-stricken by the preparations for the cannibal feast, and stood together some distance away from the *hangi*. "I stood with them," says one Te Kahu-pukoro, who was a boy at the time; "I was afraid to join in the eating, but the savour of the flesh cooking in the ovens was delightful!"

When the warriors, a little later on, were enjoying their meal of man-meat, some of the little children were heard calling out to their fathers: "*Homai he poaka mou*" ("Give me some pork to eat"). They had seen the meat carried up in flax baskets, and thought it was pork.

Now the white soldiers' funeral pyre was set alight. An old man, Titokowaru's *tohunga*, or priest, walked up to it with a long stick of green timber in his hand, an unbarked sapling with a rough crook at one end. He stood in front of the pile as the flames shot up and chanted a song. Then, when the logs with their terrible burdens were well alight, he began a strange incantation. Using his long stick with both hands he turned over the burning logs, pushed them closer together to create a fiercer heat, and forked the bodies into the midst of the blaze. And as he did so he recited a pagan *karakia*, the chant of the *Iki*, anciently repeated over the bodies of warriors when they were being cremated on the battle-field. These were the words of the incantation (the mystic meaning underlying some of the expressions would require many notes to fully elucidate them):

	Translation.
Ka waere,	Clear them away,
Ka waere,	Clear them away!

Ka waere i runga ma keretu,	Sweep them into the earth,
Ka waere i raro ma keretu,	Into the stiff and useless clay.
Kei kai kutu ma keretu,	There let them perish and decay.
Kei kai riha ma keretu,	
Whakatahia te kukakuka,	Sweep man's flesh to earth again.
Whakarere te kukakuka,	
Te roua atu,	Fork them that way!
Te kapea mai.	Haul them this way!
Roua ki Whiti,	Fork them to Whiti,
Roua ki Tonga,	Fork them to Tonga,
E tu te rou,	To the ancient homes of man.
Rouroua!	Here I hold my fork erect,
Takataka te kape;	I turn them this way, that way.
Kapekapea!	Quickly stir the funeral pile,
Ka eke i tua,	Now this way haul, now that!
Ka eke i waho,	
Ka eke i te Maru-aitu	Their spirits far have gone;
Te ihi nei,	The flesh alone remains;
	They have gone the way of Destiny.
Te mana nei,	Their courage no longer stirs them;
	Their pride and power have flown;
Nga toa nei.	Their valour's gone!
Ko tai ko ki,	In the fullness of life they fell—
Ko tai ko rea,	Like the fullness of the tide!
Ko tai takoto ki raro.	And now they lie naked before me!
Ma peruperu!	They leaped in the war-dance;
Ma whiwhi!	They were strenuous in battle;
Ma rawea!	But they fell.
Haere ake ra te ihi o nga toa,	Farewell! spirits of the brave!
Te mana o nga toa,	The pride and power of heroes!
Te whatu te ate-a-Nuku	Heart of Earth, and heart of Heaven—
Te whatu te ate-a-Rangi.	For both joined to produce you!
Huri ana te po,	Now turns the night—
Huri ana te ao,	It turns to day again.
He rangi ka mahea;	The clouds obscure the sky;
He whai ao,	We search for light,
He ao marama!	The perfect light of day!

The people sat there on the *marae*, silently watching the burning of the dead. Far above the trees of the surrounding forest rose the thick black column of smoke from the blazing pile. It went up as straight as an arrow, unswayed by any breath of air, to a great height. To the savage watchers it was verily the incense of the battle-field, rising to the war-god's nostrils. "Now and then," says Bent, "a body would burst, and the blaze of flame and the smoke would leap straight up, high into the air."

Long the Hauhaus gazed at the dreadful crematory blaze on the palisaded *marae*, replenishing the fire with dry logs as it burned down, until all the dead were consumed, and nothing but a great heap of charcoal and ashes remained.

The revival of the ancient practice of cannibalism was the most hideously savage feature of Titokowaru's method of warfare. It was not meat-hunger in this case; it was a battle-field rite. In olden Maoridom war was war to the death, and to the oven; it was no use beating your enemy unless you killed him, and no use killing him unless you also ate him. The eating of soldiers' bodies not only glutted racial revenge; but also—in Maori eyes—destroyed the prestige of the whites; it ruined their *mana* as men and as warriors.

The Taranaki Maoris tell a singular little story in explanation of those man-eating rites in Titokowaru's camps. In consuming bodies from the battle-fields they were only putting into practice the spirit of a speech made by old King Potatau te Wherowhero a decade or so before.

Potatau—grandfather of the present "king" of Waikato, Mahuta Potatau te Wherowhero, M.L.C.—was a warrior of exceeding renown three-quarters of a century ago, and a cannibal of cannibals.

Te Wherowhero Kai-tangata—"man-devourer"—he was called. Many a time he raided Taranaki with his war-parties of Waikato and Ngati-Maniapoto and Tainui. At Pukerangiora, about 1830, he slew hundreds of Ngati-Awa tribespeople, and with his warriors cooked and ate them. Nearly thirty years later he was set up as king over the confederated Maori tribes in the centre of the island.

When the Maori kingdom was first established, the then governor of the colony visited old Potatau, and discussed the Maori aspirations for independence. The governor, according to the Maori story, endeavoured to show the king the folly of opposing the sway of the white man; if it did come to warfare—which was not then contemplated by either side—the British soldiers would soon make a clean sweep of the ill-armed and ill-provisioned Maori.

"You are wrong," said Potatau; "it will take you many a year to sweep away the Maoris—you will never do it."

"But," said the governor, "suppose we fight you, and drive you into the forest, far away from your cultivations, what will you do for food?"

"Why," replied the old king, "I have plenty of food even in the bush—the berries of the *tawa* and *karaka* trees, the heart of the *mamaku* tree-fern, and the *nikau*, and other foods of the forest. We can live on those."

"And suppose I chase you with my soldiers, and fight you in the forest, and pursue you so that you cannot even get those things to eat, the berries and the *mamaku*, what then will you do for food?"

Said old Potatau, grinning, "Then I'll eat you!"[9]

This half-defiant, half-jocular speech of the venerable warrior of Waikato was repeated word for word, as it is given here, in every Kingite village and in the Hauhau *pas* of after years; but it was left for Titoko's bushmen of Taranaki to put into actual execution their old foeman's commissariat methods.

"Titokowaru heard it," say the Maoris; "and when the war began, and he became a fighting chief, he did as Potatau would have done—he fought his enemy in the forest, and slew him there, and ate his flesh for food. And, as Potatau had predicted, it was many a year before the war was ended—and even then Titokowaru was never caught."

---

[9]   "Ko koe te kai mau!"

CHAPTER XVII

SKIRMISHING AND FORT-BUILDING

Te Ngutu-o-te-Manu abandoned—On the march again—Skirmishing on the Patea—*Pakeha* in pickle—A new stockade—Bent the
pa-builder.

THE famous "Bird's-Beak" *pa*, made so memorable by the terrible scenes enact-
ed around and within its stockade, was soon deserted.

Titokowaru, not long after the Hauhau victory and the savage rites narrated in the last chapter, issued an order that the village must be evacuated, and a
new position selected for a bush-fort in which to withstand the attack that must
inevitably be delivered against him by the Government. So one day the whole of
the inhabitants of the Te Ngutu-o-te-Manu—men, women, and children, and the
solitary white man—having gathered together their belongings, marched out of
their village and tramped away through the bush eastwards. The armed men of
the *Tekau-ma-rua* preceded them, to make sure that the way was clear of the *pakeha*
enemy.

At the village of Turangaréré and at Taiporohenui they dwelt for a while, and
the warriors scouted out day after day in the vicinity of the European redoubts. A
little skirmishing occurred; some shots were fired at the Turuturu-Mokai redoubt,
now re-garrisoned, and a sniping party amused themselves, with the Manawapou
Camp as a target. Before very long Bent and his companions were once more on
the move, swagging through the bush to the Patea Valley. The scene of war was
now to be the Lower Patea and the Waitotara, whence Titokowaru, it was believed,
intended to raid the town of Wanganui.

For some weeks Titoko and his Hauhaus camped in the Oruatihi *pa*. Then
they shifted to Otoia, near the banks of the Patea, where they built a redoubt, from
which they could fire into the European position at Manutahi. The fortification
was finished in a day and a night, all hands, men and women, toiling at it, Bent
amongst them. Some dug the trenches with their spades, some carried earth in flax
baskets, and others piles of flax and fern, with which they built up the parapets.

Early in the morning the day after the *pa* was completed there was a brush
with the Government forces. A column of Armed Constabulary and Wanganui
Maoris made a reconnaissance up the cliffy, forest-fringed banks of the Patea in
the direction of the Hauhau redoubt. Titoko's men attacked them, lining both sides
of the river. The troops retired to their tea after a pretty little skirmish; and the

Hauhaus marched back to the *pa* in high jubilation, singing war-songs, waving their guns, and bounding about and grimacing like a company of fiends. Then the steaming pork and potatoes, and speech-making and howling *hakas* around the great camp-fires. From the Maori point of view, quite a pleasant day's sport.

During the two months following the bush fight at Te Ngutu-o-te-Manu no serious engagement occurred, but Titokowaru's war-parties scoured the district for many miles, laid ambuscades on the tracks between the European redoubts, burned settlers' houses, and bagged a stray *pakeha* or two.

One incident of this period illustrates the peculiar ghoulish humour of the Hauhau savage. Two friendly Maoris—Nga-hina and another—who were mail-carriers in the Government service, halted awhile at Manawapou one day, while on their way to Patea, and searched the settlement there for the wherewithal for a dinner. A cask stood beside one of the *wharés*, and on taking the top off they found it to be a barrel of brine, containing meat—apparently pork.

Anticipating a good meal of salt pork, they fished up some of the meat. They found to their disgust that it was human flesh!—"Long-pig!" Not being Hauhaus or cannibals, they dropped the man-meat—white man—back into the cask and stayed their hunger on good honest potatoes.

The question was, who pickled the *pakeha*? A Hauhau prisoner some time later enlightened the Government Maoris. A scouting party from Titoko's camp had dodged down to Manawapou, and discovered there, not far from the redoubt—which had been temporarily vacated by the troops—a new-made grave. Opening it, they disinterred a white man's corpse. In sheer devilment they cut it up, put it into a cask of brine that stood handy, and then recovered the cask and left it.

It would have been an exquisite joke, from the cannibal Hauhau view-point, had the Government soldiers unknowingly helped themselves to a joint of white man!

Titokowaru's entrenched position at Otoia was not a strong one, and shortly he, after a council of war with his principal men, decided to abandon it and build a new bush *pa*, which should be as nearly impregnable as a Maori fort could be.

So one morning a long line of Hauhaus of all ages and both sexes—the armed men in front and rear—bearing their simple belongings in flax-basket *pikaus* on their backs, left the Otoia redoubt, and marched away through the bush to a spot about twelve miles from the mouth of the Patea River and a mile and a half from the old Okotuku *pa*, which had been attacked by the troops two years previously. At this place, Moturoa—the "Song Bush," so called because of a long strip of forest which covered the plain here—the war-chief ordered that the new fort should be constructed.

The position was on partially cleared land, nearly level, surrounded by the forest. The men, after hastily constructing huts, roofed with the fronds of tree-fern and *nikau*, set to work with their axes to hew out a large clearing. Titoko marked out the lines of the entrenchments and palisades. The forest-trees quickly fell before the practised assault of many bushmen, and the shrubby cover in front of the *pa* was carefully burned.

Then came the setting up of the stockade. *Tawa* and other trees of small size were cut into suitable lengths for the palisade-posts. There were two rows of palisades; the outside one was the largest and strongest. For the heavy outside row of stockading, timbers from eight to twelve inches in diameter were sunk solidly in the ground, forming a wall some ten feet high. Saplings were cut to serve as cross-ties or rails to lash across the posts, and with supplejack and *aka* vines the whole were bound strongly and closely together.

Kimble Bent worked with the Hauhaus—toiling like a navvy, cutting timber, setting up the great posts, lashing the palisading, and digging trenches. He wore nothing but a rough flax mat round his waist—trouserless, bootless, hatless. In everything but skin a Maori.

"It was exciting," says the white man, "but none the less it was slavery. Many a night those times, when I lay down on my flax *whariki*, though I was dog-tired, I could not sleep—thinking, thinking over the past, and dreading what the future might bring me. Many and many a time I wished myself dead and out of it all."

What furious, what Homeric toil was that *pa*-building! Those wild brown men, spurred by the reports of speedy attack, laboured with incredible energy and swiftness. The Moturoa fortified hold—which later became known as Papa-tihakehake, because of the battle which befell here—was completed in three days—stockaded, trenched, parapeted, and rifle-pitted—ready for the enemy!

Behind the strong tree-trunk stockade there were trenches and casemated rifle-pits from which the defenders could fire between the lower interstices in the great war-fence; behind the trenches again was a parapet from which a second line of Hauhaus could deliver their fire over the top of the palisade. It was one of the strongest works yet constructed by the Maoris, and one that was not likely to be stormed except at the cost of many lives.

CHAPTER XVIII

THE FIGHT AT MOTUROA STOCKADE

Kātené's vigil—Attack on the stockade—Major Hunter's death—A Hauhau warrior's desperate feat—Over the palisades—Government forces repulsed—A rear-guard fight—An unanswered prayer—Scenes of terror—Tihirua's burnt-offering—A soldier's body eaten.

Just within the stockade of the Moturoa, or Papa-tihakehake *pa*[10], there was a small, roughly built *taumaihi*, or look-out stage, ten or twelve feet above the ground, high enough to allow a sentinel to see well over the sharp-pointed palisades, and scan the approaches to the fort.

In this bush watch-tower there stood, at misty dawn on a grey November morning, the Hauhau scout and warrior Kātené Tu-Whakaruru.

Kātené was cold, and he stamped his bare feet upon the unbarked logs that floored the sentry-box, and he chanted softly to himself a little *waiata* to Kopu, the morning star, which he had looked for in vain, for a heavy drizzling mist obscured everything. The thin, persistent rain penetrated the blanket that he held closely wrapped about him.

Presently a faint light began to steal over the forest, and Kātené could see the outlines of the black charred stumps and burned trees in front of the *pa*, then beyond the gloomy woods, through which a narrow winding path led to the open fern-lands of the Wairoa.

Suddenly Kātené's murmured chant ceased, and he strained his eyes into the mist. To a Maori forester the slightest sound was enough to set every faculty on the alert, asking suspiciously, *"He aha tena!"* He had heard a faint sound in the direction of the track beyond the black tree-stumps, a sound that he fancied resembled the striking of steel against steel.

Kātené hardly breathed. His eyes glared fixedly through the mist. In a few minutes his vision confirmed the evidence of his keen ears. He saw, just for a moment, a dark figure, then another, come hazily out of the wet fog where the track from the Wairoa emerged on the clearing, then disappear, as if they had suddenly dropped to the ground or vanished behind a tree.

---

[10]   This name Papa-tihakehake was given to the place after the fight, in commemoration of the defeat of the troops. Papa means a battle-ground; tihakehake refers to the dead bodies of the whites which strewed the ground.

That glimpse was enough for Kātené. He dropped from his sentry-perch, and ran from *wharé* to *wharé* and tent to tent giving the alarm.

"The soldiers are coming!" he said to those whom he awakened. "The soldiers are on us! They are by now entering the clearing. Get your arms quickly! Man the trenches! But don't make a sound!"

The fighting-men poured out of their sleeping huts, snatching up their weapons and accoutrements, and ran to their places in the pits and ditches behind the stockade. They hastily loaded their *tuparas*, their rifles, and their carbines, and, peering eagerly through the defence-works, sought to penetrate the raw, damp morning mist that shrouded their front.

The whole bush-castle was alive and ready. Every man and boy who could shoulder a gun was in the well-hidden firing lines.

The wet mist slightly lifting as the morning light came, the musketeers presently saw dim figures moving out from the dark forest on their front and right and left flanks. Moving quickly, half running, in a cautious, crouching gait, they flitted from tree to tree, and burnt stump to stump, and nearer and nearer to the stockade.

Not a sound came from the breathlessly waiting warriors, nor from the ghost-like figures that now sank to the ground, each behind a log or a great blackened stump, or the butt of a standing tree.

Gun in hand, finger on the trigger, the Hauhaus waited.

The apparitions were picked bush-fighters of the New Zealand forces, led by Colonel Whitmore, seeking to surprise Titoko in his forest-den.

Advancing silently in skirmishing order through the bush, they took cover, waiting for light enough to fight by. There were detachments of four divisions of the Armed Constabulary, many of them veteran bush-fighters, and men of the Patea Rifles and Patea Cavalry. There, too, came Kepa's Whanganui Maoris, with rifle and tomahawk, old hands on the war-trail, and eager for another brush with their ancient enemies of Taranaki.

There were two hundred Government men fronting the fort, but the fighting men behind the palisades did not, according to Maori accounts, number many more than half the number.

Amongst Titokowaru's men, however, there were some of the most renowned bush scouts and warriors in Taranaki, including—besides Kātené, the wide-awake sentry—such men as the veteran Te Waka-tapa-ruru, Paraone Tuteré, one of the best Hauhau shots, Timoti, the fiercest of the cannibals of Nga-Rauru, and the active young warrior Tutangé Waionui, he who had despatched von Tempsky on the battle-field of Te Ngutu-o-te-Manu. Tutangé says that he was asleep in a tent when Kātené gave the alarm that morning. He was with his tribe, the Nga-Rauru, most ferocious of all Maori bush-fighters, who occupied one end of the *pa*; the other tribes holding the fort were Ngati-Ruanui and Pakakohi. It was the side occupied by the Pakakohi men that was first attacked.

All at once, as the Hauhaus crouched behind their palisades squinting for a sight of *pakeha*, with impatient fingers on their gun-triggers, fifty or sixty blue and grey figures sprang from cover and charged for the stockade. Some of the assaulting party ran past the corner of the war-fence, looking for some opening or gateway by which they might charge in.

The leading files were within a few paces of the high, solidly set palisading, when suddenly the whole face of the fence flashed fire, and volleys crashed in terrifying reverberations that set flocks of sleepy *kaka* parrots flying, screaming harsh screams of fright, through the dark forest.

Nearly half the storming party of A.C.'s fell before that fearful fire.

The first man shot was their leader, a brave officer, Major Hunter, whose brother, Captain Hunter, had fallen at Te Ngutu-o-te-Manu two months previously. Tutangé says that it was Paraone Tuteré who shot the major; he fired at the leading figure, not knowing then who he was. Colonel Whitmore came running in with the stormers, but, with his usual luck, although in the thickest fighting he was never hit.

Those of the attacking column who were not hit instantly dropped to cover amongst the logs and stumps that surrounded the *pa* front. Then they returned the fire as well as they could, but one man after another was hit, without being able to see one Hauhau of the scores that occupied the *pa* and thrust the muzzles of their guns through the interstices of the palisades.

It was a foolish thing, that blind frontal charge on the strong stockade. Major Hunter was too good a soldier to have done such an insane thing of his own volition. He was obeying Whitmore's orders. Hunter was shot in the femoral artery, when within nine or ten yards of the stockade. He implored those near him to try to stop the gushing blood, and some of his comrades attempted to staunch it; but the wound was too close to the stomach to get at, and he died in a few minutes.

Captain W. E. Gudgeon, with about forty Government Maoris, tried to work round and take the *pa* in the rear. His line of charge was on Hunter's right flank, and he had good cover, but in spite of that he lost two killed and five wounded.

Now a brisk little fight went on on the flanks of the *pa* between Kepa's men and a party of warriors who had made a sortie from the stockade. Kepa was furiously assailed by the bushmen, leaping from tree to tree, yelling their frightful Hauhau cries; and it was as much as the plucky Whanganui men could do to hold their own. Their attempt to take the *pa* in the rear failed, and they at last slowly withdrew to support the shattered ranks of their white comrades.

The A.C. supports came doubling up, and a heavy fire was concentrated on the stockade, but to little purpose. It was impregnable to rifle-fire, and in their pitted works the defenders were able to pick off the white skirmishers in perfect safety.

Bullets swept the clearing in every direction, and through the infernal music of the forest-battle the white soldiers heard the loudly yelled war-cries of the chiefs and the shrill voices of the Maori women as they encouraged their warriors, husbands, and brothers, and screamed them on to slaughter with all the fury of brown tattooed Hecates.

The women were gathered in the *marae* and in the trenches, some armed, all filled with the fire of savage war.

"Ka horo, ka horo!" they shouted. *"Kia maia, kia maia! Patua, kainga! Patua, kainga!"* ("They fall, they fall! Be brave, oh, be brave! Kill them, eat them! Kill them, eat them!")

All this time Kimble Bent was walking to and fro on the *parepare*, the inner breastwork, the bullets screaming *zssh! zssh!* over his head and all about him. The air seemed filled with flying lead, yet very few Maoris were hit. One woman he saw shot dead through the head as she rose to wave her shawl and yell a fighting cry to the men at the palisades.

And here Bent was an eye-witness of the most desperately daring deed he had ever seen.

A fiery old tattooed warrior, by name Te Waka-tapa-ruru—the Hauhau mentioned in an earlier chapter as the man who had killed Charles Broughton, Government Native Agent, on the Patea River, in 1865—was in a quiver of excitement while the garrison awaited the assault, and could hardly be silenced until the attack was delivered.

When the *pakeha* storming party rushed up at the double, the old man was one of the first to open fire on them with his *tupara*. And then, when the order *"Kokiri-tia!"* ("Charge!") was given, and the Hauhaus rushed out to engage the Government men who were trying to work round to the rear of the *pa*, he led the wild charge.

Perfectly naked, except for the broad flax waist-girdle, which held his short-handled tomahawk, and gripping his double-barrelled gun, the tall old savage took a great running jump at the stockade from the inner parapet, and leaped clean over it!

Yelling a *Pai-mariré* battle-cry as he rose from the ground after his extraordinary leap, he snatched the tomahawk from his belt, and charged straight for the advancing whites.

It was a fit of *whakamomori*—sheer blind desperation, utter recklessness of death.

Possibly the furious old fanatic imagined that his Hauhau angel and his mesmeric password, *"Hapa! Pai-mariré! Hau!"* would avert the bullets of the *pakeha*. But he was killed in the very charge—the only Maori fighting-man killed that day.

Two white soldiers met him. He was in the act of striking a desperate blow when a *pakeha* ball took him square in the forehead, and with a huge convulsive bound and a half-choked barking *"Hau!"* on his lips, the old tattooed brave fell dead amongst the foremost of his enemies.

It was just the death that he desired—face to the foe, with his war-axe in his hand—the death of a true Maori *toa*!

This savage hero's son, Ratoia—now living in the village of Taiporohenui—a young boy at the time of the fight, saw his father's great leap over the palisade, and saw him killed.

Bent tells of a curious *matakité*, or prophetic dream, which Te Waka-tapa-ruru had on the night before the battle. The old man was a close friend of the white runaway, and they were accustomed to sleep side by side on the *whariki*-spread floor of one of the huts. He dreamed that he saw his face reflected in a *pakeha* looking-glass, and that he was combing his hair. This vision disturbed the old man, and deeming it a warning from the unseen world, he asked Titokowaru— just when the approach of the troops was first announced—what it might portend. The war-chief interpreted the dream as an omen of death, and warned Te Waka not to leave the shelter of the stockade during the impending engagement or he would be killed. But he disregarded this in his fit of *whakamomori*, and ran amok, and so he fell.

Finding it impossible to take such a strong and well-defended position by storm, the white colonel withdrew his forces. There were dead and wounded lying all over the place. The *pakehas* succeeded in carrying off the wounded and some of the dead, including the gallant Major Hunter. A number of dead, however, had to be left where they were lying, for it was death to attempt their removal from under the very muzzles of the Hauhau guns.

The rescue of Hunter's body from the Hauhau tomahawks, under a heavy fire, was a gallant piece of work. Captain Gudgeon was one of those who brought the dead officer out; one of his comrades was Captain Edward McDonnell, and troopers Foote and Kelly were amongst the others. Two or three men were shot in the attempt. Kepa (Major Kemp) was there, too, but he was pretty well engaged in looking·after his own men and extricating them from that place of death.

MAJOR KEMP (KEPA TE RANGIHIWINUI.)

The Colonial soldiers retired, fighting a hard rear-guard action, out to the edge of the bush. Each division of Armed Constabulary in turn halted, knelt down facing the enemy, and covered the retreat of the other divisions, thus giving time for those of the dead and wounded who had been recovered to be carried off the field. Out to the fern-lands the Hauhaus followed the troops, sometimes engaging them so closely that the fighting was hand-to-hand, and it was carbine and revolver against long-handled tomahawk. The skirmishing lasted until the whites were well clear of the bush; the Maoris would have followed them out even to their camp, the Wairoa Redoubt, had not they been recalled by orders from Titokowaru. The battle of Papa-tihakehake was over. It was a more severe repulse for the Government men than even the engagement at Te Ngutu-o-te-Manu a bare two months before. One man out of every four in the force actually engaged was on the casualty list—more than twenty killed and quite thirty wounded.[11]

THE FIGHT AT MOTUROA, 1869.

This sketch, with the one opposite, drawn by an eye-witness shortly after the engagement, depicts the defeat of the Government A.C. Force by the Maoris.

THE FIGHT AT MOTUROA, 1869.

A grim story of that hard-fought retreat through the bush is told by Kimble Bent.

After the *kokiri*, the rush out in pursuit, had been ordered by the Maori war-chief, one of the Nga-Rauru men came across a white soldier lying on the ground,

[11]   Colonel W. E. Gudgeon writes me: "For the number engaged Moturoa was the most desperate engagement fought in the Maori War. Whitmore's return did not give nearly our losses. I made it at the time fifty-two out of less than two hundred actually engaged. At Te Ngutu-o-te-Manu all did not behave well, but at Moturoa any one might have been proud of the men. No force in the world could have behaved better."

with his head pillowed against a fallen *pukatea*-tree. He had been cut off from his division by the foremost of the pursuing Hauhaus, and was lying there feigning death, hoping that the rest of the Maoris would pass on and not notice him.

The Nga-Rauru man, however, stopped and looked closely at the prostrate *pakeha*. He said to one of his comrades, "I don't think that man is dead." Going up to the Constabulary man, he put his hand on his shoulder, and said in English, "Wake up!"

The white man opened his eyes. He exclaimed, "Save my life! Let me go, and I'll never forget you—I'll repay you for it."

The Nga-Rauru man, who must have been a humorous kind of barbarian, said to his victim, again in English, "Go on your knees and pray to your God to save your life!"

The soldier knelt as he was told, and ejaculated some sort of a prayer.

Playing with his prey, the savage asked, "Well, are you saved now?"

The kneeling soldier looked up, but could make no answer. He stared at his terrible-looking captor, with horror in his eyes.

"Poroporoaki ki to Atua!" ("Say farewell to your God!") cried the Maori, and swinging his gun round in both hands, he brought it butt down with a frightful smashing blow on the soldier's head.

The man fell backwards dead. His slayer stripped him of his uniform and accoutrements, and a little later could have been seen dancing a furious *haka* in front of the stockade, his face blackened with charcoal from the charred tree-stumps, the soldier's cap on his head, and the captured carbine in his hand.

Young Tutangé Waionui was in the thick of the skirmishing. "My weapons that day," he says, "were a *tupara* (double-barrelled gun) and a revolver. The gun was a muzzle-loader; I preferred it to the breech-loaders used by the *pakeha*, because something was always going wrong with them. I could load (*puru-pu*) very quickly; but a quicker man was old Te Waka-tapa-ruru—he who was killed; there was no one so expert as he at loading a muzzle-loader."

What scenes of horror followed that battle in the bush!

The Hauhaus were in a delirium of triumphant savagery. Like frenzied things they came dancing and yelling back to the *pa*. They had blackened their ferocious faces with charcoal from the burnt tree-stumps in front of the *pa*. Singing war-songs, shouting *Pai-mariré* cries, dancing their weapons in the air, projecting their long snaky tongues and rolling their eyes till only the whites were visible, set in a petrifying glare—the grimace of the *pukana*—it was a sight that brought fear to the heart of the lone white man, accustomed though he was by this time to spectacles of barbaric ferocity.

The women were as wild and savage-looking as the men—their dark eyes blazing with excitement, their faces black-painted like the warriors, their loosened hair flying behind them, many of them nude from the waist up—waving shawls, mats, tomahawks, in welcome to the returning heroes, shouting, singing, screaming.

Outside the front fence of the *pa*, just us they fell, among the logs and stumps and on the blood-stained ground, lay the dead men whom the retreating A.C.'s had been compelled to leave on the battle-field. There were seven of them.

Upon these fallen soldiers rushed the Hauhaus. They stripped them of their uniforms. They tied flax-leaf ropes round the necks of the dead *pakehas*, and hauled them away to the gateway of the *pa*.

As they dragged the corpses off, leaping from side to side as they hauled in a fury of blood-madness, they shouted out such sentences as these:

"Taku kai! Taku kai! E hara ka kite noho koe taku kai, taku tika, taku he! Nau te kino, naku whakahoki ton kino. Taea hokitia—te mahi o te atua a Titokowaru!" ("My food! My food! Behold my food; behold the right and the wrong of it all. 'Twas you"—addressing the slain—"that wrought the evil work. And I have returned your evil. Behold the work of the god of Titokowaru!")

A young Hauhau, huge-limbed and·naked but for a very brief waist-mat of dangling flax, leaps to the side of one of the white men's bodies, just as it is harnessed in so revolting a fashion to be dragged into the *pa*.

His tomahawk flashes in the air above him as he steps over the fallen soldier—once, twice, thrice!

He thrusts in a hand into a huge gaping wound in the dead man's breast; he is searching for something. He rises with some object, all bloody, in his horrible red hand. He sticks his tomahawk back into his girdle, he comes bounding from the corpse, waving his dripping trophy in his hand, swinging it round his head. His fiendish yells ring echoing over the forest clearing.

What is it he flourishes so exultingly?

It is the white man's heart!

This is the young warrior Tihirua, the priest of the burnt sacrifice. He has torn out the *manawa* of the soldier, as a *mawé*—an offering to the God of War!

At his waist, buckled to his flax girdle, is a leather pouch, such as was generally used for carrying percussion-caps. Out of this he takes matches—*pakeha* matches! Striking match after match, he holds them underneath the bleeding heart until it is singed, and dark smoke goes up from it—incense to Uenuku, the war-god, who appears to his savage worshippers in the arch of the rainbow.

The heathen rite—the ceremony of the *Whangai-hau*—performed, Tihirua flings down his terrible trophy, and then directs the hauling of the bodies into the palisaded inferno.

Bent, standing just outside the *pa* gateway, watched the in-bringing of the bodies of his fellow-whites—prelude, he too well knew, to a cannibal feast.

He turned to enter the village, when an old Maori, tugging away madly at a flax line which he had made fast to the neck of a dead man, caught sight of him, and shouted:

"You, *pakeha*! Come and give me a hand. Help me to drag in my food!"

"What do you want?" Bent heard a rough voice ask. He turned and saw the war-chief Titokowaru standing at his side. "What do you want of this *pakeha*?"

The Maori replied that he wished the white man to help him haul the soldier's body into the *marae*.

"No!" cried the chief in his great hoarse voice. "No! you must not call upon my *pakeha* to help you. He shall not touch the bodies of his countrymen."

So the war-captain and his cartridge-maker stood by watching the frightful procession of Hauhaus and their prizes. The seven naked bodies were dragged into the *pa* and laid out in the centre of the *marae*.

The excited people all gathered in a great circle around the bodies. One after another the orators leaped out from the squatting ranks, their eyes flashing wildly in the *pukana* glare; they bounded to and fro, and cut the air with their tomahawks as they told the thrilling episodes of the fight.

All the clothes, arms, and accoutrements taken from the dead and wounded were laid before Titokowaru.

"Whose was this?" the war-chief would ask, picking up a carbine, or an ammunition-pouch, or a soldier's tunic from the heap.

"Mine," replied the man who had taken it on the battle-field.

"Take it away, then," said Titokowaru. "Whose is this?" picking up another trophy.

"It is mine," a young man would reply; "it is my first spoils of war, a *tanga-ika*."

"Burn it," was the chief's order.

Then the human bodies lying on the *marae* were apportioned one by one, to each tribe, as piles of food are served out at a ceremonial Maori gathering.

"Nga-Rauru, this is yours! Tangahoé, this is yours!" and so on, till the seven bodies were all disposed of.

A woman sat weeping on the *marae*. She was Te Hau-karewa, wife to one Te Rangi-whakairi-papa and a sister of Te Waka-tapa-ruru, the old warrior who had fallen in his desperate rush upon the white enemy that morning. Though old, she was a tall, fine-looking woman, with a mass of black curly hair.

Ceasing her *tangi* for the dead, when the bodies of the soldiers were laid out on the ground, she rose, and, taking a stick in her hand, she walked along the row of the dead men and struck each a blow on the head.

"*Upoko-kohua!*" she cried vehemently, with hate flashing in her eyes; "*Upoko-kohua! Ka taona koe ki te umu, he utu mo taku tungane kua mate, ko Te Waka-tapa-ruru! Mehemea ko au i tata i taku tungane i te takiwa i mate ai, ka kainga au i te karu o te tangata nana i whakamatea Te Waka!*" ("Boiled heads! Cursed heads! Soon ye'll be cooked in the oven, as payment for the death of my brother, Te Waka-tapa-ruru. Had I but been near my brother when he fell, I would have swallowed the eyes of the man who slew him!")

Then, throwing away her stick, she sat down again, and fell to weeping in the very abandonment of woe, for the savage woman of the woods loved her grim warrior-brother greatly.

Some of the Maoris proposed that the bodies of the slain whites, the "Fish of Whiro," should all be burned or buried.

But up leaped Timoti, wildest of all the wild Waitotara tribe, the cannibal Nga-Rauru, a thin, savage-faced fellow, very dark of complexion, as active and agile as a wild cat. He ran up and down in front of his slain enemies, turning from one side to the other, *pukana*-ing—only the whites of his eyes showing—and his tongue protruded in derision and defiance. He flashed his tomahawk in the air; he yelled, "We must have one body—one body to cook in the *hangi*!"

"Yes," said another of the clan, "the customs of our fathers must be observed. What is the use of killing so many *pakehas* if we cannot have one to eat?"

No man making objection, several Hauhaus jumped up and ran to the heap of slain Constabulary men. They selected a body, and dragged it off to the cooking-place at the rear of the *marae*. "He is the fattest of the *pakehas*," said the saturnine Timoti.

All eyes watched them, but no man said a word.

Bent, after a while, rose with some of his Hauhau companions, and walked over to the cooking-*hangis*, and watched the cooks at their horrible work.

They were roasting the white man's body on the great fire of hot stones, in a hollowed-out earth-oven. "It was being cooked," says Bent, "much as you would roast a piece of mutton; they turned it over and over until it was thoroughly done, and then they cut it up for the feast."

When the cannibal meal was ready, it was brought on to the *marae* with much ceremony in flax baskets. Potatoes had been steam-boiled in other *hangis* at the same time, and these were carried to the assembly-ground, to be eaten with the man-meat. Bent saw the flesh of the soldier eaten. The man-eaters, he says, all belonged to the Waitotara tribe. Ten of them consumed the *pakeha*, or as much of him as was borne to the *marae*; the rest of the people did not share in the feast. Titokowaru himself would not eat human flesh, because of his *tapu*.

"I noticed," says the *pakeha*-Maori, "Timoti and Big Kereopa, each with a basket before them, enjoying the meal of human flesh. Timoti grabbed up his portion of meat from his basket, and ate it just as if he were eating a piece of bread."

Then Titokowaru rose and, crying in a loud voice, ordered the people to burn the rest of the corpses, so that they should not defile the *marae*.

The bundles of clothing from the dead lay on the *marae*. The Maoris gave Bent three pairs of soldiers' trousers, four shirts, and some boots. "I tell you I was pleased," says the old *pakeha*-Maori, who had no inconvenient scruples on the subject of dead men's clothes; "for a long time I had been wearing only Maori-made garments of flax."

A great pile of wood was collected, heaped up six or seven feet high, and in the evening, as darkness fell, the bodies of the *pakehas* were placed on this funeral pyre and cremated.

The people squatted round—as they had sat at a similar ceremony in the "Bird's Beak" *pa*—and watched the flames devour their fallen foemen. And by the light of the great fire roaring away there on the *marae*, Titokowaru *taki*'d up and down, addressing his followers, and bounding and parading to and fro, his sacred feather-plumed *taiaha* in his hand. He recited incantations, and chanted songs, and exhorted the Hauhaus, bidding them be of good heart and fight to the bitter end.

Then Titokowaru turned to the body of the slain warrior Te Waka-tapa-ruru, lying on a blanket on the *marae*, with gun and tomahawk by his side. Gazing upon the silent, tattooed features of the dead *toa*, his comrade in many a wild foray and forest battle, he cried the old farewells to those whose spirits have passed to the *Reinga*, and he chanted this lament:

> *"Ki konei ra, e Waka e!*
> *Ka wehe koe i au.*
> *Ka riro i a koe*
> *I nuku-maniapoto,*
> *E ngakinga mate.*
> *Aue, e Waka e!"*

("There thou liest, O Waka!
Parted from me for ever.
Thou'rt borne away to the fields of night,
In revenge for other deaths.
Alas, O Waka!")

And the wild *korero* went on. *Tangi* songs were chanted, and there were speeches of savage, boastful jubilation made—"great swelling words." But from a lone little thatched hut on one side of the crowded parade ground came a long-sustained crying sound, a sobbing heart-breaking dirge, rising and falling like a Highland coronach—a keening for the dead. Te Hau-karewa made lamentation for her slain warrior.

CHAPTER XIX

THE TAURANGA-IKA STOCKADE

Another fighting *pa* built—Scouting and skirmishing—The watcher
on the tower—McDonnell and Titokowaru—How Trooper Lingard won the New Zealand Cross—Hairbreadth escapes—Pairama
and the white man's leg.

On the edge of the great forest, some miles to the south of the Waitotara River,
was the site of the olden Maori village, Tauranga-ika. In front fern and grass lands
stretched away to the sand-dunes of the sea-coast, with here and there a small
shallow lake; in the rear was the dense and roadless bush, a perfect and safe retreat
for the Hauhaus in the event of defeat. The country hereabouts was dotted with
the white man's farmsteads; but the whites had been driven off before Titokowaru's victorious army, leaving their homes, the labour of many years, to go up in
smoke, and their sheep and cattle to feed the Hauhau bands. Wanganui town was
only a day's march away, and Titokowaru's council of chiefs, eager to follow up
their victory at Moturoa, proposed to assault the town and massacre every soul
in it.

This old-time village was fixed on by the Hauhau war-chief as the site of his
new fighting *pa*, for he abandoned Papa-tihakehake soon after the repulse of the
white forces at that strong stockade. With the wariness of the Maori strategist, he
avoided a second attack in any one entrenchment, and sooner than risk another,
and possibly disastrous, engagement at Papa-tihakehake, he took the trouble to
construct an even stronger fortification, a splendid example of native military en-
gineering genius.

In the building of this new *pa*, Kimble Bent and his Hauhau comrades toiled
early and late until it was completed. It was of large size, fully defended with palisading, trenches, parapet, and rifle-pits. It was between two and three chains in
extreme length at the rear, with a somewhat narrower front. The ground in front
was bare of forest, but carried high fern cover; on the flanks were burned clearings,
dotted with blackened tree-stumps and cumbered with logs; then the forest, with
some beautiful groves of *mahoé* on its outskirts. Two rows of palisades, high and
strong, were erected around the position; the posts, solid tree-trunks, were from
six to twelve inches thick and ten to fifteen feet high; the rows were four feet apart.
The spaces between the larger stockade-posts were filled in with saplings set up-
right close together, and fastened by cross-rails and supplejack ties; these saplings
did not rest in the ground, but hung a few inches above it, so that between them

and the ground a space was left for the fire of the defending musketeers, who were enabled to pour volleys from their trenches inside the war-fence on any approaching enemy with perfect safety to themselves. Behind the inner stockading was a parapet about six feet high and four feet wide, formed of the earth thrown out of the trenches. The interior of the *pa* was pitted everywhere with trenches and covered ways, so that in the event of attack the defenders could literally take to the earth like rabbits, and live underground secure from rifle-fire, and even from artillery. The place was a network of trenches with connecting passages, roofed over with timber, *raupo*, and *toetoe* reeds and earth. To any assault that could be delivered by the Government forces then available, the fort was practically impregnable.

At one angle of the *pa* the Hauhau garrison erected a roughly timbered watch-tower, about thirty-five feet in height. This tower, or *taumaihi*, was a feature of the ancient *pas* of Maoridom; on its upper platform a sentinel was posted, day and night, to give warning of the approach of the enemy. In front of the *pa*, outside the palisades, a tall flagstaff was set up, and on this staff the Hauhau war-flags were hoisted. There were two gateways in the rear stockading, giving access to the bush. In one end of the *pa* near the rear was a small tent occupied by Titokowaru. Bent, the cartridge-maker, lived in a little rush-built *wharé* towards the other end, near one of the gateways.

When the stockade was finished the Hauhaus constructed a *tekoteko*, a great marionette-like figure of a man, cut out of a *pukatea*-tree. It was so placed that its head stood about fifteen feet above the ground, well above the front stockade, and it had loose-jointed arms, to which flax ropes were fastened, leading down to the trench below. By manipulating these ropes the arms of the wooden warrior were made to move in the actions of the *haka*, just as if some painted Hauhau were dancing a dance of defiance on the fortress walls.

When the fort was finished the garrison gathered in their food supplies, saw to their arms, and for many weeks waited for the *pakeha*. Hauhau scouts and small war-parties daily sallied out from the fort, seeking game in the shape of stray *pakehas*.

One of these savage man-hunters was a Ngati-Maniapoto man from the King Country, whose name was Pairama, and who had married a Nga-Rauru woman. He used to go out by himself, looking for some one or something to kill. Te Pairama returned to the stockade in huge jubilation one day, bearing as a trophy of his prowess on the trail a white man's leg! He had, says Bent, scouted down until he was close to Kai-iwi. There he spied a white settler in a grass paddock, carrying a rifle.

Down he crouched at once, and stealthily stalked the *pakeha*. Just as the unsuspecting settler came to the paddock gate, the Maori leaped out from behind the fence, with a furious snatch tore the rifle from the man's grasp, and shot him dead with it. He cut off one of the *pakeha's* legs with his tomahawk, and brought it home as proof of his success on the war-path as proudly as any Indian ever flourished his take of scalps. Up and down the *marae* of the *pa* he bounded, exhibiting the captured rifle and severed limb, yelling his war-song, and loudly boasting that he would that night cook the *pakeha's* leg and eat it all himself.

But the warrior's braggadocio received a sharp check from Titokowaru. The war-chief disapproved of this sort of thing on the part of irresponsible young free-lances. "No man must bring white man's flesh into this *pa*," he said, "unless he is one of the *Tekau-ma-rua*, the war-party sent out by me. Take that *pakeha* leg back again at once and place it alongside the body." And soon thereafter the dis-gusted scout, his ardour for "long-pig" so unexpectedly damped by Titoko's code of cannibal etiquette, was to be seen trudging back along the track to the *pakeha* farm, with sulky visage and reluctant gait, and a white foot and leg—raw—pro-truding from a flax basket strapped to his shoulders.

By day the scouting parties of the Hauhau "Twelve Apostles" scoured the country; by night the people gathered round the fires on the *marae* or in the big sleeping *wharés*, and talked and sang and danced the *hakas* of which they never wearied. Wild night-scenes those on the stockaded *marae*, with the crowds of blan-keted or flax-cloaked men and women, their wild faces illumined by the leaping flames, squatting in great circles round the camp fires, while more than half nude figures leaped and stamped and slapped their limbs and chests with resounding slaps, and expelled the air from their lungs in wolfish "Ooh's!" and "Hau's!" as they trod the assembly ground in all the fury of the war-dance. A warrior orator would rise, weapon in hand, and throwing off his blanket for freedom of action, go bounding along the *marae* in front of the assemblage, shouting short, sharp sen-tences as he *taki*'d to and fro, his athletic figure untrammelled except for a waist-shawl or short dangling mat, fire in his movements, and ferocity in every gesture and in every cry—the embodiment of belligerent Maoridom in its savage prime.

Like defiant replying shouts from some hidden foe in the blackness of the forest that rose in a solid wall above the rear stockade came the clear echoes of the roaring *haka* choruses.

And so the wild night passed, until the camp fires died down, and the tribes-people sought sleep in their packed *wharepunis* and their rush-strewn burrows; and the melancholy "*Kou-kou!*" of the "hundred-eyed" *ruru*, the bush-owl, was heard, as the bird-sentry of the night hours cried his watchword from the forest or a perch on some tall palisade-post. Yet not all eyes were closed in the *pa*, for the Hauhaus, grown wise by much hard experience, did not neglect the posting of sentries, and a sentinel watched from the platform in the angle-tower. At intervals he cried his watch-cry, or raised his voice in a night-song that rose and fell in mea-sured cadences like a *tangi* wail.

The most dreaded hour in Maori warfare was the dark, dank hour just before the dawn, and then it was well to be on the qui vive, for Kepa's dusky forest-rang-ers and their white comrades the A.C.'s had a truly unpleasant fashion of attack-ing their enemies at most unholy, shivery times, when man slept soundest. So the watchmen in the tower were enjoined to extra vigilance in the early morning hours. And, as in the olden Maori days, out rang the voice of the high sentinel, chanting his ancient "*Whakaara-pa*," his "All's well" song, to Tarioa and Kopu, the first and morning stars.

This is one of the songs he cried, an old watch-chant of the Ngati-Toa tribe of Kawhia:

	Translation.
Kia hiwa e!	Now watchful be,
Kia hiwa!	O watchful be,
Kia hiwa e tenei tuku,	On this side and on that!
Kia hiwa e tera tuku;	Bend ears to every sound,
Kia, whakarongo koe	High up, high up
Ki nga kupu.	The surf rolls in
Whakapuru tonu,	On Harihari's cliffs,
Whakapuru tonu	And loudly sounds the restless sea
Te tai ki Harihari,	
Ka tangi tere	On Mokau's coast.
Te tai ki Mokau.	Now yonder, lo! the sun—
Ka ao atu te ra,	The sun leaps up
Ka ao mai te ra	Above the mountain-tops.
Ki tua o nga pae ra.	
E—e! I—a—we!	

Late one night, as the Hauhaus lay behind their palisades, Colonel Thomas McDonnell—a man who spoke Maori like a native—rode boldly up to the *pa* wall with his escort, and asked for Titokowaru. He called out in the native tongue, "O Titoko—where are you?"

Titoko, summoned from his tent, went down to the stockade. "I am here!" he shouted.

The white officer cried: "Titoko, I have been trying to discover your *atua*, the god which guides you in your battles. Now I have found it—I know the source of your *mana*. When the wind blows hard from the *whakarua* (the north-east), I know it is the breath of your god, the wind of Uenuku! But your *atua* is only a *tutua*—a low fellow!"

Spoke Titoko angrily, and said: "McDonnell, go! Depart at once! If you do not ride away directly, there will be a blazing oven ready for you!"

McDonnell rode away, and the angry chief returned to his tent. Why McDonnell should have paid this daring night visit to the stockade is not quite clear, but the incident is given just as Bent narrates it. He and his companions on the *marae* heard the dialogue, and Bent says the old fear struck to his heart when he heard Titokowaru menacing the white officer with the oven. The Taranakis seem to have been particularly addicted to the "ordeal by fire."

"The oven is gaping open for you!" was their customary threat. Their tribal history abounds, too, in tales of how some obnoxious neighbours or others, Ngatiso-and-so, had been effectively disposed of by the simple process of surrounding their huts while they slept, fastening the doors, and then setting fire to the *wharés*. The only objection from the Maori point of view to this summary method of obtaining *utu* was that it "spoiled the meat!"

Colonel McDonnell was so conversant with Maori *tikanga*—customs, rules of life, and ways of thought—that he was by way of being a *tohunga*-Maori himself, and his dramatic twitting of Titokowaru with the fact that the reputed source of his fighting *mana* was within his (McDonnell's) knowledge was a circumstance that hugely annoyed the old war-chief.

It was just as if so much of his *mana-tapu* had passed to his white foeman—to the rival maker of strong "war-medicine."

Occasional skirmishes with the white cavalry patrol-parties enlivened the three months' sojourn in Tauranga-ika. In one of these rencontres a young Wanganui trooper—now a resident of Wellington—won his New Zealand Cross. This was William Lingard, a member of Captain John Bryce's troop of Kai-iwi Cavalry.

A HAUHAU SCOUT, TUTANGÉ WAIONUI, OF PATEA.

Out scouting one day, Bryce took a party of his men boldly up to the front of the stockade on a reconnaissance. The place was unusually quiet, and a white flag was flying on the flagstaff in front of the *pa*. One of the cavalrymen, Sergeant Maxwell, leaping a ditch and hedge that intervened between the farm lands and the *pa*, raced right up close to the stockade, and fired at it. Trooper Lingard, also leaping the obstacles, with the rest of the detachment, rode up past the *pa*. Lingard, though he could see nothing of the Maoris, raised his carbine and fired a shot. The next instant the whole palisade front—just above the ground, where the interstices were left for musketry—was a blaze of fire, and a storm of lead sang over the little troop. The Hauhaus, hidden in their trenches, and preserving complete silence, had waited till the patrol was within murderously close range. Maxwell was mortally wounded; but he sat his horse till it carried him out of range. Several horses were shot, and fell. One trooper, H. Wright, was pinned to the ground by his horse falling on his leg, and was unable to extricate himself, but, nevertheless, drew his revolver, and kept popping away at the palisades.

The whole *pa* was now in a roar of battle-excitement. The Maoris, as they fired, raised their fearful yells and war-shouts, an infernal din that almost drowned the cracks of the firearms. Kimble Bent was there, sitting on the parapet inside the stockade, and watching the encounter. A burly framed Hauhau, a herculean savage known as Big Kereopa—one of those who had shared in the cannibal feast at Papa-tihakehake—dashed out from the rear of the stockade, armed with a long-handled tomahawk, and rushed at the helpless *pakeha*. Trooper Lingard instantly put his plunging horse at the Hauhau, and cut at him with his sword. Another trooper, Tom D. Cummins (now of Wanganui) took a hand in the combat, and with a shot from his carbine stopped the charging Hauhau. He put a bullet into Kereopa, and the big fellow clapping a hand to his wound—which was in his posterior parts—bolted back into the *pa* nearly as quickly as he had come, yelling "I'm shot! I'm shot!" Lingard, leaning over, got Wright by the hand, and, though almost dismounted himself, succeeded in dragging his comrade from under the fallen horse. Then, noticing a white horse—which was usually ridden by one of the Maori scouts—tethered to a *tutu*-bush a short distance from the palisades, Lingard galloped at it, cut the tether-line with his sword, and soon had Wright mounted again and riding down the hill out of range, with the Hauhau bullets whistling close around their heads. Lingard's rescue of his comrade was a remarkably plucky bit of work.

An incident of Hauhau life at this period, illustrative of the pitilessly savage character of the olden Maori, is told thus by Kimble Bent:

"While we were living in the *pa* at Tauranga-ika, a Hauhau fighting-man named Taketake quarrelled with his sister. She threatened that she would run away to the *pakehas*, and tell them of the cannibal practices of the rebels. He warned her that if she did he would shoot her. That evening she left the *pa*, and started for the white soldiers' camp. Taketake loaded his gun and followed her. Overtaking her on the road, he shot her through the back and killed her. He returned to the *pa* and reported what he had done. A party of men went out and brought back the murdered woman's body, and that was all there was about it. No one interfered with Taketake, or considered what he had done was a crime. All they said was '*Kaitoa!*' ('Serve her right')."

While the *pakeha* attack was awaited, Bent and his companions spent much of their time in the forest at the rear of the fort, catching eels in the creeks, hunting wild pigs, and gathering wild honey for the garrison food-supplies.

CHAPTER XX

A SCOUTING ADVENTURE

The passage of the Okehu—A night's vigil—Mackenzie the scout—"Maoris in the bush!"—The watchers in the fern—A race for life.

A CLEAR, bright, moonlight night of summer; a moon that silvered the sharp hill-tops of the broken Maori country, but left black mysterious shadows in the gorges and river valleys that every few miles cut deeply into the rolling fern lands; valleys full of danger and death, for in their depths crept the war-parties of the savage, laying ambushes, planning murder and mutilation. On a gently sloping rise on the open fern lands a hundred white tents, the camp of the *pakeha* troops, glittered in the full moonlight. The sweet bugle-calls of "Lights out" and the "Last post" rang out for miles across the wilderness, and except for the piquets and sentries the camp was soon asleep. But away on the forest edge, a mile from the safely entrenched camp, a little band of men, half a dozen scouts, crouched hiding in the fern, carbines in their hands, watching, listening. They were the eyes of the army. Their wits, their keenness of vision and hearing, were pitted this night against the savage men of the forest, born bushmen, with the cunning of the Indian.

It was the 17th of January, 1869, nearly three months after the repulse of the Colonial troops at the Moturoa stockade. All this time Titokowaru and his victorious *Tekau-ma-rua* had everything their own way on the West Coast, scouring the country-side, burning settlers' houses, killing cattle, and strengthening their palisaded position at Tauranga-ika. The East Coast campaign following on the Poverty Bay massacre had necessitated the diversion of nearly all the Constabulary from the West Coast, until the storming and capture of Te Kooti's hill-fort Ngatapa and the flight of the rebel chief to the forests of the Urewera Country enabled attention to be again given to the Taranaki and Waitotara Hauhaus. Now, well on in the month of January, 1869, Colonel Whitmore, with Colonel Lyon—a brave one-armed soldier, veteran of the Crimea—as his second in command, advanced from Wanganui with a strong force of Armed Constabulary, about eight hundred in number, besides a large body of *Kupapas*, or friendly Maoris, mostly of the Whanganui tribe, under Kepa te Rangihiwinui. The force encamped at the end of the first day's march near the right bank of the Kai-iwi stream, about ten miles from Wanganui, and prepared to march the next day through the Okehu Gorge and on to Nukumaru and Tauranga-ika.

This country around the Kai-iwi was mostly open fern land, but some of the river gullies were filled with a dense growth of forest. A short distance to the north of the camp there was a deep gorge, the valley of the Okehu stream. Through this gorge a road had been cut some years before, and the river had been bridged, giving access to Nukumaru and the Waitotara, and this was the route by which Colonel Whitmore intended to approach the Hauhau stronghold. It was, however, plainly a dangerous place, where the Maoris might easily lay an ambush. The little colonel was too old a soldier to run risks of this sort, and he determined to have the gorge carefully scouted before he took his column into it.

That afternoon he selected half a dozen of his most active men, some of them Constabulary, some volunteers, and as soon as night fell despatched them to the Okehu, with orders to spend the night on the fern-covered right bank of the gorge, and find out if the Maoris were laying an ambuscade in the bush below. Trooper William Lingard, of Bryce's Kai-iwi Cavalry—the young trooper who had distinguished himself at the Tauranga-ika skirmish described in the last chapter—was placed in charge of the scouts. With him were Chris. Maling, a young surveyor—his father had been killed by the Maoris years before, and he often declared that he would never rest until he had killed a Maori with his own hands in revenge; a Frenchman called Peter the Guide; three men named Herri, Powell, and Williamson; and an old Indian soldier named Mackenzie. It is with this Mackenzie that this story of a night's scouting expedition is chiefly concerned.

It was the calmest of nights, a still night when sounds travelled far, and in silence the little squad of armed scouts set out from the tented camp in single file towards the dark gorge of the Okehu. They marched as silently as Indians, for they were shod exactly like Indians, in moccasins that felt the ground as soundlessly as a wild cat's pad.

The making and wearing of those moccasins was Mackenzie's idea. This veteran soldier was a man who had been brought out from India by Sir Henry Cracroft Wilson, when that gentleman settled in Canterbury. He was, as one of his scouting comrades says, a fine-looking, resolute man, something over forty years of age, with hair beginning to turn grizzly, and a bold, fearless eye. He was partly of Gurkha blood, and his senses were wonderfully keen. He had marvellous escapes from death, and had even been partly scalped. Once when he was overpowered and felled in a mêlée, a savage had passed his knife around his head and underneath the scalp, and was about to "lift his hair" when a timely bullet from one of Mackenzie's comrades knocked his assailant over, and the soldier was rescued. His companion ran to his aid, pressed down the torn scalp into its place, and bound it firmly with bandages. Mackenzie saved his hair, but to his last day bore the scar of the scalping-knife running round his head. He carried besides his carbine a remarkable weapon, a two-ended steel knife, or dagger, of Afghan make, which he wore in a sheath at his back with a flap of skin over the top. One end of the dagger was a stiletto and the other was a double-edged cutting and thrusting blade, ground as sharp as a razor. It had the handle in the middle. With this knife he would perform some wonderfully dexterous feats. He would throw it up into the air thirty or forty feet and catch it by the middle as cleverly as a juggler as it came whizzing down. He would stick a piece of paper on a post and, retiring twenty or thirty yards, hurl the shining weapon at it and transfix the target in the exact centre, the knife quivering several inches deep in the post.

The moccasins the scouts wore were made by Mackenzie from the skin of a horse. Immediately the party had been organised the old soldier went out with his carbine and shot one of the numerous ownerless horses that roamed the hills. Cutting out suitable pieces of the skin, he fitted them while still warm to his comrades' feet, with the hair inside; then cut thongs and laced the horse-skin shoe firmly to the foot. In a few hours these moccasins took perfect shape, and made the most suitable foot-gear for bush-work that could have been devised. "If we wear ordinary boots out scouting we're sure to lose our lives," said Mackenzie; "we can't scout noiselessly in them, or run fast enough when it comes to running."

An old Maori war-track wound through the high fern above the Okehu Gorge. Along this the scouts marched to take up their night's vigil. Two were posted at the end of the gorge nearest the camp, two more about two hundred yards away, and the third couple about the same distance farther on, above the middle of the gorge. The men made themselves nests in the fern alongside the track, and close to the edge of the slope that fell to the impenetrable blackness of the bush below. The leader, as he posted the men, told them to keep a sharp watch and listen for any sounds, and to give a signal if any of them heard Maoris in the gorge. The signal was to be the thrice-repeated sharp cry of the *weka*, the night-roving wingless bird that haunted these forests and gulches.

After posting his comrades in their several positions, young Lingard rejoined his companion Maling in a little nook in the thick fern just on the gorge side of the narrow foot-track, and stayed a while with him conversing in whispers. In half an hour's time he cautiously patrolled the track again to visit the others. When he came to Mackenzie, the old soldier was sitting up reading a pocket Bible by the bright moonlight.

"What are you reading?" asked Lingard, as he squatted down quietly in the fern by Mackenzie's side.

"Look and see," said the soldier, and Lingard saw, and wondered, for not many a rough old soldier like Mackenzie was seen with such a book. And he wondered still more when Mackenzie, closing the book, asked him to look at it again. There was a clean-cut hole in it, right through one of the covers and penetrating many of the leaves.

"That book saved my life," said the veteran. And he told the story. It was the comrade who had bowled over the Indian who was about to scalp him that gave Mackenzie the little Bible. "'You say you will always be grateful to me for saving your life,' he said. 'Well, I want you to do just one thing for me; it's a little thing. I won't ask much.'

"He was so insistent," said Mackenzie, "that I gave him the promise he asked. 'Well,' said my friend, 'just take this little book of mine and read something in it every night; or, if you won't read it, take it out and look at it and open it. And always carry it with you. It will save your life.'

"I did so, and I read it, more to please my old friend than anything else. I carried it in my jumper pocket, for it was small and light. And in those dangerous days I carried something else night and day—this dagger that I wear at my belt. About midnight one night I was lying alone in my tent, half-asleep, when I heard something—no, smelt it! It was pitch dark, but I knew there was something or some one close to me. As quietly as I knew how, I loosened my dagger and gripped it firmly. The next moment I felt a terrible thud on the chest, and a figure hurled itself on me. I brought round the knife with a swift sweep, and nearly ripped the side out of the fellow—killed him dead. It was a native who wanted to kill and rob me. He had jumped at me with a knife, but the point of his blade struck the Bible in my breast pocket as I lay on my back, and that saved my life. See! It's the sort of thing you used to read about in little Sunday-school books, isn't it? I wonder how many people would believe it? But it's absolutely true. That old comrade of mine saved my life twice. And it's these two I put my trust in, my Bible and my dagger. That knife's the best weapon I've ever had. It's more to me than carbine or revolver."

Then Mackenzie put his hand on his fellow-scout's arm, and spoke in an earnest whisper of a presentiment that filled his mind.

"I feel," he said, looking straight into his friend's eyes, "that this is my last night on earth. I have a conviction that I won't see another sun rise."

"Nonsense!" said young Lingard, beginning to feel creepy. "Don't talk like that, old man; you'll unnerve me. You're not going to die."

"Why should I unnerve you, my boy?" asked Mackenzie very quietly and gently. "There's nothing to be afraid of in dying. I can face death with perfect calmness; and I know I'm to die very soon."

There was silence for some moments. Suddenly Mackenzie started, turned in a listening attitude, and put up a hand in warning.

"Don't you hear them?" he whispered. "Don't you hear them? There are Maoris moving in the bush below. I heard the pat of a naked foot just now and the breaking of a twig."

The young leader of the scouts listened with utmost intentness for the next few minutes. The two comrades could hear each other's hearts thumping, so still they crouched. But not another sound came except the occasional call of the melancholy morepork.

After a little while Lingard bade Mackenzie good-bye for the time, and, with his carbine at the "ready," crept back along the track and visited the other men. Joining Maling, he told him of his strange conversation with Mackenzie.

"He's a real good fellow," said Maling, "a good comrade. I hope that presentiment of his is all bunkum. But if he says there are Maoris moving in the bush, we'll have work before morning."

In half an hour's time Lingard went the rounds again, stopping every now and then to listen for sounds of the enemy. He found Mackenzie still reading, bare-headed, by the clear moonlight in his little nook in the fern. Mackenzie's mate was sound asleep.

The old soldier's senses were wonderfully acute. Quietly as Lingard stole up on his moccasined feet, he had heard him. He was listening while he read.

"Lingard," he said, "I've been reading for the last time. I know it's my last night of life. To-day I was so sure of this that I settled my account at the canteen, and paid my last instalment on a horse I bought from John Handley, and I've written to my wife. I won't see to-morrow's sun rise. This came to me yesterday morning.

"Lingard," he went on again, in a whisper, "there are Maoris about! Can't you smell them? They're in the bush below, waiting. But you'll stay, I suppose, till daylight, unless something happens before then."

In a few minutes Lingard, after vainly listening for sounds in the bush, cautiously rose and walked back along the track. He left Mackenzie sitting there, with the moonlight streaming down on his earnest face, still reading his little book. Returning to Maling, Lingard sat with his companion listening, until it was within perhaps half an hour of full daylight.

Then, all at once, they heard a fearful sound. A rifle shot, followed instantly by a terrific yell, the war-yell of the Maoris from the bush behind them. The bush flashed fire, the flashes of many guns, accompanied by reverberating bangs; then the pattering and thudding of many naked feet along the track.

The ambuscade had been unmasked. One of the scouts—so it was learned afterwards—had cautiously worked his way down the valley, far enough down to see that the bridge over the Okehu had been set on fire, and by its light he saw a large party of armed Hauhaus. He hurried back to give his comrades warning, but before he could reach them some of the prowling natives discovered Mackenzie and Williamson and fired on them, wounding Williamson in the back when he started to run.

The scouts had done their work, but would they ever reach the camp alive?

The whole of the war-party were on the white men's heels, racing through the fern and along the narrow track and firing as they ran. The moon had gone down, and it was too dim to see very far, but the dawn was spreading over the eastern sky.

"They're on us!—they're on us!" exclaimed Maling. "It's no use to run now; we wouldn't have a show. Let's hide here in the fern."

The scouts were crouching in the fern within a yard or so of the Maori track. The fern was very high here, over a tall man's head in height, and was very thick and matted, and lying in a slanting direction. The two men, knowing that it was certain death to venture out, for the Maoris were rushing along the track in force, crept underneath the thick masses of ferns, and pushed it up over them so that they had room to move and were perfectly screened from the enemy's eyes in that early morning light. They made ready their Terry carbines, bit their cartridges ready for reloading, and put their percussion-caps in their mouths for instant use. Just before they did so, Maling turned to his companion and said:

"Lingard, old man, promise me if it comes to the worst you won't leave me, and I'll do the same by you. Don't let us leave each other," and he put out his hand.

The young leader of the scouts gripped Maling's hand. "We'll stick by each other," he said.

The next moment there was a thundering rush of feet past the very muzzles of their carbines. A mob of Hauhaus, yelling and shouting, raced past them, following up the leaders who had been fired on by the scout, and who had come dashing after the white men.

The two hidden scouts could hear nothing of their comrades, but they well knew the odds were greatly against any of them reaching the camp.

Presently they heard firing from the direction of the camp. The troops had turned out on hearing the shots at the bush edge, and were covering the retreat of the scouts.

Then another thing happened. Maling and his companion heard and felt something now and then swishing and cutting through the fern just above their heads. They were under the fire of their own comrades.

"Maling," said Lingard, "this is getting too warm! It's not good enough to stay here and be shot by our own men. Let's make a run for it."

Creeping out from their place of concealment, and giving a quick look backwards to make sure that no more Hauhaus were coming, the two scouts ran along the track in the direction of the camp. Close by on their left they could hear the enemy yelling and firing.

Just as they turned a bend in the path they came upon a terrible sight. Mackenzie lay on the ground, face downwards; his head smashed in and his brains spattering the ground. His carbine and ammunition and Afghan sheath-dagger were gone.

This they saw at one horrified glance, then they dashed on, taking a short cut across the fern to the camp. They could see the white tents now in the morning light. They ran towards the troops shouting, "Don't fire!—don't fire!"

The two scouts reached camp safely, and Lingard immediately reported the result of the night's work to the colonel. All the others excepting poor Mackenzie turned up. One of them had fallen shot, wounded in the back, close to the camp, but was rescued by the surgeon, Dr. Walker, who pluckily ran out and carried him in.

Mackenzie, one of the survivors said, was running well, and would have escaped, but he suddenly fell prone on his face without any apparent cause. A Hauhau came running along next moment, and, putting his gun close to Mackenzie's head, blew his brains out.

Then came another strange development of the morning's adventure. Surgeon Walker, on examining Mackenzie's body, said he believed the scout had died suddenly of heart disease, and that he was quite dead before even the Hauhau shot him.

The brave old Gurkha soldier's presentiment of speedy death was only too true a foreword from the Unknown.

It was fortunate that this Hauhau ambuscade had been unmasked. The camp was already astir, and the troops were having their early morning coffee, and in another half-hour would have begun the march by the Okehu Gorge route, when the first shots were fired. Once down in the narrow gorge and the presence of the enemy undetected, they would have been practically at the mercy of their active and well-concealed foes in the thick bush above and on either side of them.

After this little morning skirmish the Hauhaus, numbering probably a hundred and fifty, quickly retired through the bush to the Tauranga-ika *pa*, taking with them as trophies the dead soldier's arms. The white troops were soon on the move. Four divisions of Armed Constabulary, the Volunteer Cavalry, and the *Kupapa* Maoris marched through the Gorge unmolested, and took up a position near the great Hauhau *pa*, which Whitmore now prepared to storm. First he tried artillery in an endeavour to breach the stockade, and Kimble Bent and his Maori comrades in the crowded fort now stood target for cannon-fire.

CHAPTER XXI

THE FALL OF TAURANGA-IKA

Shot and shell—The fort abandoned—Flight of the Hauhaus—The chase—The fight at Karaka Flat—Mutilation of the dead—The ambuscade at the peach-grove—The sergeant's leg—Rewards for Hauhau heads.

Skirmishing up over the fern slopes of Tauranga-ika came Whitmore's Armed Constabulary and Kepa's kilted guerillas from the Wanganui. Some of the A.C.'s advanced to within about two hundred yards of the stockade, and took cover in a ditch which ran parallel with the front palisading; here they opened fire. The main body had pitched camp about half a mile from the *pa* front. At the same time Armstrong guns were brought up and posted on the left front of the stockade, and shell-fire was opened on the rebel position at a range of five hundred yards.

But most of the Hauhaus were safe in their trenches and their covered ways, and the shells and bullets passed harmlessly over them. A few of the young bloods danced and yelled defiance from above-ground. On the stockade was the Hauhau *tekoteko*, the dummy figure which they worked in marionette-fashion by means of ropes that led into the trench below. This dummy was intended to draw the *pakeha* fire, but it had hardly deceived the veteran A.C.'s and Kepa's *Kupapas*, versed in all Hauhau ways that were dark and tricks that were vain. Bent was underground, listening to the bang of the Armstrongs and the whistle of the shells, and now and again squinting through the palisades at his adversaries.

One Maori, who was standing in an angle of the *pa*, was wounded in the head by a splinter knocked off one of the palisade-posts by a shot from an Armstrong gun. The same shell, whizzing through the *pa*, ripped a hole in Titokowaru's tent.

When night fell, no appreciable breach had been made by the shell-fire. It was now decided to storm the *pa* at daybreak. Some of the A.C.'s crept up with their entrenching tools to within fifty yards of the stockade, and dug out shelter-trenches.

The fort was remarkably quiet during the night. It was reconnoitred when daybreak came, and found—empty. The Hauhaus had for some mysterious reason deserted it under cover of darkness, and taken to the bush. So fell to the *pakeha* the very strong Tauranga-ika *pa*.

Bent explains this unexpected abandonment of Titokowaru's most formidable entrenchment.

The eternal feminine was at the bottom of it all.

The chief of blood and fire, with all his *mana-tapu*, was vulnerable to the artillery of a dark *wahiné's* eyes and soft *wahiné* blandishments. He was detected in a liaison with another man's wife. This misdemeanour was, in Maori eyes, fatal to his prestige as an *ariki* and a war-leader. He had trampled on his *tapu*, and his Hauhau angel, who had so long successfully guided his fortunes, now deserted him. His run of luck had turned.

A council of the people was held to discuss the *cause célèbre*, and many an angry speech was made. Some of the chiefs went so far as to threaten Titokowaru with death. At length a chieftainess of considerable influence rose and quelled the storm of violent words. She appealed to the aggrieved husband's people not to attempt Titoko's life; but urged that the garrison should leave the *pa*—it would be disastrous to make a stand there after their *tohunga*, their spiritual head and their war-leader, had lost his *mana-tapu*. This met with general approval, and on the night of the attack the people packed their few belongings on their backs and struck quietly into the forest for the Waitotara. Titokowaru, with forty warriors, covered the retreat. "Afterwards," says Bent, "when we had taken safe shelter in the Upper Waitara, Titokowaru regained his *tapu* by means of incantations and ceremonies performed by another *tohunga*. But by that time the war was over."

So to the forest fled Titokowaru and all his people, and hard on their trail, when the *pa* was found deserted, came the A.C. scouts and Kepa's Maoris, in lightest marching order for the chase.

The Government troops overtook the Hauhau rear-guard at Te Karaka flat, on the descent to the Waitotara River. At Te Karaka Major Kepa, the fighting chief of the Whanganuis, was leading the advance-guard of the pursuing force, when he was hotly attacked by the Hauhaus who had planted an ambush in the bush. Kepa was closely pressed. Captain T. Porter, who commanded No. 8 Division of Armed Constabulary—consisting of Arawa and Ngapuhi Maoris, with a few good European bushmen—was close up when Kepa was fired on, and he promptly extended the supports across the flat. Kepa, after a sharp hand-to-hand fight with the enemy, burst through them and fell back on Captain Porter. The *Kupapas* and their white comrades fought the Hauhaus till dark, and had to leave them dead and wounded on the field. Next morning they found the mutilated bodies minus hearts and livers, which the cannibal enemy had cut out and taken away. The Hauhaus had also beheaded one of the slain, a Whanganui soldier named Hori Raukawa.

The grief of the friendly Maoris at this mutilation of their dead was intense, and was given vent to in weeping and furious threats. Kepa was in a terrible rage, and determined on retaliation in kind.

This feeling was intensified a few days later, when a strong force of Hauhaus ambuscaded and slaughtered seven out of a party of ten white Constabulary men at the Papatupu peach-grove on the banks of the Waitotara River. The Constabulary detachment was in charge of Sergeant Menzies of No. 2 Division. The men, who belonged to Colonel McDonnell's force at Te Karaka, had obtained leave to forage for peaches in a grove at Papatupu, on the opposite (north) bank of the

Waitotara, and crossed the river in a canoe. They were gathering the fruit when a volley was suddenly poured into them by a large body of Hauhaus, who were lying close by waiting for *pakeha* game. They at once seized their arms and rushed for their canoe, pursued by two or three score of Maoris, led by Big Kereopa. The rest of the story was told the author lately by Tutangé Waionui, of Patea, he who had distinguished himself in the repulse of the white troops at Te Ngutu-o-te-Manu the previous year. This is Tutangé's account:

"I was one of the Hauhaus who ambushed the Constabulary men, under Sergeant Menzies, at the peach-grove at Papatupu. Some of them had got into their canoe, and would have escaped, but the others held on to it in an attempt to board it, and so we caught and killed seven of them. The sergeant was a big, tall man, and stout. I killed him. He was stooping down at the time. I slew him with no other weapon than a canoe paddle of *manuka* wood. I snatched up a paddle from the canoe and struck him a slanting blow on the side of the temple with it, the fatal blow called *tipi*, as delivered in sideways fashion with the edge of a stone *mere*. The white sergeant fell, and a Maori named Toawairere slashed off one of his legs with a tomahawk. This was done for the sake of getting the boot on the *pakeha's* foot for one of our men, a one-legged fellow named Paramena, who wanted the boot. The leg was taken away into the bush."

Next day Colonel Whitmore sent the *Kupapas*—the Maoris of No. 8 Division under Captain Porter and the Whanganui under Kepa—across the river in pursuit of the enemy, and Colonel McDonnell's division of Constabulary followed them in support. Porter and his men, during the skirmish which followed, came across the fire in which Sergeant Menzies' leg had been roasted. The remains of the bone of the leg were there, and it was evident that Big Kereopa[12] and his fellow-savages had once more feasted on the flesh of the *pakeha*.

It was now that Colonel Whitmore agreed to a request made by Kepa and offered rewards for Hauhau heads. He said he would give £5 a head for ordinary men and £10 for chiefs killed. This gave a fillip to the bush-whacking chase, into which the Government Maoris entered with ferocious zest.

––––––––––

[12]   Kereopa, in the days before the war, had been a pupil at the Kai-iwi mission school.

CHAPTER XXII

THE FOREST FORAGERS

Fugitive Hauhaus—Hard times in the bush—The eaters of *mamaku*—
Bent's adventure—Lost in the woods—Rupé to the rescue—The
tapu'd eels.

"AFTER we deserted Tauranga-ika," says my old *pakeha*-Maori, "we led a miserably rough life in the bush. We were as near starvation sometimes as we could well be. Kepa's *Kupapas* and the white scouts were hunting for us, stalking us like wild beasts, and we were hiding in the forest and living on what we could pick up. We scattered in parties. I and some of the Hauhaus selected a safe spot in the deep bush, built *wharés* to shelter ourselves, and then went out to the edge of the forest digging up fern-root for food. We scoured the bush for the *mamaku* fern-tree,[13] and cut out the white pith of the tree; it was one of our principal foods at that time. It has a peculiar effect on any one who eats much of it—it makes him strangely drowsy and sleepy. Sometimes, too, we had to eat *whara-whara* and similar mosses, and the mushroom-like *haroré* that grew on the *tawa*-trees, and *hakeke*, or wood-fungus. We became very weak and feeble for want of food. We did not dare to light a fire in the daytime, for fear the smoke rising above the forest trees would betray us. At night we would kindle a small fire, just enough to keep the pipes going as we sat round and smoked and talked in low voices."

Titokowaru's warriors, too, ran short of ammunition. For his cartridges, Bent sometimes had to use small pieces of hard wood cut to the proper size instead of lead bullets. The natives were also often short of percussion-caps; they used to save the exploded ones, and cut off match-heads and insert them. A box of caps was a great prize to a Hauhau in those days. This ingenious use of match-heads was a common practice in the later days of the war, and many a box of *pakeha* matches found its way through supposedly "friendly" Maori hands into the rebel camps.

For three or four weeks the Hauhaus concealed themselves in the forests between the Waitotara and the Patea Rivers, their warriors making occasional sorties and laying ambuscades for straggling whites.

[13]   The Taranaki Maoris used to cultivate the mamaku fern-tree for the sake of the edible pith. The natives point out one of the olden mamaku grounds just to the north of Keteonetea (near the present township of Normanby), where the old Whakaahurangi track went in towards Mount Egmont. Here there were two or three miles of mamaku forest. The Maoris used to cut off the upper parts of the trees and plant them in the ground, thus making two mamaku grow where only one grew before. The old tree so decapitated always sent out a new head.

Not only was Bent in daily and nightly danger of death at the hands of his enemies, the Government men, during this period of hiding and starving in the bush, but in one of his adventures he narrowly escaped the tomahawks of his own companions, the Hauhaus.

Bent and a party of about twenty Maoris set out one day from their camp at Oteka, away inland of the Weraroa, on a food-hunting expedition into the great trackless forests in the rear of their hiding-place. They travelled half a day's journey into the rugged bush-country, a lone region where no booted foot had ever trod. They fished for eels in the creeks, and climbed for wild honey wherever they saw the bees buzzing round their hives in the hollow trees. They carried with them *taha* (calabashes made from the *hué,* or vegetable gourd); these they filled with the honey. When they had collected as much as they could carry, they started on their return tramp to the *kainga.* Bent's *pikau,* or back-load, consisted of about thirty pounds weight of honey in *taha* and two large eels, all in a flax basket.

When the party left their camping-place the white man went on ahead, and was soon out of sight of his companions. After a while he found that he had missed the route by which he had come the previous day.

He pushed on and on, hoping every moment to catch sight of a broken branch or a footprint or a tomahawk blaze on a tree that would indicate the trail. He wandered about, up and down hill, crossing creeks, and tearing what little clothes he wore in the tangled bush, until he had not the least idea where he was.

He was lost in the forest.

Night came on while the lonely white man was still toiling bewildered through the dense woods. He spent the hours of darkness crouched up under a tree, sleeping little, and shivering with the cold, for he was thinly clothed and had no blanket, and no matches or flint and steel with which to light a fire for warmth and cooking.

Early next morning Bent climbed a tall *rata*-tree near his bivouac and scanned the wild country round. Nothing but forest, forest everywhere—vast waves of deep verdure sweeping away and away as far as the eye could see. No sign of human life—no guiding landmark. Somewhere beneath that impenetrable pall of green that clothed everything were his people. But where?

Ah! What is that blue, thin coil rising slowly out of the forest far ahead, westward?

A curl of smoke! A Hauhau camp; perhaps some hunting-party cooking their morning meal.

The white man joyfully descended from his tree-perch, and quickly getting into his *pikau* straps again, set out at as fast a pace as his load would allow him, steering in the direction of the smoke.

He toiled on and on, breaking through jungles of undergrowth and clinging vines, over logs and through watercourses, until suddenly he found himself at the foot of a rocky wall which rose perpendicularly above him for about thirty feet.

He endeavoured to clamber up the precipice, assisting himself by the forest roots and creepers which hung in trailing coils down its face, but they gave way under his weight when he had ascended but a few feet, and he found himself at the base of the cliff again, debating whether to try the climb again, or make a long detour, and perhaps lose the run of the point for which he was heading.

Suddenly, high above him, a voice cried, "Who's there?"

The startled white man, peering through the tangle of foliage and creepers, saw a man standing on the cliff-top—a Maori girt with a flax mat, a gun in his hand. It was Rupé, his chief and owner.

The Maori was gazing intently down the cliff. With him was a woman, the old chief's daughter Rihi, who was Bent's wife. He had heard the noise made by Bent in his attempt to scale the cliff, and he noticed the shaking of the bush-vines and leaves that screened the lower part of the wall, but the white man was so far hidden from his vision, Bent called to him: "Don't fire, Rupé! It is I, your *pakeha*—Tu-nui-a-moa!"

"*E tama!*" cried the old chief. "I am glad indeed! I came out searching for you, for your life is in great danger."

The *pakeha*, changing his position so that Rupé could see him, explained his predicament.

"Remain where you are," said Rupé, "and I will lower a rope to you."

In a few minutes a line, made of split leaves of the *harakeke* flax, knotted together, and strengthened with *aka*, or bush-vines, was thrown down the cliff to Bent. The upper end of the hastily made bush rope the old man had made fast to a tree on the cliff-top.

"Send your *pikau* up first, and you can follow," ordered Rupé.

Bent tied his flax basket of eels and honey to the line. Rupé hauled it up, lowered the line again, and Bent tied it round his body below the arms. Then the chief and his stalwart daughter hauled the light-weight *pakeha* safely to the summit of the wall.

Rihi and her father both wept as they took Bent's hands, so great was their relief at finding their *pakeha* safe and sound. Rupé told the white man that he had feared he was dead.

"Why?" asked Bent.

"Why? There are a score of armed Hauhaus searching the forest for you, and had they found you before I did they would have killed you."

The old chief explained, further, that when Bent did not return to the bush-village the previous night, his fellow-eelers had come to the conclusion that he had given them the slip on the journey home, and had made off to the white men's camp. So at daylight a party set out to scour the forest round the *kainga*, fully intending, if they found the deserter in hiding, to summarily execute him. Old Rupé, too, had taken to the forest with his daughter—before daylight—but for a different reason: he did not believe his *pakeha* would desert him, and as he concluded Bent had lost himself in the bush, he had kindled a fire on the most prominent hillside in the forest, in the hope that the wanderer would see it and make his way towards it. His bush-craft was successful, and no doubt it saved Bent's life, for had he gone wandering on he would most probably have run into the arms of his hunters.

So the three of them—the *rangatira* and his "tame white man" and the Maori girl—travelled homeward as quickly and as quietly as they could, seldom speaking to one another for fear some prowling Hauhau should hear them. "Even now, if they find you out in the forest," said Rupé, "I may not be able to save you. Be cautious, for this may be your last day!"

Late in the afternoon the camp of the fugitive rebels was reached, and Bent was safe.

Titokowaru, just back from a scouting expedition to the forest-edge, was in the village. The grim war-chief was genuinely pleased to see the white man back again, and safe.

"*E tu!*" said he; "it was fortunate indeed that Rupé met you in the forest. Had any of the others found you—my young men of the *Tekau-ma-rua*—then you had been a dead man!"

Now came an illustration of that many-sided law, the *tapu*. Titokowaru took the two eels which Bent had carried home on his back and hung them up as an offering to the *atua*, the heathen gods. They were under the ban because they had been borne on the white man's back, which was temporarily *tapu*; therefore they could not be eaten.

The honey, however, was not wasted. Titokowaru, having no doubt a sweet tooth, sagely decided that it would be sufficient to hang up the eels for the gods; he *whakanoa*'d the honey, that is, he repeated *karakia*, or incantations, over it, by which the maleficent powers of the *tapu* were nullified or averted and the food made fit for consumption.

CHAPTER XXIII

A BATTLE IN THE FOG

The surprise of Otautu—An early morning attack—Kimble Bent's
dream—*"Kia tupato!"*—A gallant defence—Brave old Hakopa—
Flight of the Hauhaus.

A MISTY morning in the forest. A little Maori hamlet, just a collection of
thatched huts, in a small clearing enclosed on all sides by the dense woods. In the
rear a deep ravine, jungly with thick undergrowth, then the winding snag-strewn
Patea River. This was Otautu, Titokowaru's refuge-camp. It stood on a plateau—
now a richly grassed farm; scattered over the clearing were potato-gardens. There
was a frail stockade of stakes, but there were no trenches or rifle pits; it was an
ordinary residential *kainga*; the fugitive Hauhaus trusted to the tangled forest as
their best defence.

Grey dawn. The raw morning fog hung low on the sleeping village—a mist
so thick that it shrouded from the view objects even a few yards distant. It lay like
the winding bank of smoky mist that marks the course of a forest stream early
on a summer morning; the black tree-tops stood out clear above the white pall of
damp, cold vapour.

Not a sound from the slumbering *kainga*, where some three or four hundred
Hauhaus—Kimble Bent amongst them—lay packed in their *nikau*-roofed huts.

At the edge of the clearing a solitary Maori sentry, a man armed with a revolver, sat, keeping a semi-somnolent guard.

Suddenly, out of the dark forest, appeared a body of armed men. They came
in Indian file; they broke into a stealthy run as they left the shadow of the trees;
their bodies were bent eagerly forward; they carried their rifles at the trail; they
uttered not a sound.

They were the Maori advance-guard of Colonel Whitmore's expeditionary
force of four hundred A.C.'s and *Kupapas*. After weeks of bush-scouting a Government column had at last happened on the Hauhau hiding-place.

The Maori sentinel—he was a man of the Puketapu tribe named Te Wareo—
was all in an instant wide-awake. The moment he jumped up he was fired on by
the advance-guard. Leaping into cover he raced for the village, firing his revolver
as he ran.

The discharge of the rifles rolled crashing through the forest. Startled *kaka* parrots flew from their tree-perches, screaming discordantly at their rude awakening. The clear notes of a bugle rang out —it was the "Advance" and "Double!" The active little colonel rushed his men up at top speed, extended them, and advanced on the hidden camp, and a strange combat began.

At the first crack of the firearms the *kainga* was awake; and what a scurry there was! The Maoris poured out of their *wharés* just as they leaped from their sleeping-mats—some wearing only a shawl or ragged mat; others entirely naked. Some of the women rushed out of their huts without a shred of clothing on, screaming and shouting, and running for their lives. The men snatched up their guns and tomahawks, and their cartouche-belts; and quickly took post to defend their position, and give time for their women and children to retreat in safety.

According to Kimble Bent the attack was not entirely unexpected. At any rate, it had been foreshadowed in Maori fashion by one of the Hauhau "medicine-men."

"The day before this attack," says Bent, "I had a strange dream, which Titokowaru's priest and reader of dreams interpreted as an omen of misfortune. I dreamt that I saw a strange Maori village in which each house was cut in two length-ways, leaving only half the dwelling standing, in the shape of a shed or lean-to, such as we called *tiheré*. I described this vision to the Hauhau seer. He gathered the people in the meeting-house that night, and after speaking of the dream I had had, he cried in a loud voice to them these words of caution and warning:

"*Kia tupato! He po kino te po; he ra kino te ra!*" ("Be on your guard! This is a night of evil and danger, and the morrow also will be a day of evil!")

"The prophet then said to me: 'Be ready for flight in the morning! Get your belongings ready packed in your kit, and, if you hear a suspicious sound, fly from the *pa* at once.'

"So, when the first shots were heard in the early morning, I was ready to make a bolt for it. The moment the alarm was given I jumped up from my sleeping-place in one of the huts, grabbed my kit, and bare-footed and with nothing on but my shirt and an old piece of a tent-fly girt round my middle, I ran to the bank at our rear, and jumped down the cliff. I went tumbling and scrambling down to the river, and then travelled up along the banks for a considerable distance as fast as I could go. All I had saved from Otautu was what I had in my kit—some papers, a little money, needles and thread, and so forth. As I ran up along the river banks I fell in with some of our people. We went on until we found a canoe tied up on the bank, and we crossed the Patea in her, ferrying four across at a time until all were safely over. Those who were with me were non-combatants, like myself, mostly women."

While the unarmed people of the camp were making good their escape, the Otautu clearing was the scene of severe fighting. The Hauhau warriors took post just at the edge of the little plateau where the thickly timbered ground suddenly fell away to the ravine at the rear. Sheltered by the fall of the ground, they swept the clearing with their rifles and smooth-bores. Some of them climbed into the branches of the *rata*-trees and delivered their fire; some extended in bush-skirmishing order on either flank; and both sides—*pakeha* and Maori—peppered away briskly at each other for half an hour or more.

It was a singular skirmish, for the dense fog still shrouded the hill-top; and the Government men, who were being punished severely by the Hauhau fire, could for a long time see nothing of their enemies. Many A.C.'s dropped, some shot dead.

The Government Maoris, the *Kupapas*, under the celebrated Kepa, advancing from tree to tree round the edge of the clearing, came to close quarters with the Hauhaus. One of Titokowaru's veteran warriors performed a deed here which is still told and retold with loving admiration by the old Taranaki Hauhaus.

He was the old man Hakopa (Jacob) te Matauawa, the Maori who had taken a friendly interest in Kimble Bent at Te Ngutu-o-te-Manu, and saved the white man from the two savages who stalked him there, as narrated in a previous chapter. Hakopa was a tall, athletic man, of spare frame, and well tattooed. He was about seventy years of age, a true type of the olden Maori *toa*—the hero of the war-trail, the brave. He was a curious figure, in his military cap, tunic, and trousers—stripped from a dead Constabulary man after the fight at Papa-tihakehake.

Hakopa dodged from tree to tree out on the flanks of the clearing, making good use of a recently captured carbine. In the uncertain light it was difficult for the Government men to tell friend from foe, and Hakopa's *pakeha* uniform seems to have completely deceived some of the *Kupapas*. As he leaped from tree to tree and stump to stump, he shouted *"Raunatia! Raunatia!"* ("Surround it!") to induce the belief that he was one of the Government force.

At last all Hakopa's cartridges but two were gone. A prudent warrior would have retired at this stage—but not Hakopa. He did not like the idea of retreat while he had a shot in his locker, and he determined to bag something in the way of a *Kupapa* or a *pakeha* with his last charges. He waited until the leading men of Kepa's party were within close "potting" distance, and, as one of them unsuspectingly approached him, he quickly threw up his gun and put a bullet into his enemy, then turned and bounded into cover, and rejoined his comrades in the defile, unhurt, hugely delighted with his exploit.

"You young men waste your cartridges," he said reprovingly, after the fight, to some of the youthful braves of Ngati-Ruanui. "Look at me! I know the worth of good powder and lead too well to fire them away for nothing. For every cartridge I used I hit a man!"

It was a determined, plucky stand, that defence of the Otautu clearing by Titokowaru's warriors. Every minute they held out, they knew, was giving their women and children and old people a better chance of safety.

At last the fog lifted, swept away from the clearing by the morning breeze, and the sun shone out.

Now for the first time the Government soldiers saw the village. The bugle sounded the "Advance" again, and at the double the A.C.'s swarmed into the empty *kainga*, to find, to their astonishment, that it was neither rifle-pitted nor parapeted.

The Hauhaus, their resistance broken, took to the forest, racing down the steep gully in rear of the village and up along the banks of the Patea. Kepa's Maoris went in hot pursuit, and shot two or three of the fugitives. The main body crossed the Patea safely, and rejoined their womenfolk and children, camping, hungry, weary, and with limbs and body torn and bruised in their flight, in a well-hidden nook deep in the forest on the north bank of the river.

CHAPTER XXIV

THE HEAD-HUNTERS

The skirmish at Whakamara—Hauhaus on the run—Government
head-hunters—Major Kemp's white scout—Sharp work in the
bush—Barbarism of the Whanganui—*Kupapas*—Smoke-drying the heads—A present for Whitmore—The heads on the tent
floor—End of the war.

THE deep and roadless forest was now the scene of sharp, barbaric war. The
Hauhaus, after the abandonment of Tauranga-ika, built no stockades, but trusted to their most ancient of refuges, the *nehenehe-nui*, the great woody wilderness.
From one hiding-place to another they fled, with the Government bush-fighters
on their heels.

"After our surprise and defeat at Otautu," to continue Kimble Bent's narrative,
"we were safe neither night nor day. Even when far in the depths of the bush we
were always on the look-out for danger, for we never knew when we might have
a sudden volley poured into our midst. Kepa and his friendlies were continually
scouring the country for us. We retreated north and west through the forest till we
reached a settlement called Whakamara. Two nights we were on the track; all we
had to eat was a couple of potatoes each. At Whakamara we found many pigs, and
were able to fill our stomachs once more.

"But early one morning the soldiers were on us again. Two of our men, young
Tutangé and the warrior Kātené Tu-Whakaruru, who were out scouting on horse-
back, discovered the troops lying in ambush just outside, waiting to attack the village. They turned and galloped back to us, Tutangé waving his sword and whack-
ing his horse along with the flat of the blade.

"So off we went again, running for our lives, with Whitmore's troops close behind us, firing as they ran. Titokowaru and all his men fled, after a very short fight.
We took to the bush just like wild pigs racing before the hunters. I and a few others
kept together, running for all we were worth, half-naked, foodless, tumbling over
logs, scrambling in and out of creeks, and made no halt until we found ourselves
once more at Rimatoto, my old home of 1866."

From Whakamara village the Maoris fell back on a little fortified *pa* in the rear
of the camp. This position they abandoned after a brief skirmish, and then the forest chase began. Whitmore ordered an immediate pursuit, and a flying column of
sixty white Armed Constabulary, under Captains Northcroft and Watt, and about

one hundred and forty Maori *Kupapas*, under Major Kepa and Captain Thomas Porter, all in light marching order, took to the bush after the retreating enemy.

A CONSTABULARY OFFICER IN BUSH-FIGHTING COSTUME.

(From a photo of Colonel T. Porter's taken in 1869.)

The advance-guard of the pursuing force numbered twenty-five Maoris, about equally divided between the Whanganui and Arawa tribes. Captain Porter was the only European officer with them, but one or two white scouts and bushmen accompanied the Maoris. As the column's march was necessarily in single file through thick and tangled bush, it was difficult to bring a large number of men into action when any skirmish or ambuscade occurred, and the consequence was that practically all the fighting was done by the advance-guard.

It was a picturesquely savage chapter of the war, that chase of Titokowaru and his scattered Hauhaus. There was more than a touch of the barbaric in it, for some of the Government forces reverted to the primitive war-methods of the Maori himself.

Between the moccasined hero of the war-trail in Fenimore Cooper's and Captain Mayne Reid's romances of Red Indian days, and Kepa's Maori guerilla and some of his white comrades, there was, after all, only this difference: one took the trail hunting for scalps, the other for heads!

As mentioned in a previous chapter, Colonel Whitmore had agreed to a request made by Major Kepa after the fighting on the Waitotara, and had offered rewards of £10 a head for Hauhau chiefs killed and £5 for ordinary men. Kepa's *Kupapa*, Maoris, recruited from the Whanganui, Ngati-Apa, Ngati-Raukawa, and other "friendly" tribes—only friendly to the *pakeha* by reason of their deadly animosity to the Taranaki tribes—were little less savage than the Hauhaus themselves, and this manhunt under the *mana* of the Government was just the work that delighted them. They were "stripped to a gantlin'" for the bush chase—simply a waist-mat or shawl and cartridge-belts and a pouch for their percussion-caps. And some of the white bushmen-scouts were just as eager on the head-hunting trail, and added to their service arms a tomahawk.

With the Whanganui men marched a European scout and bushman about whom some remarkable stories are told. This was Tom Adamson, Kepa's *pakeha*-Maori, a big, powerful fellow who surpassed the Maoris themselves in bushcraft and endurance. He marched bare-footed, like his Maori comrades. Another of the white scouts and Hauhau-hunters was a man who, in after years, became celebrated for his pioneer exploration work in the vast wilderness of Milford Sound, an old John-o'-Groat's sailor and soldier named Donald Sutherland, whose name has been given to the immense waterfall that is one of New Zealand's natural wonders.

It was a wild, picturesquely unkempt column, that little armed force of *pakehas* and Maoris, as it filed off under its active and daring young officers into the gloomy, danger-haunted woods, the unknown and trackless forest through which the Patea and its tributaries flowed. The bush-fighting costume of many of the whites as well as Maoris was simple, not to say brigand-like. Officers and men of the Constabulary and other corps who had to do much bush-marching discarded the trousers of civilisation and took to the "garb of old Gaul," worn alike by the Scottish Highlander and the Maori; this kilt was usually a coloured shawl, strapped round the waist and falling to the knee.

Through the huge and tangled woods they scrambled—hunters and hunted. Now along some narrow trail, hardly discernible to the untrained eye; now crawling through networks of supplejacks and brambly shrubs and great snaky lianes that looped tree to tree in bewildering coiled intricacies. Down into steep and narrow watercourses, swinging down one after another by the hanging vines and tough tree-creepers; up rocky gorges and jungle-clad cliffs. For endless miles upon miles the great solemn woods covered the face of the rugged land; beneath the shadows of the thick, dark foliage loped the blood-avengers.

In the afternoon of the first day of the chase the column descended into a deep, thickly wooded gorge. Suddenly from both sides a fire was opened upon the centre of the force, the main body of the A.C.'s. "Clear the bush!" was the order. The advance-guard and A.C.'s quickly circled round and enfiladed the enemy, who bolted like Red Indians through the thickets; and the chase went on.

Three Hauhaus were shot and decapitated on the first day of the chase. Every man killed, in fact, on this and the succeeding days of the pursuit had his head cut off.

The first Maori decapitated was a young chief, who was shot while in the act of climbing a steep cliff in the bush. Being a *rangatira*, his was a £10 head. This man was a prominent Hauhau named Matangi-o-Rupé. He belonged to Titokowaru's own immediate clan, or *hapu*, Ngati-Manu-hiakai—"The Tribe of the Hungry Bird." It was a Ngati-Raukawa soldier in Kepa's contingent who took off the Hauhau's head with his tomahawk; later he duly delivered it at the *pakeha* camp. Matangi's son, Kuku—now living at the village of Taiporohenui—on learning of his father's fate, swore to have *utu*—revenge—and vowed to Bent that if he ever encountered the man who beheaded his parent, he would "slice him to pieces like a piece of beef."

Some years after the war, Bent, while on a visit to a Maori settlement at Oroua, in the Manawatu district, met this Ngati-Raukawa head-hunter—"an ugly, tattooed old villain," as he describes him. The *pakeha*, by way of imparting an interesting bit of news, informed the old warrior of Kuku's threat, but the tattooed veteran only smiled. The days of the *lex talionis* were over. That *utu* account has not been squared; but only because of the inconveniently peaceful rule of the *pakeha*. Kuku has by no means forgotten or forgiven the man who sold his father's head to the white man.

Later on in the bush chase the advance-guard, hurrying along at the double, came upon a Hauhau family—a grey-haired, middle-aged man, his wife, and two or three children. They had not been able to travel so fast as their friends, on account of the tired children, and so had been left behind. The old warrior was fired on by one of the Arawa Maoris, and was severely wounded. He fell, but struggled to a squatting position, with his empty gun across his knees. The Arawa rushed at him, with tomahawk raised, to finish him off. The old Hauhau sprang up with a great effort, gripping his tomahawk. He was too badly wounded, however, to strike a blow, and the Arawa seized him and his tomahawk. Just at that moment a white man, dressed like a Maori in a waist-shawl, and bare-footed, rushed up, tomahawk in hand. He seized the Hauhau by the hair, and, with a couple of furious strokes, chopped off his head, and dropped it, all bloody as it was, into the flax kit he carried slung at his back, and in which there were already other heads.

The Arawa by no means liked being done out of what he considered was his head, seeing that he had captured the Hauhau, and there was a savage squabble between the two as to its ownership. The white man "bluffed" the Maori out of it, however, and prepared to add the heads of the rest of the family to his collection. He rushed at the weeping *wahiné* and her children, and their heads would have come off also had not Captain Porter, fortunately for them, just come up. The poor, terrified woman clung to his knees, beseeching him to save her and her children. He told them they would be safe, and ordered the white scout forward. The Arawas took charge of the widow and her children, and she was sent to Rotorua when the campaign was over.

The Whanganui *Kupapas* were fully as savage as any wild rebel. No quarter was given to any Hauhau warrior, and no Hauhau thought of asking for any mercy. Of one frightful scene Porter was an eye-witness. After killing and beheading two or three men in a little valley in the forest, the Whanganui Maoris tied flax ropes to their ankles and hung them up to the branches of the trees, eviscerated them and thrust sticks into them to keep them open, just like animals in a slaughter-yard. Then they danced round the bodies like fiends, flourishing the tattooed heads of the dead by their long hair and shouting and yelling war-songs, and making the hideous grimaces of the *pukana*. They were quite beyond control, mad with the lust of killing.

Porter at last managed to put a stop to this mutilation, but he was powerless to prevent the head-taking, except so far as his own men were concerned. He did not allow any Arawas to decapitate an enemy, much as some of the warriors from the Hot Lakes Country would have liked to. He asked the Whanganui natives to bury the heads, and, if necessary, take only the ears with them if they wished to claim Whitmore's reward. But the warriors answered, "No, Witimoa said 'heads,' and if he doesn't get the heads he may not pay us."

The pursuit of the Hauhaus continued for several days, until Titokowaru's warriors finally scattered in the dense forest, and the pursuers had exhausted their food. It was then determined to make for the coast again, but owing to the density of the bush the Government men lost their bearings. They were far in the tangled, jungly forest, without a guide, for they had killed their prisoners. The column accordingly divided, each division marching independently for the open country, food, and tented camps.

The night before the divisions of the pursuing column separated, Major Kepa ordered one of his *tohungas*, a wild-looking, tattooed old warrior, learned in all the savage arts of Maoridom, to *whakapakoko nga upoko*, that is, to dry or preserve the heads of the slain Hauhaus. Porter and the other Europeans in the Maori contingents now for the first time witnessed the ancient process of smoke-drying human heads. The heads had up to this time been carried in flax kits on men's shoulders through the bush, and it was necessary, if they were to be taken out to the camp, that they should be preserved from decay.

The old medicine-man went into the bush and returned with armfuls of branches of the *mahoé*-tree, and made a fire, which he kept burning until all the wood was reduced to glowing embers. The earth was heaped up around this fire, and the head, neck downwards, was placed over it, and all openings at the sides were closed, so that the fumes from the charcoal oven would pass up into the head. The brains had previously been removed and the eyes stuffed up. As the smoking went on, the old man smoothed down the skin of the face with his hands to prevent it wrinkling and wiped off the moisture, until the head was thoroughly smoke-dried and quite mummified. For several hours the head-smoking went on, and in the morning the trophies of the chase were packed for the final march.

Half-starved, ragged and weary, the Constabulary and their Maori allies at last reached the open country; from the top of the range of wooded hills they had seen the white tents of Colonel Whitmore's headquarters at Taiporohenui. That evening they were in camp, and there they enjoyed the first square meal they had had for days. Kepa and Porter and their contingents had been nine days in the bush.

Captain Porter went to Colonel Whitmore's quarters as soon as he arrived, and reported the result of his expedition. While he was giving the commanding officer an account of the forest chase, the Whanganui men who had taken the Hauhau heads came up in a body and opened the tent door, and poured in head after head upon the ground, exclaiming as they did so, "*Na, Witimoa, to upoko!*" ("There, Whitmore, your heads!")

The little colonel was thunderstruck. He stared with consternation in his eyes on the ghastly heads, most of them tattooed, with grinning teeth and long blood-stained hair, strewn about the floor where they had rolled. There were eleven of them, some at the colonel's feet, some beneath the table; some had rolled under the camp bedstead.

He had forgotten all about his promise of a reward for heads. Anyhow, he now told the Maoris, he did not mean that the heads should actually be brought in to him in camp, but that a reward would be paid for each Hauhau killed in the pursuit. But he kept his word to Kepa, and each head was paid for.

The white scouts, too, brought in their kits of heads, and received their blood-money. These and certain other Taranaki heads brought in were not personally delivered, but were all paid for, mostly in orders for clothes, boots, and other necessaries.

"No more heads," was the colonel's order. He realised that this barbarous fashion of squaring affairs with the enemy would arouse a howl of condemnation from those who did not understand the sharp and savage necessities of frontier-fighting.

These facts may not please the mild or gentle variety of reader. The idea of a New Zealand Government force decapitating its enemies and smoke-drying those heads for purposes of reward is too, too savage for the refined humanitarian to contemplate without a shudder. Nevertheless, these are facts. Many an ugly incident happened in the bush-fighting of those days. It was no kid-glove warfare. In this case the Government Maoris were inflamed by anger and revenge, and indeed some of them were little better than the cannibals they were chasing. And they were wild with a desire to *ngaki mate*, that is, to seek vengeance, payment, for their dead—blood for blood.

But while it was barbarous, it was thoroughly in accord with the spirit of gue-rilla warfare that was forced upon the troops, and it served its purpose, for it struck terror into the hearts of Titokowaru's warriors, and they never fought again.

The Hauhau war-chief's *mana-tapu* was gone, and there was nothing for it but to fly to the depths of the wilderness. He and his men gathered in a few days at Rimatoto, but made a very short stay there. They marched through the forest to the island-fastness in the Ngaere swamp, where they were very nearly caught by Whitmore and his Constabulary, who made a rough *tête-de-pont* over the quak-ing morass with hurdles of supplejack and bush-vines. Then they made off for the Ngatimaru Country, on the upper waters of the Waitara, thirty or forty miles away, over terribly rough country and through an almost trackless forest.

"A party of forty or fifty of us," says Bent, "remained in our little settlement at Rimatoto, always on the alert against surprise by the troops, until the anxiety of our position became too much for us. We packed up our belongings, and swagged them inland to Rukumoana, on the Patea River. In this lonely spot, far in the bush, we camped, and made a little clearing in order to plant food. When we had felled the bush with our axes, twenty men travelled across to the Upper Waitara to pro-cure seed potatoes from their friends, and we planted our crops and waited."

In this remote valley of refuge, far in the forest, the white runaway and his Hauhau companions—he was still with his chief Rupé—remained for many weeks, living the loneliest life conceivable, hearing nothing of the outside world, and existing precariously on the foods of the forest.

Titokowaru was safe in his bush retreat in the Ngatimaru Country, his last battle fought, his once godlike *mana* in the dust.

CHAPTER XXV

THE LAND OF REFUGE

The flight from Rukumoana—Retreat to the Waitara—The Kawau
pa—Life in the Ngatimaru Country—Rupé and his white man—a
Maori Donnybrook fair—a tale of a *Taniwha*.

ONE day two Hauhaus, exhausted and half-starved, entered the little bush-
camp at Rukumoana. One of them was Bent's old *rangatira*, Tito te Hanataua. They
had passed through many perils and hairbreadth escapes, and they warned the
white man and his Maori comrades that Kepa te Rangihiwinui and his Whanganui
Maori scouts were still hunting for them, and would have their heads to a certainty
should they happen on the trail to the refuge place.

The old feeling of terror came over Bent and his companions at the mention of
Kepa's name. That night Hauhau piquets kept watch on the edge of the clearing,
and more than once they imagined they heard stealthy footfalls, the breaking of
branches, and the whispers of enemies in the woods. These dangers, however,
were things of the imagination. Nevertheless, it was an anxious night in the lonely
kainga, and when morning came the people decided to abandon their camp and
bury themselves still deeper in the wilderness.

In a very short time the men and women of the settlement were on the march,
laden with their flax *pikaus*, containing such belongings as they thought worth re-
moving. They took to the forest in a due northerly direction; bound for that Alsatia
of rebels and Hauhaus, the remote and rugged Ngati-Maru Country, up on the
head-waters of the Waitara—Titokowaru's hiding-place.

The utmost caution was observed on the march. No fires were lighted. So that
there should be no clue to the direction of the flight, care was taken to leave no broken branches or other bushmen's signs; not a leaf was turned or a twig displaced
if the refugees could help it until they were well into the ranges. Wherever possible they took to the creek-beds and walked in the running water, so that no trail
should betray them. They could have spared themselves that anxiety and trouble,
however, for the Government troops had at last abandoned the chase.

Two days Bent and his friends spent on that terrible trail—the roughest, wildest part of the Taranaki hinterland. Fording rivers, pushing through matted jungles, climbing wooded precipices, lowering their swags down perpendicular cliffs,
and swinging themselves down by forest vines and creepers—they emerged at
last, a weary little band, on the banks of the Waitara, about thirty miles from the

mouth of that river. All around towered the densely forested blue ranges; the high banks of the winding Waitara fell precipitously to its rapid-whitened waters.

On the cliff-top where they left the forest there was a little Maori camp. Here the fugitives were ordered to the main Hauhau camp, the Kawau *pa*, where Tito-kowaru and his followers had established themselves, weary of war, but neverthe-less resolute to die "fighting like the shark," as the Maori has it, if attacked in their last hiding-place.

The Kawau *pa* stood in an admirable position for defence, in a great bend of the Waitara River. The winding rapid river here swept round a long tongue of steep-banked level land, protecting it on three sides; in the rear was the dense forest. The banks of the river were from twenty to thirty feet high, and could be climbed only in a few places. On this high tongue of land, about a quarter of a mile long, there stood a large village of well-built *raupo* and *nikau* thatched houses; between the village and the forest were the cultivations of potatoes, *kumara*, and *taro*. On the opposite side of the river, in the direction of the Taramouku Range, wild horses and cattle abounded in the bush. A short distance below the village there was a large *pa-tuna*, or eel-weir, consisting of two rows of stout *manuka* stakes set closely together and sunk into the river-bed and converging in a $\mathbf{V}$, at the lower end of which *hinaki*, or eel-baskets, were set for the purpose of catching the *piharau*, or lamprey, which abounded in the Waitara, and which were a great Maori delicacy.

As Rupé and his *pakeha* Bent and their companions marched slowly into the *marae* of the war-chief's camp, their eyes on the ground, they were welcomed with the ancient ceremony of the *powhiri*. The village women and girls waved green branches and shawls as they retired before them, singing all together the famous old greeting song, *"Toia Mai te Waka!"* ("Oh, haul up the canoe!") likening the guests to a canoe-party of visitors arriving from a distant shore.

Then as the women fell back the whole force of Titoko's warriors leaped to their feet, and swinging their firearms this way and that, threw themselves with martial fury into all the thrilling action of the war-dance. The ground shook under the mighty tread of many scores of brown feet, and the forest rang with the chorus of the war-song and the reverberating volleys of many guns. And then, when the dance was ended, the *hongi* of long-severed friends, the pressing of nose to nose, and the pitiful weeping for the dead. For quite two hours the great *tangi* lasted. When it ceased one of the head-men of the river-tribes sent the new arrivals to his own camp, close by the Kawau; the village women came in procession, to the lilt of the *tuku-kai* song, bearing their baskets of food, steaming hot from the *hangi*, and the half-starved white man and his friends were soon enjoying a bountiful feast after their long-enforced existence upon the meagre rations of the bush.

Kimble Bent lived in this securely hidden place of refuge, and at Paihau vil-lage, near by, from the end of 1869 until about 1876. He was now a Maori in all his ways; he planted food-crops and harvested them, snared birds, fished for eels, cut out canoes, and paddled his canoe on the river, joined the Hauhaus in their songs and their sacred chants, and danced with them in their *hakas*; he wore as little clothing as any native in the camp.

Life did not go too easily with the white man during those days on the Waitara. He was still Rupé's bond-servant; and his master and owner sometimes took fits of ungovernable passion. In one of these paroxysms of anger Bent had a narrow escape.

Rupé one day ordered his white man to go down to a creek, which ran into the Waitara near the Paihau *pa*, and clear out the little dam in which the household were accustomed to steep their Indian corn, their *kaanga-pirau*. Bent was working away cleaning out the steeping-pool when his chief came up and found fault with him because he was not working hard enough. "I made him some answer which didn't please him," says Bent, "whereupon he flew into a terrible rage and rushed at me like a tiger. I stooped and caught him by the leg, and he fell into the muddy pool. Up he jumped in a foaming passion, and ran to the *pa*, got out his gun, and loaded it to shoot me. But his wife rushed at him, took the gun out of his hands, and told me to hurry down to the other village, where I would be safe. So I ran to the river-bank, loosed a small canoe, and paddled down the river to the lower *pa*, where I was kindly received and taken into my old friend Hakopa's house, and I lived and worked there for some months."

Another incident of those wild old days on the Waitara, narrated by Bent, is worth the telling, as an illustration of the whimsically variable temper of the Maori and of his truly Hibernian love of a "free fight."

The war had long been over, and some *hapus* of the tribes on the upper river talked of selling their lands to the whites. Certain of the chiefs had been down at Waitara township and in New Plymouth, and there they had been approached by the agents of the Government. In the end they sold their lands for eighteen-pence an acre. But the more conservative of the Hauhaus stoutly held out against land-selling, and against any dealings with the hated *pakeha*; and the difference of opinion led to frequent quarrels.

One day a council of the people was held on the *marae* of the Paihau village for the purpose of discussing the land-selling proposals. Long and bitter were the speeches; speaker after speaker *taki*'d up and down the *marae*, and worked himself up into a fury of excitement.

Two old chiefs, tattooed veterans of the war, their long hair adorned with feathers, weapons of wood and stone in their hands, angrily assailed each other. One was Rupé, the other was Horopapera Matangi. One advocated the sale of surplus lands, the other vigorously opposed it, and insisted on the principle of "Maori land for Maori men." Then there arose a dispute about the ownership of a *tangiwai* (greenstone pendant). From argument they came to hurling abusive threats at each other.

At last Rupé furiously hurled his weapon—a sharp wooden spear—at Horopapera, who dodged it, and cleverly caught it near the butt end as it whistled past him. He instantly smartly returned it to its owner, spearing him through the leg.

Next two women went at it. Women of rank these, who considered themselves entitled to equal debating voice with the men-folk. Their powers of rhetoric and invective exhausted, they fell on each other very literally "tooth and nail," biting, hair-pulling, scratching, screaming. In their struggle they tore each other's clothes off, and two nude Amazons raged round the *marae*.

One of the wild women, a young chieftainess, her long hair streaming behind her, her pendant breasts quivering, her shoulders bleeding, seized a canoe paddle and struck her antagonist a blow across the naked back with it. The other grabbed a *tokotoko*, or walking-staff, and, thrusting it between her opponent's legs, neatly up-ended her, in the "altogether," on the green *marae*.

By this time the whole tribe were into the battle, with sticks, paddles, spears, and any weapon they could lay their hands on—men and women alike. It was a real faction fight. Fortunately, the people had left their guns in their *wharés*, and were too intent upon their hand-to-hand encounter to run for their firearms.

Kimble Bent stood on one side watching the squabble. He was close to the river-bank, where the canoes were tied up. Presently, one of the Maoris ran down to the water-side with an axe, and began furiously cutting away at his antagonists' canoes. Others ran to the cooking *hangis*, and with burning sticks from the ovens set fire to some of the thatched houses in the *kainga*. Soon there was a pretty blaze, and half the village was burned down in a few minutes.

In half an hour's time the people had cooled down, and the trouble was over. Then—a Hibernian people the Maoris, surely!—they began to weep over their quarrel, and fell on each other's necks—or, rather, pressed each other's noses—to make up for the hard words and blows they had just exchanged, and set to work to rebuild the dwellings they had destroyed in their hasty anger.

Meanwhile, Titokowaru wearied for the trail again, unable to rest in this secluded wilderness of the Waitara. His *tapu* status had been restored by a Waitara priest, with the appropriate *karakias* and invocations. Gathering together a band of his warriors—the remnant of the once ever-victorious *Tekau-ma-rua*—he paraded them in the *marae* of the Kawau *pa*, and farewelling his people, took his old place at the head of the *taua* and led them off in a grand war-dance. A truly savage figure, that stern old chief, as he leaped to the van of his war-party and danced, his sacred *taiaha* in the air; his waist girt with a coloured shawl, a rich feather cape of native make fastened over the left shoulder and under the right; his grizzled head decked with white plumes. And with loud cries of "*Haere, ra! Haere ra!*" the villagers farewelled the great war-chief as he marched his armed men out of the *pa* and struck into the forest of the Taramouku, bound for the open lands of South Taranaki and his ancestral home. But it was no longer the war-trail, for Titoko and his henchmen fought no more, but betook themselves to the great camp of Te Whiti the Prophet, who preached peace, and prophesied sundry supernatural ways by which the Maori would come into his own again.

The minds of these isolated forest-dwellers were saturated with superstition, with strange beliefs that were a reflex of the vast untrimmed places of nature in which they lived. The white man, too, almost came to believe in the tales of saurian-like *taniwhas* and water-demons, in the *patupaiarehe* and *maero*, the forest-fairies and forest-giants, in the occult malevolence of the *tapu* and *makutu* spells.

A story related by Bent is illustrative of the Maori belief, up to quite modern days, in malignant beings which made their homes in lonely waters and in caves—the dreaded *taniwha*.

The tale of the "Taniwha" of the Kopua:

One day—this was in the early "seventies"—an old man named Te Maire left the Kawau landing in his canoe, and paddled down the Waitara to a place called Te Kopua, the site of an ancient village. The object of his expedition was to procure dry resinous strips of the *rimu*-pine for the purpose of making torches to be used in catching *piharau* (lampreys) in the river at night. After getting the wood he required he started on the return paddle to his home. On the way to the Kawau he disappeared, and was never seen again alive; no doubt he overbalanced and fell into the river while poling his canoe up one of the small rapids near the Kopua.

That afternoon five men from the Kawau, including Kimble Bent, were paddling their canoe down the river to a settlement a few miles distant, when they caught sight of the old man's empty canoe drifting down with the swift current. As they approached it it sped away rapidly before them, and at last stranded on a shingle-bank in a bend of the river. In it they found Te Maire's gun and a young pig, which the vanished man had evidently caught in the bush while on his torch-making expedition.

Bent's Maori companions immediately explained in their own way the mystery of their tribesman's disappearance.

"There is a *taniwha* there," they said, "a fearful water-monster that dwells in a deep, still pool under Te Kopua's banks. He has stretched forth his long claws and dragged the old fellow down to his den."

The Maori canoeists made haste to quit the dead man's craft, and plied their paddles with unusual energy until they reached their destination on the shore below. They told their story, and that evening a meeting of the village people was held in the *wharepuni* to discuss the mystery.

For hours the wiseacres of the bush-hamlet solemnly debated the circumstances, and each canoeist in turn had to give his account of the affair and advance his theory. At last it was decided that there was no possible doubt that the *taniwha* of the river had seized Te Maire and drowned him. There must, of course, be a reason, for no *taniwha* of any repute would take such an extreme step without some good cause.

The verdict was that Te Maire had violated the *tapu* of the deserted village; he had in all probability taken some dry *rimu* from an old house that stood there, and which was sacred because a chief had died in it—goodness knows how long ago. The river-god had very properly punished him with death—it was the penalty of infringing the law of *tapu*.

The next day and for some days thereafter canoe crews hunted the river for the old man's body, but found it not. At last a woman at the lower settlement, on going down to the river one morning to get a calabash of water, spied the body of the missing man hanging in the branches of a prostrate *kahikatea*-tree on the opposite side of the river, about four feet above the water.

The question was, how did the body get there, entangled in the branches that height above the river, for there had been no flood, no noticeable rise or fall in the level of the river.

The answer was plain to the mind of the Maori. He summed it all up in two words:

"Te taniwha!"

The river-monster, after grabbing Te Maire from his canoe and detaining him a while in his watery grave, had dragged the body away down-stream and hung it up in the tree-branches opposite the village, so that the dead man's people should have no difficulty in recovering it, and in giving it decent burial.

A truly thoughtful and considerate *taniwha!*

CHAPTER XXVI

BUSH LIFE ON THE PATEA

The return to Rukumoana—The forest-village—Bird-snaring and bird-spearing—Bent the canoe-builder—His third wife.

At last—about the year 1876—the Upper Waitara was sold to the Government. The white man and his Maori people cried their farewells to Ngati-Maru and journeyed back over the ranges and through the forests to their old lands in the valley of the Patea. Bent was still Rupé's servant. The old chief and his household and some Hauhau relatives, armed, and carrying their belongings on their backs, trudged through the wilderness until they reached Rukumoana, their old-time shelter-camp on the banks of the Patea, about thirty miles from the sea. Here they halted and built their hamlet of saplings and thatch, and an old overgrown clearing was burnt off and planted with potatoes and maize. The party was but a small one. Besides Bent, there were Rupé, his wife, and their two sons; old Hakopa and his wife; and their niece, a girl named Te Hau-rutu-wai ("The Breeze that shakes the Raindrops down").

It was an even lonelier spot than the refuge-camp in the Ngati-Maru country; life here was simple and primitive in the extreme. The people tended their little plots of food-crops, shadowed by the dark forest; they snared and speared the forest birds, they hunted the wild pig, and climbed the hollow trees for wild honey. For nearly two years the *pakeha*-Maori lived with his little tribe in Rukumoana.

The ancient customs of the Maori fowler's cult were observed by these bush-dwellers, brown and white. For instance, the first *kaka* parrot or *tui* or other forest creature snared or speared in a day's birding was not eaten, but was left, as an offering to the gods of the forest, beside an old *tapu* canoe which was lying in the bush close to the river-bank. It was a hoary relic, this ancient *waka-tapu*, a carved dug-out covered with long grey moss. It was a small canoe, eight or ten feet long, and had lain there for years and years filled with water. Somewhat similar canoe-shaped troughs, filled with water, stood in various places in the forest; these were filled with water, and were generally placed in spots remote from streams or pools. Above them slip-knot snares were arranged, so that the pigeons and *tui* and other birds, flying down to quench their thirst after feeding on the *miro* or *hinau* or *tawa* berries, were caught in the nooses, and hung there, flapping and helpless, until the fowlers went round to collect the day's bag. This canoe was called a *waka-whangai*, or *wai-tuhi*.

When spearing birds with the long barbed spear of *tawa*-wood, the hunter would take great care to avoid getting any blood on his hands in withdrawing the weapon from the bird's body. Should blood stain the hands—"*kaore e mana te tao*"—the spear would lose its bird-killing powers; it would be an unlucky affair altogether, and the forest-man might as well throw it away. Such were the beliefs of the dwellers in those dim forest-places.

At the end of the first harvest season Rupé led his white man out into the forest one day, and, halting before a tall, straight *totara*-pine that grew near the steep bank of the Patea, he said:

"This is my canoe! Hew it down and carve it out! In it we will paddle down the river to Hukatéré, and you shall look upon the faces of your fellow-*pakehas* again."

So now behold Bent the canoe-builder. There above him towered the tree—Tane the Forest-god personified. In his hand was his broad-axe; with it he must make his *rangatira's* river-boat.

He felled the tree, and, lopping off the upper part, began the laborious work of dubbing out the *waka*. The upper side of the trunk he levelled off with his axe, and then he gradually cut it into hollowed shape, an art he had learned on the Waitara. For this portion of the work an adze was chiefly used, a steel blade lashed to a wooden handle in the old Maori fashion. He trimmed and shaped the ends into bow and stern, and day by day the canoe assumed more shapely proportions, until at last it lay complete—a craft of about twenty-five feet in length and three feet in beam, rough and undecorated, it is true, but still a ship of the Maori, fit to carry cargo and paddlers, and run the rapids of the swift and broken Patea. Ropes were made of stout supplejack vines, and with Rupé and his family the white man lowered the canoe down the high bank to the water-edge. *Te Riu-o-Tané* lay ready for its crew—the Hollow Trunk of Tané.

Then paddles were shaped out, and Bent and his companions set to work catching and drying eels and gathering wild honey, in preparation for the voyage down the river to Hukatéré village, where the main body of Rupé's tribe resided.

About this time the white man entered upon his third matrimonial experience. His chief's granddaughter, a good-looking girl of about eighteen, came to the little village with a visiting party of Ngati-Ruanui. She had already a husband, but he had quarrelled with her, and attempted to kill her; she, therefore, returned to her old *tupuna*, Rupé, who now gave her to Bent; and the white man and his young Maori wife lived happily there in well-hidden Rukumoana.[14]

[14] This name Rukumoana originated thus, according to the Maoris: About the year 1830 a war-party from the Waikato attacked and slaughtered a number of Taranaki people here. One of the Taranakis saved his own life and that of his brother in a remarkable manner. These two men were cousins of Hakopa, the old warrior who befriended Kimble Bent in Te Ngutu-o-te-Manu pa in 1868, and later on the Waitara. One of the men was wounded, and in another moment his head would have been slashed off by a Waikato savage, but his brother seized him in his arms, and leaped over the steep bank of the Patea into the river below. He dived to the bottom, and still holding his brother, crawled along the bottom until he reached a place under the banks where the overhanging shrubs concealed them from view. The pursuers failed to find the brothers, who presently escaped to the forest. The Taranaki people commemorated this heroic deed by naming the spot where Hakopa's

CHAPTER XXVII

HIROKI: THE STORY OF A FUGITIVE

Hiroki, the slayer of McLean—Strange faces at Rukumoana—A forest chase—A meeting and a warning—Hiroki's wild bush life and his end.

MORE than one outlaw from the white country outside took refuge in the Taranaki bush even in those *post-bellum* days. One of these was Hiroki, the Maori who killed McLean. Hiroki ("The Lean One") had quarrelled with a survey-party who had camped on his land away out near the coast in the year 1878; the cause of the trouble, as he said, was the killing of his pigs by McLean, who was the survey-or's cook. Hiroki remonstrated with the *pakehas*, but they jeered at him; and when his last pig had disappeared he sat down and wept, then loaded his gun, went to the survey camp, and shot McLean dead. Wherefore he was a hunted man, with a price on his head.

One day, as the *pakeha*-Maori (Kimble Bent) and his Maori companions were sitting smoking in their lonely little bush-village at Rukumoana, far up the Patea River, they heard a loud hail across the river. They looked at each other in astonishment and a little alarm, for they imagined that no one knew their hiding-place. Bent went to his hut, and loading a revolver, put it in his belt, then walked over to the river-bank. On the other side of the stream there were six natives standing. They called to Bent to bring a canoe over and ferry them across.

Bent, always on the *qui vive* for danger, was dubious about the wisdom of trusting himself alone with a party of strangers, who, for all he knew, might be after his head, for he was still an outlaw. But he dropped into his canoe, and with a few strong strokes sent the dug-out across the river. He knelt in his canoe, holding her nose into the bank, and interrogated the strange Maoris. The leader was a tall young half-caste. They were all armed with revolvers, and one or two had tomahawks stuck in their belts.

"Where do you come from, and what do you want here?" asked the white man.

"We have come seeking a man who has committed a crime," replied the half-caste, speaking, as Bent had done, in Maori.

Bent shoved the canoe a stroke off from the bank and said determinedly, with a hand on his revolver:

"If you have come to capture me I will not be taken; I will spill the blood of the first man who attempts it. I will kill my enemy first and then kill myself." ("*Ka maringi i ahau te toto a te tangata tuatahi. Ka mate taku hoariri nei, maku e whakamate toku tinana.*")

"It's all right, friend, we don't want you," said the half-caste; "we are looking for a Maori called Hiroki, who has murdered a surveyor's cook, named McLean, out yonder on the plains. We have traced him up here, and we want to know where he is, because there is a price on his head, and we are Government Maoris."

"Come along, then; I'll take you across," said Bent. The strangers stepped into the canoe, and the white man paddled them over the Patea; then took them up to the village and into Hakopa's house.

To the old chief and his Maori companions the half-caste explained the mission that had brought his party to lonely Rukumoana.

"We have not seen your man Hiroki," said Hakopa. "He may have swum the river and passed through here by night. Who knows? If he has passed this way he has no doubt gone to Te Ngaere, which is a very difficult place to reach and a good refuge-place for men like Hiroki."

"We do not know the trail to Te Ngaere," said the half-caste. "Will any of you guide us there?"

Bent offered to go as guide, saying he knew the track to Ngaere very well and had frequently been there in the war-days. "But," he asked, "will you guarantee my safety if I trust myself with you? How do I know that you will not cut my head off when you get me out alone in the bush, and take it out to get the Government reward?"

The half-caste laughed. "You're quite safe, *pakeha*. Not a man of us will touch you. I tell you we only want Hiroki."

A young man named Pakanga, of the Ngati-Maniapoto tribe from the King Country, happened to be in the village on a visit to the forest-dwellers. He was sitting alongside Bent. "Friend," he said quietly, "I will go with you, and see that they don't attack you treacherously."

So Bent agreed to go as guide, and, after a meal of pork and potatoes, set before them by the women of the *kainga*, the armed party of man-hunters set out along the bush-track leading in the direction of the swamp-defended Ngaere, the place where Colonel Whitmore and his force of Colonial soldiers just failed in surprising and capturing Titokowaru in the last days of the war in 1869.

Bent leading, the party filed along the narrow overgrown trail until they were close to the banks of a small stream, the Mangamingi. A little distance back from the creek the white man asked his companions to halt, saying that he and Pakanga would go on to reconnoitre.

The half-caste and his five men sat down and lit their pipes, and Bent and the King Country Maori went off cautiously, saying one of them would come back at once if they caught sight of the fugitive.

The white man and his friend had gone only a short distance when they came upon a fire burning just alongside the track, in an old camping-place beneath the shade of a giant *totara*-tree, whose great branches overhung the little dark river that flowed close by. A few roasted potatoes, still warm, lay alongside the fire. Evidently it had been deserted only a few minutes.

"Now," said Bent to his companion, "let us settle quickly how we shall act. Hiroki—for it can be no one else—must be close by; he must have only just left this spot. Shall we betray him to the Government, or shall we let him escape? He had a just grievance against the man whom he shot. We have heard all about it, and we know that he was a peaceable man, who was provoked into a fit of passion. He is a lonely and a hunted man, and for me my sympathies are with him, for is he not a fugitive like myself?"

"*E tika ana*," said the young King Country Maori. "That's right. We won't give him up to the Government head-hunters."

"Let me tell you now, friend," said Bent, "that I have had suspicions for some days that Hiroki has been in hiding near our village. One morning lately, when I went to look in my *pataka* (store-house) across the river, where I keep my seed-potatoes for the new season's planting, I found that some of them had been taken. Then half a mile up the river the next day I saw a place where some stranger had been fishing for eels, for there were heads of the eels lying there where he had cut them off. There was a fire there, and some of my seed-potatoes had been roasted in it. I told old Hakopa and no one else about it."

The two men descended the bank to the river. Just where the track entered the slow-moving, muddy stream they saw the fresh prints of naked feet. Wading across, they quickly mounted the opposite bank and set out at a noiseless, easy lope, their bare feet making hardly a sound, along the trail that wound into the glooms of the bush.

Suddenly, at a turn in the track, they came upon Hiroki.

The fugitive was standing there, waiting, for the low growling of his dog, a white, savage-looking animal, had given him warning of pursuit. The hunted man menacingly presented a short-barrelled gun at the *pakeha* and his companion. He was a fellow of middle stature, lean, as his name implied, but strong and hard-limbed, with a dark determined face and a short black beard.

"Where are you going?" cried Hiroki.

"Oh, nowhere in particular," Bent replied; "just strolling along" ("*ki te haer-eere*").

The Maori looked puzzled and suspicious, and kept his gun at the ready.

"Listen to me, friend," said Bent quickly; "you are in danger. There are six Government Maoris close behind you, and they want you dead or alive. Now, go on, and go quickly. And don't venture back, lest you die!"

"*Ka pai koe!*" ("You are good!") was all Hiroki said. Turning, he went quickly at a half-trot along the path, with his gun at the trail, and his wild-looking, mongrel dog close on his bare heels, and in a few moments both disappeared in the dark forest.

Bent and Pakanga returned to the pursuing party, who were becoming impatient at the long absence of their guide and were hot with questions.

The white man and his companions managed to quiet the suspicions of the man-hunters. They declared that there were no signs of any one having passed that way, and that it would not be much use going on to the Ngaere, which was a long and very toilsome journey. Fortunately for them, the half-caste and his men had not troubled to go on as far as the big *totara* on the river-bank, where the tell-tale fire was not yet cold.

After some debate the whole party returned to Rukumoana, and the hunters, giving up the chase in that direction, made out to the open country, and that was the last Bent heard of them.

Three years later Bent met Hiroki in Parihaka, the village of the prophet Te Whiti. The slayer of McLean had had a wild and anxious life of it after his escape from Rukumoana. He told Bent of his lonely existence in the great forests of the back-country, living on eels, wild honey, the young shoots of fern-trees, and such-like rough fare of the bush. After he came out into the open country and was making his way across the Waimate Plains in the direction of Parihaka he was chased by several Government men (one of whom was Mr. William Williams, a Plains settler), and was fired at and wounded, but escaped. Te Whiti sheltered him and condoned his crime, which, being a semi-agrarian one, was counted a patriotic deed by the people of Parihaka. He spoke gratefully of what Bent had done for him, in giving him timely warning that day in the Mangamingi bush, and offered him a money gift as some measure of *utu*. This Bent promptly refused, saying, "Keep your money, and thank the *Atua* for your escape, not me."

Hiroki was a wild figure in Parihaka those lawless days of 1878-81. On meeting-days and feast-days, when the faithful of the Maori tribes gathered to hear the prophet expound the Scriptures after his fashion and prophesy many strange happenings, the Lean One used to head the procession of the *tuku-kai*, the bringing of the food for ceremonious presentation to the visitors. A double line of gaily dressed girls, bearing baskets of potatoes and pork and fish hot from the *hangi*, marched in time to a lively song into the *marae*, and in front of them paraded Hiroki, stripped to a loin-mat, a loaded and cocked double-barrelled gun in his hands, white feathers stuck in his hair, red war-paint on his cheeks and forehead, leaping from side to side, eyes rolling, tongue defiantly protruded, the embodiment of Maori savagery and ferocity. But when John Bryce, as native minister, invaded Parihaka in 1881 with his force of 1,700 Armed Constabulary and Volunteers, and arrested the two prophets Te Whiti and Tohu, Hiroki was also captured, and shortly thereafter he was tried for McLean's murder and was hanged.

To this day the Maoris of the Patea tell stories of Hiroki's solitary and savage life in the bush. One place in particular—at Orangimura, between three and four miles above Rukumoana—is pointed out as a hiding-place of the refugee. Here a large, hollow *rata*-tree grew near the top of a high bank; the Patea River flowed below. Hiroki had camped here in order to get wild honey from a hive in the hollow tree, and after he had filled a couple of calabashes with the honey he lit his nightly fire and went to sleep close to the cliff-top, first tying his dog up to a bush with a flax rope. In the night the dog bit through the flax that held him, and jumping on his master so startled him that he forgot he was so near the verge of the cliff, over which he promptly rolled in the darkness; he fell with a mighty splash in the river below, together with his astonished dog. The spot where this night adventure occurred is called by the Maoris Te Pari-o-Hiroki, which means "Hiroki's Precipice."

CHAPTER XXVIII

OUT OF EXILE

Canoeing on the Patea—The voyage to Hukatéré—The white man's world again—Bent the medicine-man—*Makutu*, or the Black Art—Bent's later days—The end.

ALL was ready for the voyage, and the *pakeha*-Maori and his companions loaded their canoe and embarked for Hukatéré—thirty miles down-stream, not far from the sea-coast. The Patea was a very winding stream, flowing between high forest-covered banks; its course was impeded by frequent rocky shoals and accumulations of sunken logs, which formed rapids. Aboard the canoe, besides Bent, were Rupé, Hakopa and his niece, and a man named Te Rii, who was an *urukehu*, or "fair hair."

The white man and his Maori companions paddled along merrily for seven or eight miles, lightening their labours with canoe-songs. Then, in shooting a rapid, the canoe struck a rock, swung broadside on to the swift current, and immediately capsized.

The crew reached the shore safely, and hauled the canoe up on to a shingly bank. Fortunately all the cargo—the baskets of dried eels and the calabashes filled with honey—had been made fast to the thwarts, as a precaution against such an accident, and so was saved; but old Hakopa lost a little kit—his bush savings-bank—containing a sum of money which he had acquired at the Waitara. On the bank a fire was kindled by means of flint and steel—commonly used amongst the Maoris in those days, and still occasionally seen in use in remote forest districts, such as the Urewera Country. By the blaze of the great fire the wrecked canoeists dried themselves and their garments, and they camped there that night.

At daylight next morning they embarked again, and another day and a half at the paddles took them down to the Hukatéré *kainga*, a large settlement of *raupo*-thatched houses, standing on the left bank of the Patea, in a beautiful bend, with the lofty, forest-fringed cliffs of Pariroa jutting out abruptly on the opposite shore.

The approaching canoe, its four paddles flashing in the sun and dipping again all together, was seen from the *kainga* while still some little distance up the river, and the men and women of the Hukatéré gathered on the water-side and cried and waved their welcome to the long-absent people of the bush.

"*Kumea mai te waka!*" they chanted, and the women waved shawls and green branches in the poetic greeting of the *powhiri*. "*To-o-ia mai te waka!* Oh, haul up the canoe! Draw hitherwards the canoe. To the resting-place—that canoe! To the sleeping-place—that canoe! Oh, welcome, welcome, strangers from the forest-land! Urge swift your paddles, for home darts your canoe!"

So, chanting their ancient song, the villagers received the new arrivals, and, still waving their garments and their leafy branches, retired slowly before them as they landed and walked up the sloping banks until the open *marae* in the centre of the *kainga* was reached. There the guests from Rukumoana were received by a dignified chief, white-bearded old Nga-waka-taurua (Double-canoe). Now the *powhiri* was succeeded by the doleful sounds of the *tangi*, and one after another the Hukatéré tribespeople pressed their noses to those of Rupé and his household; and they wept long and unrestrainedly for the dead, for those who had passed away since they last met.

And then the feasting. The bush-family and their "tame white man" enjoyed a meal of truly huge proportions and variety in comparison with the meagre forest-fare to which they had been confined so long. And when the *pakeha* tobacco and *pakeha* grog came out—unwonted luxuries to the *mohoao*, the bush-people— old Rupé and his household were indeed in the Promised Land for which they had longed for many a month; they had all that the heart of the Hauhau could desire.

The feast over, the dried eels and honey, conveyed with so much toil from distant Rukumoana, were brought up to the *marae*, and ceremoniously presented to old "Double-Canoe," who distributed the food amongst the people of the village. The canoe itself was similarly presented to the chief as a gift of *aroha* from Rupé. In return, the men of Hukatéré placed before the visitors their gifts—£5 in money (representing the sum total of the *pakeha* cash in the village), and blankets, shirts, and other articles of clothing, of which Bent and his companions were in much need after their rough life in the bush.

"While I was in the *kainga*," says Bent, "the local chief went down to the town of Patea, a few miles away, to get me some European clothing. He informed some people in the town that Tu-nui-a-moa, the *pakeha*-Maori, who had been with the Hauhaus for twelve or thirteen years, was in his *kainga*, and next day about twenty Europeans rode up to the settlement out of curiosity to see me. We had a long talk, and they gave me some articles of clothing, and told me all about the white man's world from which I had cut myself off. This was about the end of the year 1878.

"After a month's stay we returned to our own village, in a canoe belonging to the Hukatéré natives, loaded with goods and 'tucker.' Five days' paddling and poling up-river took us to Rukumoana. Planting season came round again; then we whiled away the time in Maori fashion—hunting wild pigs, snaring and shooting birds, catching eels, and getting honey—until the crops were harvested. And not long after that we bade farewell to our old *kainga* for ever, loaded our canoe for the last time, and once more paddled down to Hukatéré."

KIMBLE BENT, THE PAKEHA-MAORI.

(From a photo taken in 1903.)

From Hukatéré the *pakeha*-Maori and his girl-wife went to Taiporohenui—Bent's old home in the war days. There he lived for a year or so, blanketed like a Maori, and working in the cultivations. Here, too, in the long nights he was much with the old men of the *kainga*, and from such learned men as Hupini and Pokau—true *tohungas*, or priests, and soothsayers—he learned much of the strange occultism of the Maori. He saw singular ceremonies, the rites of the *makutu*, the black art. He learned scores of *karakias*—incantations useful in Maori eyes for all sorts of purposes, all conditions of war and peace time. Some of these were *makutu* spells by which the wizard could slay an enemy, by witchcraft and the power of the evil eye. Many a case of death from *makutu* came under Bent's observation during his life among the Maoris. Old Hupini, says the *pakeha*-Maori, undoubtedly killed men with his *makutu*—a combination of three factors: projection of the will force, the malignant exercise of hypnotic influence, and sheer imagination and fright on the part of the person *makutu'*d.

Many Maoris believe that the witchcraft can be wrought by an adept or *tohunga* by taking some of the hair or clothing or even remains of the food of the person intended to be slain, and pronouncing the appropriate powerful *karakias* and curses over it. The enemy's *hau*—his life-essence, his vital force—then lies in the hollow of the *tohunga's* hand.

A *tohunga* can take the *hau* of a man's footprints and thereby *makutu* him; he can even *makutu* an enemy's horse so that it will fall sick and not be able to travel!

Amongst the prayers and ceremonies which old Hupini taught Bent were the *karakia* for combating the evil spell of the *makutu* and for restoring a bewitched and ailing person to health and safety—to the Land of Light and Life, the *Ao-marama.*

One of these rites Bent describes in true Maori fashion:

A person is taken seriously ill; it is the *makutu.* The wise man is called in; he divines that the illness is caused by another *tohunga's* witchcraft. At daylight in the morning the sick man is carried to the water-side. The wise man then takes three small sticks or twigs (*rito*)—fern-sticks will do—and sets them up by the side of the river or the pool. One of these sacred wands represents the invalid, one the tribe to which he belongs, and one the mischief-working wizard (*te tangata nana te makutu*). A charm is said over them, and then two *rito* are taken away, leaving only one—that for the wizard—the "wand of darkness."

An incantation, beginning:

"Toko i te po, te po nui, te po roa" ("Staff of the night, the great night, the long night"), etc., is repeated over this wand. When this is said the priest conducts the sick person to the edge of the water and sprinkles water over his body, repeating as he does so a charm to expel the *makutu* spirits from his body, ending with a curse upon the malevolent wizard—"Eat that *tohunga makutu*, let him be utterly eaten and destroyed."

When this is ended the patient is taken back to his house. He is told that the wise man has, by virtue of his very strong charms, seen the rival *tohunga makutu*, and that it will not be long before that evil man dies. The curse falls, the wizard is himself *makutu'*d, and the invalid—perhaps—recovers.

About the year 1881 Bent—now able to venture into the towns of the *pakeha* again in safety—left Taranaki, and travelled to Auckland and up to the Waikato. Then he went on to the west coast, and spent some months amongst the Maoris of the Ngati-Mahuta tribe, living in the historic old settlement Maketu, on the shores of Kawhia Harbour, close to the legendary landing-place of the Tainui canoe—the Waikato Maoris' pilgrim ship.

Tawhiao, the Maori King, was then living at Kawhia, and he asked Bent to remain with him and be his *pakeha* and interpreter. The white man was now, however, wearying to be back in his old home, Taranaki.

"Tawhiao," says Bent, "insisted on me remaining with his tribe, but I repeated a Maori incantation which I had been taught by the *tohungas* in Taranaki, a *karakia* used as a charm by strangers (*tangata tauhou*) who may desire to leave the place where they are staying on a visit and proceed to a new *pa*, and who fear obstruction. The charm begins:

> "'*Ka u, ka u, ki tenei tauhou,*
> *Ki tenei whenua tauhou.*'

"When the old king heard me repeat the incantation he exclaimed:

"'Ha, so you are a *tohunga*!'

"'Yes, I am,' I replied.

"Then the old man said, '*Kua tuwhera te rori mou*' ('The road is open to you.') He permitted me to return to Taranaki, and sent four of his men to escort me through the King Country to Waitara."

The last quarter-century of Kimble Bent's life has not carried much adventure. Living amongst the Maoris, he acquired some reputation as a "medicine-man." During his wild life in Maoridom he had become expert in the rude pharmacopœia of the bush, and learned to extract potent medicines from the plants of the forest. Native herbs and tree-bark and leaves, prepared in various ways, are exceedingly valuable remedies. The knowledge of these herbal remedies, gained from many a *tohunga* and wise woman of the bush tribes, the white man now turned to practical account. His fame as a doctor reached Parihaka, the village of Te Whiti, the Prophet of the Mountain. The prophet's people sent for the white medicine-man to come and heal the sick. He spent a week in Parihaka, and returned to his Taiporohenui hut with more money in his pocket than he had possessed since he left his old home-town of Eastport to see life in England. "And I was luckier than most *pakeha* doctors," says the old man, "for none of my patients died!"

And so the tale of "Tu-nui-a-moa" is told, and we take our leave of the old *pakeha*-Maori—Kimble Bent, sailor, soldier, outlaw, Hauhau slave, cartridge-maker, *pa*-builder, canoe-carver, medicine-man, and what not—sitting smoking his pipe in the midst of his Maori friends. He is still living with the natives; working in their food-gardens, fishing with them, house-building for them. A grey old man, of mild and quiet eye, who might easily be taken for some highly respectable shop-keeper who had spent all his life in city bounds. Yet no man probably has lived a wilder life, using the term in the sense of an intimate acquaintance with primeval, passionate savagery, and with the ever-near face of death. He is the sole living white eye-witness of the secret Hauhau war-rites; the only white man who has survived to tell of those terrible deeds in the bush, to tell the story of the last Taranaki war from the inner side—the Maori side.

Bent has reached the age of seventy-three; and now the old man's thoughts go to his boyhood's home in the far-off State of Maine, and he sometimes expresses a wish to reach his homeland again. "If I could only get a berth on some American sailing-vessel bound for New York or Boston, I'd even now try to work my passage home," he says. "I'd like to die in my mother's land." But that can never be. He is for ever beyond the pale; and he will die as he has lived, a *pakeha*-Maori.

APPENDIX

TITOKOWARU, THE TARANAKI WAR-CHIEF

THE following interesting supplementary particulars concerning Titokowaru, one of the leading figures in this book, were supplied to the writer by the Rev. T. G. Hammond, of Opunake, Wesleyan missionary to the Taranaki Maoris:

"It was Titokowaru's right eye that had been destroyed by a bullet in some engagement. He was about five feet nine in height and somewhat spare and muscular, with fine bone, an alert, active man, but by no means good-looking. His skin was rather darker than the general run of Maoris, and his nose low in the bridge, with wide nostrils. His face rarely lit up pleasantly, and he was of reserved manner. His knowledge of tikanga Maori was considerable, and during the war he conducted the usual ceremonies to make the war-parties successful.

"The late Rev. Stannard, of Wanganui, told me that Titokowaru's name given him in baptism was Hohepa (Joseph), and I have heard from Tairuakena and others that Tito was one of the young men who accompanied the Rev. Skevington on his last visit to Auckland. (This was long before the Maori War.) They journeyed overland from Te Waimate to Auckland, Mr. Skevington going to attend the Auckland Synod. While in the old High Street Church, Auckland, he died suddenly. Titokowaru and the other young men returned to bear the news to the people, as he (Tairuakena) put it, 'Ka hoki mai matou tangi, haere ki tena kainga, ki tena kainga.' Mr. Woon succeeded Mr. Skevington at Heretoa, Te Waimate.

"I had one interview with Titokowaru which I shall never forget. I think it was in 1876, and before I knew Maori. Mr. William Williams, of Manaia, Taranaki, was going to visit Titokowaru at Omuturangi, on the Waimate Plains, and, as I was on my way to New Plymouth, he persuaded me to delay a day and go with him—a most unwise thing, as the Maoris had said they would shoot any one who crossed the Wai-ngongoro. We went from Hawera to Normanby, and then picked up old Kātené Tu-Whakaruru, who was just then acting as a Maori policeman. We rode along over these vast plains, with the cocksfoot brushing against our knees as we sat in our saddles. We came to a house on the edge of the bush, and found only one woman, whose face was deeply scarred; she had lately lost her child, and had been cutting herself in her grief. This woman told us that Titokowaru and the men were in the bush planting potatoes, and pointed out a narrow path, along which we galloped for a good distance, perhaps a mile.

"Suddenly we came upon about eighty Maoris, all men, and Titokowaru with them. They gathered round us as we dismounted, and Titokowaru came and took my right arm, and a big burly fellow my left. They sat me between them, holding me fast, while the smoke from the fire close by almost smothered me. An old bald-headed Maori began to speak in an excited manner, and when he had done a very rascally looking young fellow made a speech, coming up to me and smacking his thigh, and letting out an angry grunt at the end of every period. When he finished, Kātené spoke, and did his best to turn away their anger; reminded them of the good the missionaries did in getting them released from bondage in the Waikato and the Ngapuhi Country.

"Then Williams spoke, and at the close of his speech a fine man in a piupiu (flax waist-mat) orated, and then came forward to hongi (rub noses) with me. After which there was a little fraternisation, and we came away. Even old Kātené looked very white while the row was on, but I did not know enough to be scared. It was a narrow escape; I, of course, know now what I did not know then. I thought at the time Titokowaru was protecting me, but I think now he was making sure that I did not get away."

Titokowaru died at his village near Manaia, on the Waimate Plains—the scene of his olden battles against the whites—towards the end of 1889. To the end he was a sturdy enemy of the Europeans, and though he did not actually fight against them after 1869, he was the leader in many obstructive movements against white settlement, surveying, and road-making.

REWARD FOR TITOKOWARU'S HEAD

Under address and date Downing Street, February 26th, 1869, the Right Hon. Earl Granville, K.G., Secretary of State for the Colonies, wrote to Sir George F. Bowen, G.C.M.G., Governor of New Zealand:

"I see it stated in the newspapers that you have offered a reward of £1,000 for the person of the Maori chief Titokowaru—I infer alive or dead—and £5 for the person of every Maori rebel brought in alive. I do not at present pronounce any opinion as to the propriety of these steps, but I must observe that they are so much at variance with the usual laws of war, and appear, at first sight, so much calculated to exasperate and extend hostilities, that they ought to have been reported to me by you officially with the requisite explanation, which I should now be glad to receive."

In the course of his reply to this despatch Governor Bowen said:

"It is contended that this passage implies that the Maoris now in arms ... are foreign enemies, or at all events belligerents, with whom the usual laws of war must be strictly observed."

On this, Earl Granville remarked in a despatch of November 4th:

"I think you would have done well to point out to those who thus argue that my despatch nowhere hints that the Maoris are foreigners, a doctrine which I had never heard of before I perused the Attorney-General's opinion; and that the legitimate inference from my despatch is the direct contrary to that which is drawn from it.... I do not clearly understand how you justify this notice as a matter of law. I understand you to disclaim the application of martial law; and viewing Titokowaru merely as a notorious, but untried and unconvicted rebel and murderer, I am not aware of any Colonial enactment which would make it lawful for any chance person to shoot him down."

Lector House believes that a society develops through a two-fold approach of continuous learning and adaptation, which is derived from the study of classic literary works spread across the historic timeline of literature records. Therefore, we aim at reviving, repairing and redeveloping all those inaccessible or damaged but historically as well as culturally important literature across subjects so that the future generations may have an opportunity to study and learn from past works to embark upon a journey of creating a better future.

This book is a result of an effort made by Lector House towards making a contribution to the preservation and repair of original ancient works which might hold historical significance to the approach of continuous learning across subjects.

HAPPY READING & LEARNING!

LECTOR HOUSE LLP
E-MAIL: lectorpublishing@gmail.com